Rivalry and central planning

Historical Perspectives on Modern Economics

General Editor: Professor Craufurd D. Goodwin, Duke University

This series contains original works that challenge and enlighten historians of economics. For the profession as a whole it promotes a better understanding of the origin and content of modern economics.

Rivalry and central planning

The socialist calculation debate reconsidered

Don Lavoie
George Mason University

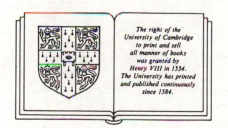

The right of the
University of Cambridge
to print and sell
all manner of books
was granted by
Henry VIII in 1534.
The University has printed
and published continuously
since 1584.

CAMBRIDGE UNIVERSITY PRESS

Cambridge
London   New York   New Rochelle
Melbourne   Sydney

Published by the Press Syndicate of the University of Cambridge
The Pitt Building, Trumpington Street, Cambridge CB2 1RP
32 East 57th Street, New York, NY 10022, USA
10 Stamford Road, Oakleigh, Melbourne 3166, Australia

First published 1985

Printed in the United States of America

Library of Congress Cataloging in Publication Data
Lavoie, Don, 1951–
  Rivalry and central planning.
  (Historical perspectives on modern economics)
  Based on the author's thesis (doctoral), New York
University.
  Bibliography: p.
  Includes index.
  1. Marxian economics. 2. Central planning.
3. Austrian School of economists. 4. Neoclassical
school of economics. I. Title. II. Series.
HB97.5.L292 1985   335   84-17659
ISBN 0 521 26449 9

For my mother,
Ruth Evelyn Knight Lavoie,
for instilling in me the love of reading

Contents

Acknowledgments   *page* ix

1. **Introduction**   1
   Purpose, scope, and procedure   1
   The standard account of the debate   10
   An alternative account of the debate   20
   Rivalry and central planning   22

2. **Marx's socialism: the critique of rivalry**   28
   Beyond utopian socialism   29
   Consciously ordered versus
   anarchic social production   39

3. **Mises's challenge: the informational
   function of rivalry**   48
   The nature of economic calculation under capitalism   48
   Economic calculation under socialism   60
   Difficulties with the labor time solution   67
   Mises's anticipatory critique of market socialism   74

4. **The diversion of the debate into statics:
   rivalry assumed away**   78
   From "formal similarity" to "theoretical possibility"   79
   The limitations of static analysis   100
   The static answer to Mises reconsidered   114

5. **The market socialists' "competitive" response:
   rivalry ignored**   117
   Lange's extension of the
   "formal similarity" argument   118
   The crucial ambiguity of "trial and error"   125
   Variations on the Lange theme   132

6. **The Austrian rejoinder: learning from rivalry**   145
    Robbins and Hayek: retreat or restatement?   145
    Robbins's and Hayek's early critique of
    the competitive solution   158
    Hayek's later rejoinders to the market socialists   166
    Mises's own rejoinder   173

7. **Conclusion**   179

    References   184

    Index   201

Acknowledgments

My deepest debt in the writing of this book is owed to Israel M. Kirzner, who served as chairman of the original dissertation committee (with Fritz Machlup, James Becker, Elizabeth Durbin, and Gerald O'Driscoll) at New York University. From the first paper that I wrote on the calculation debate in his course on the history of economic thought to the final draft of the dissertation, he provided incisive criticism and constant support. His example of thorough scholarship in the history of thought and his way of making old ideas come alive serve as a constant inspiration.

A special acknowledgment is due to the late Fritz Machlup, whose well-known concern for precision in the choice of words had a substantial effect on the book and whose extraordinary warmth and generosity had a substantial effect on its author. Of the other members of my committee, James Becker helped me to appreciate the importance of Marxism and introduced me to Makoto Itoh, whose approach to Marxian scholarship had a significant impact on this book; Elizabeth Durbin provided extremely useful background information on the English market socialists, including (but not only) her father, E. F. M. Durbin; and Gerald O'Driscoll showed me the importance of monetary theory for understanding the Austrian calculation argument.

In addition, the early encouragement and guidance of Ludwig M. Lachmann, Walter Grinder, and Roy A. Childs, Jr., kept me working on economics at a time when I was ready to settle for a comfortable life as a computer systems analyst. Although my income has not benefited from this advice, my subjective standard of living most certainly has.

Valuable research leads were supplied by my friends Richard Ebeling and John Battalana, as well as by the members of the weekly colloquium in Austrian economics at NYU. The extent to which my ideas were shaped by innumerable and lively discussions with these people is beyond estimation.

The transformation of the dissertation into a book has been greatly facilitated by the editors of Cambridge University Press including copyeditor Christie Lerch, and in particular by an anonymous reader who provided me with very valuable comments. The Center for the Study of Market Processes and especially Wayne Brough and David Prychitko at George Mason University provided some helpful research services at the final stages of the project.

Finally I must express a profound personal debt to my wife Mary, who has supported me in every way throughout the production of this book.

CHAPTER 1

Introduction

Purpose, scope, and procedure

The socialist calculation debate of the 1930s is widely acknowledged to have been the most important theoretical controversy in the history of the field of comparative economics. Alexander Eckstein (1971, p. 2) was not exaggerating when he referred to the debate as a "theoretical controversy . . . of far-reaching importance in the study of comparative economics" that "focused on a range of problems that had a profound impact on the development of the field."[1]

References to the debate (or at least to some of the writings of which it is composed) can be found not only in most texts in comparative economics but also in many treatments of socialist economics, welfare economics, and general histories of economic thought. Significantly, many of these works take the debate as their theoretical starting point, and even those discussions of socialist economics that fail to refer to the debate explicitly nonetheless focus on issues that were first systematically examined in the calculation debate. Oskar Lange's famous contribution to the debate is considered the definitive precursor of "market socialism," the dominant trend in modern central planning theory. The whole character of socialist economics has changed dramatically since the time of the controversy, largely, to be sure, because of subsequent practical experience with central planning but also because of the impact of this theoretical exchange. Thus it may well be that a clearer understanding of this controversy could prove an invaluable aid in explaining, and possibly correcting, the problems encountered in socialist practice today.

Moreover, it can be argued that this debate has an importance that

---

[1] John Elliot (1973, pp. 232–3) calls the Mises-Hayek argument "probably the most predominent and 'fundamental' of the post-Marxist critiques of the economic theory of socialism" and stresses the important effect that contributions to the debate such as that of Oskar Lange had on later theories of socialism. Loucks (1957, pp. 257–8) says that the debate raised "theoretical problems involved in the operation of a socialized order which go to the very heart of economic process, and which up to the present time have not been solved satisfactorily by the proponents of socialism."

transcends the issues that were consciously in dispute. A better understanding of the controversy could lead to a substantial advance in our
investigation into the proper role of and methods for economic theory
in general. Despite the indisputable impact of the calculation debate,
some of the lessons to be learned from it have yet to be incorporated
into the body of what could be called the modern mainstream of
economic thought. The reason for the debate's incomplete influence
may be rooted in an inadequate understanding, by the participants as
well as by later historians of thought, of the original arguments.

The purpose of this book is to make a contribution to the history
of thought in economics by reexamining this classic debate. I will
concentrate on the articles and books that are widely agreed to be
the major primary sources in the controversy. On the critical side,
arguing that there is a fundamental flaw in the economics of central
planning, were the Austrians Ludwig von Mises ([1920] 1935; [1922]
1936), Friedrich A. Hayek ([1935] 1948e; [1935] 1948f; [1940]
1948a), and Lionel Robbins (1934a).[2] Defending one variety of economic planning or another from this challenge were the "market
socialists," Oskar Lange ([1936] 1964), H. D. Dickinson (1933; 1939),
Fred M. Taylor ([1929] 1964), Abba P. Lerner (1934b; 1936; 1937;
1944), and E. F. M. Durbin ([1936] 1968).[3] The most commonly
referenced secondary sources in this important episode in the history of economic thought have been the discussions by Joseph
Schumpeter ([1942] 1950; 1954) and Abram Bergson (1948; 1967).
Leading scholars such as Frank Knight (1936) and Benjamin N.
Ward (1967b) have endorsed this standard interpretation.

It is the main thesis of this study that these standard accounts of
the debate have been profoundly mistaken.[4] The debate as well as its
implications for comparative economic systems have been, I believe,
almost completely misunderstood. Although this book cannot attempt to offer the final word on this complex controversy, my hope
is that it will clarify many of the confusions in the debate and perhaps even serve as a stimulus for its rekindling.

Why is it, then, that historians of thought of the stature of Schumpeter and Knight, and esteemed economic theorists in the compara-

[2] Other early contributions that made arguments similar to Mises's include Pierson
  ([1902] 1935), Weber ([1921] 1978), and Brutzkus ([1922] 1935). This study concen-
  trates mainly on the central Austrian contributions, both because the market socialist
  responses did so and because I find them to represent a more complete argument.
[3] The related literature on market socialism that has emerged since the debate will be
  examined briefly, but the central focus will be on these pioneering works.
[4] I have tried elsewhere (1981) to explain just how this standard account came to
  dominate secondary sources in the history of thought of the debate.

tive study of economic systems such as Ward and Bergson, have all failed to comprehend the essential nature of this controversy? It is indeed significant that so many interpreters seem to have independently come to the same views upon reading the primary sources, a fact that lends great plausibility to the standard view. One might not expect the coincidence of numerous respected minds erring in precisely the same way.

But it should also be noted that these interpreters share a very similar training in economics within the neoclassical tradition of Walras and Marshall and that the intellectual background of Mises, Hayek, and Robbins is substantially different.[5] No economist can expect to be able to set down his whole theoretical world view unambiguously. The economist, rather, depends on the reader to relate the specific ideas expressed to his or her implicit understanding of economic theory in general. Each analytic statement, to be rendered complete, must be integrated within the wider framework of economic theory to which it is intended to be a contribution. The fact that the neoclassical interpreters of the calculation debate shared this essential analytic background only with the economists on one side of the debate may be sufficient reason to suspect that the other side has yet to have been adequately understood. Differences between the neoclassical and Austrian interpretation of such key concepts as "economic theory," "equilibrium," "competition," "rational economic calculation," "efficiency," "ownership," and "price" led the neoclassical chroniclers of the debate to consistently misinterpret the arguments that the Austrian economists were trying to make, and to do so in remarkably similar ways.

To be sure, the Austrians must accept part of the responsibility for failing to make themselves understood. A more critical attitude toward the neoclassical approach early in the debate could have prevented much of the confusion that developed later on. The early Austrian theorists were too eager, in my view, to embrace neoclassical economists as marginalist allies against the threat of resurgent classical value theory in the form of Marxism. This kept them from realizing that on some issues they and the Marxists had more in common than either did with the sort of neoclassical economics that underlies the market socialist proposals.

Another reason why the debate has been so widely misunderstood

---

[5] Actually the case of Lord Robbins is less clear-cut. He initially received a somewhat classical economic training under Edwin Cannan at the London School of Economics but was profoundly influenced by the Austrian economists early in his career and for the most part took a thoroughly Austrian position in the debate.

is that the opponents seemed to change their arguments significantly in the course of the debate. This contributed to the confusion of the debate since neither side believed that the other was maintaining a logically coherent position. The debate evolved gradually, over the course of time, as the central points of contention shifted. Misunderstandings and lack of clarity on both sides characterized the initial confrontation, and this led to some revisions in at least the expression, if not the substance, of the arguments. Each side perceived its own evolution as a theoretical advance or clarification and its opponents' as a retreat, but whatever viewpoint one adopts the changes themselves have made the debate complex and its essential nature difficult to unravel. With each side aiming at what it believed to be a moving target, it is not surprising that in many respects the arguments missed.

But the primary reason for the confusion that surrounds the controversy lies not so much in the fact that the opponents moved as in their divergent perspectives. Neither advocates nor critics of central planning seemed to comprehend the fundamental paradigm of their adversaries, and both consequently walked away from the exchange quite convinced that they had won.

That historians of thought have not yet succeeded in understanding this debate is best illustrated by the fact that both sides still claim to have won. There are highly respected contemporary protagonists of each position who to this day refer to the debate as an unambiguous theoretical victory for their side − that is, a victory for or against central planning. It would be difficult to imagine two more divergent interpretations of a controversy than those implicit in the following statements by Hayek (1978b, p. 235) and Drewnowski (1961, p. 341). According to Hayek,

the great debate of the 1920s and 1930s turned mainly on the question of the justification of the socialist hopes of increasing productivity by substituting central planning for marketplace competition as the instrument for guiding economic activity. I don't think it can now be gainsaid by anybody who has studied these discussions that those hopes were shattered and that it came to be recognized that an attempt at centralized collectivist planning of a large economic system was on the contrary bound greatly to decrease productivity.

But in Drewnowski's view,

Mises, as everybody agrees now, was wrong in his main contention that economic calculation under socialism is theoretically impossible.

And each of these comments is immediately followed by an indication that later events in central planning practice have further corroborated each theoretical position. Thus Drewnowski says we can forgive Mises for his lack of faith in central planning because he lacked sufficient data about the Soviet Union to see that central planning is now working there in practice, but Hayek points to the reintroduction of competition in socialist countries as evidence that Mises was correct. What is most striking about these assessments of the debate is not just that they are diametrically opposed but that each discussant believes that he can cite overwhelming scholarly support for his statement and that each is in a sense correct about the consensus in the scholarly community that he confidently refers to.* The resolution of this paradox will require a careful examination of both the way in which the debators are alleged to have "retreated" as well as of the underlying differences in paradigms that concealed some of the basic disagreements.

As Thomas Kuhn has shown, in his *Structure of Scientific Revolutions* (1962), often in the history of ideas a controversy emerges that is belatedly found to represent a clash of basic paradigms. Each side makes interesting points, but since it tries to translate its adversaries' arguments into the framework of its own system, each side fails to come to grips with those arguments effectively and convincingly. In the calculation debate, the failure to comprehend opposing positions was especially striking, for here there were not two but three fundamentally different paradigms – which I will loosely designate "Marxian," "Austrian," and "neoclassical" – none of which successfully engaged in critical confrontation with its opponents.[6]

Of the three possible confrontations among these paradigms, this study will limit its scope primarily to the clash between the Austrian perspective from which Mises's challenge was born and the neoclassical perspective from which the market socialist responses were formulated. In addition, some of the issues that the calculation debate raises concerning the debate's potential as an Austrian critique of the Marxian paradigm will be discussed. (Unfortunately, in the debate

---

* To avoid awkward wording, the masculine pronoun "he" will often be used in the generic sense to mean "he or she."

[6] It should be made clear at the outset that these categories are not completely consistent with common usage. For example, Schumpeter is not considered an Austrian for the purposes of this study, despite the Austrian flavor of much of his work, since on the issue of the calculation debate he adopts what I call a "neoclassical" view. Similarly the "flaws" in the neoclassical perspective cannot be attributed to every contemporary theorist who considers himself an heir to Walras and Marshall and indeed may not have been contained in the original neoclassical theorists either. Rather I am referring to a tendency of many economists, notably the market socialists themselves, to, in a sense, take the formal equilibrium theory too seriously. Those neoclassical economists who see this formal theory as providing only heuristic aids to economics may be closer to what is being called the "Austrian" point of view.

itself these research programs never came into any fruitful confrontation.) Little will be said directly about the differences between the Marxian and neoclassical perspectives.

I am primarily concerned with examining the underlying differences between the positions of the Austrian and neoclassical participants in the debate. Most histories of thought treat the Austrian tradition of economics, including the work of Menger, Wieser, and Böhm-Bawerk, as a branch of neoclassical economics parallel to the Marshallian and Walrasian branches, and it seems that this was the view of the Austrian economists themselves at the time of the debate. I will argue, however, that what appeared to be subtle differences of expression within one school have evolved into major issues of contention between distinct Austrian and neoclassical perspectives. Theoretical developments in both academic traditions that have taken place since the debate will be used on occasion to help clarify some of these differences, but the central subject of research will be the articles and books, already cited, that comprise the initial debate.

Although a closely parallel debate in German in the 1920s and 1930s[7] and somewhat related controversies in Russian over the applicability of the "law of value" to socialism are of interest, this study will concentrate almost exclusively on the English-language controversy. The German debate in almost all respects involves the same arguments that have reappeared in the later English discussions, and the Russian debates (for example, Felker 1966), although fascinating in their own right, have rarely focused on the central issues of the calculation argument as set out here.

This study's scope will also be limited in that it will refer almost exclusively to economic theories of socialism and very little to socialist

---

[7] I have had to rely on the English-language account of this literature that is found in Baldwin (1942), Hayek ([1935] 1948e, pp. 119–147), Halm (1935), and Hoff (1949). Before Mises's challenge, several Marxists proposed moneyless planning schemes: e.g., Bukharin and Preobrazhensky ([1919] 1966) and Neurath (1919), and at least one socialist, Eduard Heimann (1918) began to take up the question of price fixation under socialism. Many of the earliest responses to Mises attempted at first to salvage the Marxian moneyless economy by arguing for "calculation in kind"–e.g. Tschayanoff (1923)–whereas others rejected this but proposed some form of calculation on the basis of labor hours–e.g., Leichter ([1923] 1932). These positions were soon abandoned, in some cases,–for example, in Marschak (1923) and Karl Polanyi (1922; 1924), in favor of a rather vague decentralized syndicalism, but in most cases–e.g., Heimann (1922), Tisch (1932), and Zassenhaus ([1934] 1956) in favor of a neoclassical market socialist position closely resembling that of Lange. Rejoinders defending Mises's argument were submitted by Weil (1924) and by Mises himself (1923; 1928). See also Landauer (1923; 1931) and Kaldor (1932).

practice. Even where real-world socialism is examined,[8] the purpose will be primarily to develop an appropriate theoretical framework for (rather than to offer any particular historical evidence about) socialist experience. The prevailing view in comparative economics today – and in many ways this reflects an attitude of modern economics in general – is that the kind of "theoretical" disputes of which the calculation debate is a prime example are necessarily sterile. If we wish to learn something significant about the relative strengths and weaknesses of socialism and capitalism, it is argued, the thing to do is conduct empirical investigations of each, rather than postulate and compare unrealistic models of hypothetical systems.

But although the importance of empirical work cannot be doubted, in order for such investigations into the facts to be productive some essential theoretical issues must first be clarified. The most obvious of these is the question, Just what is meant by *capitalism* and *socialism?* As I have indicated in my references to Hayek and Drewnowski, each side of this controversy believes that the empirical evidence is consistent with its viewpoint. In my view, these different assessments of empirical evidence are not rooted in either side's reluctance to consider the real world but their divergent interpretations of facts that in themselves are not disputed. As the famous philosopher of science Sir Karl Popper has ably demonstrated (1972), all facts are to one degree or another theory-laden and must be placed into a conceptual framework to be rendered meaningful. Many of the fundamental issues of contention in comparative economics are more matters of alternative theoretical analyses of facts than disputes over the facts themselves.

Moreover, the common conclusion that economic theory is barren is itself a reaction to a particular concept of economic theory – that of neoclassical economics – which is not shared by Marxian and Austrian approaches. Neoclassical economic theory may indeed be sterile, but other theoretical frameworks may be able to go further than neoclassical theory can go in yielding substantive conclusions about the real world. When "economic theory" appears barren, perhaps our response ought not to be to abandon explicit theorizing in order to study the facts (thereby necessarily relying on unexamined implicit theoretical concepts) but rather to develop better economic theories that may be more useful in equipping empirical researchers with the conceptual tools that they require for their important studies.

---

[8] See Chapter 6 for some discussion of the relationship between the calculation argument and the historical experience of central planning.

This book is exclusively concerned with the microeconomic rather than macroeconomic aspects of central planning theory. Although during the calculation debate itself very little was said about macroeconomic planning (the main exception being some contributions of Maurice Dobb), subsequently macroeconomic planning has become a substantial if not the dominant part of the theory of central economic planning. But since this study must confine itself to the main arguments of the rivals in the calculation debate, space will not permit an examination of the subsequent flourishing of macroeconomic themes in the literature. Enough will be said, however, to suggest that recourse to macroeconomic arguments will not leave central planning advocates completely immune to the Misesian challenge.[9]

Although participants on both sides of the controversy repeatedly introduced issues that had little to do with the calculation arguments per se, this study will concentrate on the central issue raised in Mises's challenge in 1920. Thus little will be said here about the controversy between Dobb and Lerner over the extent to which a free market in consumer goods is desirable or about the claims by Mises and Hayek that attempts to bring about socialism necessarily lead to political tyranny. Only issues that bear directly on the calculation argument will be addressed.

The outline of the standard account of the debate that is presented in the next section of this chapter (followed by a summary of my "alternative" account of the debate) serves as the point of departure for the rest of the study. In my analysis of the standard account, I emphasize six specific elements that are of special importance for understanding the debate. The selection of topics and the placement of emphasis in the entire book is shaped by the discussion here of the standard account. The last section of this chapter will tie these various points of criticism together under a single theme concerning the nature of economic rivalry.

There is one aspect of the standard account with which I have no quarrel. This is the assumption that all of the contributions to the debate were intended as either answers to or defenses of the argument that Ludwig von Mises articulated in his 1920 essay entitled "Economic Calculation in the Socialist Commonwealth" ([1920], 1935). Thus it is necessary to begin by examining the concept of economic planning that dominated economic thinking at the time

---

[9] In chapter 4 of my forthcoming book on national economic planning (1985), I apply the central argument of this book to the notion of aggregative or macroeconomic planning.

when Mises's challenge was first issued and toward which it was primarily aimed – that is, the notion of central planning that is contained in Karl Marx's critique of capitalism. Chapter 2 is therefore an examination of the concept of the socialist economy that is implicit in Marx's critique of capitalism.

Chapter 3 describes Mises's original challenge, mainly as it pertains to Marx's system. Although the Marxist notion of planning is drastically different from the market socialism that emerged in the course of the debate, Mises's initial statement of the "calculation problem" can be seen as posing a serious challenge to all proposals for planning.

According to the standard account, Mises denied that socialism could allocate resources rationally, even under the assumption of static economic conditions. This, I contend, has been a complete misunderstanding. Chapter 4 takes up arguments for, against, and irrelevant to the question of the practicality of central planning that emerged during the debate and that, by making certain basic assumptions about the "data" being "given" for the use of central planners, essentially begged the question raised by Mises's challenge. Whereas the standard account of the debate views these arguments that assume static economic conditions as either unheralded precursors of or effective responses to Mises's challenge, I regard them as an unfortunate detour from the main issue at hand. Besides differentiating the various "static" arguments that have been associated with the debate in Chapter 4, I discuss the reasons why none of these approaches captures the essence of Mises's calculation argument.

According to the standard account, the main advocates of Mises's position, F. A. Hayek and Lionel Robbins, faced with the unassailable logic of some of the static arguments, retreated to a less extreme formulation, which in turn was answered by the market socialists, notably Oskar Lange in his famous 1936 essay, "On the Economic Theory of Socialism" ([1936] 1964). In Chapter 5 I argue that on the contrary it was Lange and his school who retreated, and that although many tried, they did not succeed in extricating themselves from the constraints of static analysis.

All of this is not to say that the complete argument against central economic planning was contained in that original 1920 essay. Later participants in the controversy benefited from having to answer a variety of proposals for planning that were far more fully developed than the proposals that Mises was evaluating. As a result, the calculation argument has undergone some very important elaboration since its first articulation. Chapter 6 will take up the attempt by the Austrian economists – Mises, Robbins, and Hayek – to direct the argument at the "competitive" solution. This work inspired some of the most important analyses òf the nature and function of economic competition, viewed as a dynamic process. Unfortunately some of the clearest articulations of this dynamic perspective, although contained in embryo in earlier writings, were clarified by Hayek only later in his seminal work on knowledge in the 1940s and 1960s and have not yet had much impact on the economic profession's view of the calculation debate.

The final chapter briefly summarizes the results of this reexamination, concluding that although the calculation debate raised many important issues, its participants tended to talk past each other. Since, by all accounts, the debators were focusing upon the initial challenge to central planning by Mises, and since, by my account, his challenge has been fundamentally misunderstood, my conclusion is that the Mises's argument should be seriously reconsidered.

The standard account of the debate

Central planning theory before 1920

Before the debate, it is generally agreed, very little attention had been paid to the economics of socialism.[10] Much of what did exist in such literature failed to take into account the fact that some form of market prices and some use of money were indispensable for rational planning. The failure of the War Communism period in the Soviet Union (1918–21) is often cited as evidence that many early socialists erred by underestimating the importance of prices for central planning. Although the fact that War Communism failed is rarely denied, many accounts blame this on exogenous causes rather than on the deliberate policy of the Lenin regime to destroy market relations and the use of money. Köhler, for example, refers to War Communism as "a period of general confusion, civil war, and popular unrest about the widespread use of brutal force" (1966, p. 124). But the view that is more often expressed is that at least with respect to the attempt to abolish money, the Soviet regime was in error. Thus in Dobb's view "it can be taken as tolerably certain that the difficulties of 'war communism,' amounting in some cases almost to disaster, which were so vividly in evidence in 1920, were not merely

---

[10] Lekachman's comment that early Marxism "gave no notion of how the future socialist society would be organized" (1959, p. 394) reflects the standard view on this issue.

incidental to the system." He regards the destruction of money as a key factor in this failure (1928, pp. 130–1).[11] The view is occasionally expressed that the concept of socialism without prices was a straw man fabricated by Mises and Hayek and never seriously held by socialists. Lavigne, for example, contends that the idea that "plan and market are mutually exclusive . . . was developed mainly by contemporary liberal economists during the early period of socialism in Soviet Russia" and refers to Mises and Hayek in this regard (1974, pp. xii, 377).[12] The more common view, however, is that at least some early socialists had to be taught their economics by neoclassical economists. In any case, few modern socialists believe that prices, money, and markets for at least consumer goods and labor can be dispensed with until scarcity itself is eliminated.

Mises's critique of central planning

Mises's calculation argument is generally credited with having shaken socialists out of their neglect of the economics of planning, but few commentators on the debate are willing to grant him much more than this stimulative accomplishment.[13] His argument is usually interpreted in neoclassical terms, as a denial of what Schumpeter ([1942] 1950, p. 185) calls the "logical credentials" of socialism. The usual method of interpreting Mises's argument is first to summarize it and then to offer a detailed digression on equilibrium theory and welfare economics to explain what he meant. Thus Sherman (1969b, pp. 262–3, 268) writes:

An evaluation of Mises' objection requires a brief explanation of how economists define "rational" prices and "rational" planning. Rational prices are defined as those which lead to an "optimal" pattern of outputs and utility of each output and the marginal cost of each input. As early as 1897 the economist Pareto made explicit the conditions necessary to obtain an

[11] Other writers who were not at all sympathetic to the Mises-Hayek argument nevertheless admit that a completely moneyless economy cannot work and cite this period in Russian history to illustrate the point. See for example, Wootton (1935) and Misra (1972, p. 139).

[12] Lavigne, Mandel (1970, pp. 632–3), Lange (1934; 1945), Sweezy (1936, p. 423), and others have denied that this model of socialism is implicit in Marx, but the next chapter will suggest that their arguments are not very convincing.

[13] An exception to this common view is Blodgett (1979, pp. 133–47), who argues that Mises's claim that planning without a market would be arbitrary has become accepted by "ever so many economists." It seems that Blodgett has in mind one retreat – from Marxism to market socialism – whereas most commentators on the controversy are referring to a second retreat – from Mises's "theoretical" to Hayek's "practical" argument against socialism – when they say Mises was wrong.

optimum welfare situation for all individuals, given the existing technology and the existing distribution of income.

We should be aware that Mises and Hayek attack the actual or realized operation of an imperfect planned socialist system from the viewpoint of a pure and perfect competitive private enterprise system.

Lerner similarly asserts that "Mises . . . assumes the pricing system transformed unaltered from a perfectly competitive economy" and contends that this "dogmatic" viewpoint considers "sacrilegious" any attempt to "improve on a 'perfect' price mechanism" (1934b, p. 55). Bliss (1972, p. 91), Landauer (1947, pp. 56–7), and Sweezy (1936, p. 423) translate Mises's argument into Walrasian-Paretian terms, whereas the perfect competition assumption that all agents are price takers is attributed to the Mises-Hayek position by Köhler (1966, p. 72) and Misra (1972, pp. 140–5). The word *efficiency* is invariably understood by neoclassical theorists to mean "Pareto-optimality," for example in Eidem and Viotti (1978, p. 96), Koopmans and Montias (1971, p. 44), and in Tangri (1967, pp. vi–vii). Thus Mises's argument is read as an assertion that rational economic calculation without private ownership of the means of production is not only "impracticable" but is "theoretically" impossible even under static conditions.[14] The impulse to interpret Mises in this way is so strong that it sometimes persists alongside powerful contradictory evidence. Thus Snavely includes in his fine textbook on comparative systems a clear essay by Armentano (1969, p. 134) that contains an accurate description of Mises's position: "Mises notes . . . that economic calculation ceases to be a problem in the stationary state or in equilibrium. But he considers this fact to be quite irrelevant to the problem of economic calculation under socialism, since 'equilibrium' is an imaginary construct and certainly not obtainable in a real world where economic data change and uncertainty exists." Nonetheless Snavely proceeds to repeat the same neoclassical version of Mises's position ten pages later in the book: "Lange next turned his attention to the arguments of Hayek and Robbins who, unlike Mises, accepted the theoretical possibility of Barone's approach."

Similarly Goldman (1971, p. 11) repeats the standard account, despite his inclusion four pages later of an excerpt from Mises ([1922] 1936, pp. 119–22, 137–42) in which the latter expressly states that socialism could work in theory under static conditions.

[11] See, for example, Bergson (1948), Dahl and Lindblom (1953, pp. 210–11), Dobb (1955, p. 74), Drewnowski (1961), Elliot (1973, p. 243), Knight (1936, p. 263), Köhler (1966, p. 68), Landauer (1947, p. 52), Schumpeter ([1942] 1950, pp. 172–86), and Tangri (1967, p. vi).

Some discussants say that the practical experience of socialist planning in the USSR refutes Mises's claim;[15] many contend that either Lange's or Barone's argument answers Mises; but there is a remarkably wide consensus that Mises was wrong. Elliot (1973, p. 293), for example, refers to this consensus, citing Schumpeter ([1942] 1950), and concludes: "Private ownership is not now regarded as a *logically necessary* system as a social process for economic calculation." Referring to Lange's model, Dahl and Lindblom (1953, p. 211) say that "as an analytical model in economic theory, this picture of a socialist price system is valid; the consensus of economists is that Von Mises was wrong in not granting at least this much." Köhler (1966, p. 69) agrees, asserting that "clearly . . . Von Mises had gone too far." In fact it is generally stated that Lange and his school not only answered Mises but answered him on his own terms[16] and thoroughly proved that Mises's argument was invalid. Harris (1949, p. 4), and Pickersgill and Pickersgill (1974, p. 306), use the word *demonstrated* to describe Lange's answer to Mises's argument; Seligman (1971, p. 109) calls the market socialist approach "the definitive response"; and Rima (1972, pp. 350–1) refers to Lange's "proof." Little (1950, p. 253) contends that "at a logical level Mises's challenge was completely answered by socialist economists, principally Mr. Lange and Professor Lerner."

Lekachman (1959, pp. 396–7) writes:

Oskar Lange . . . proved that a Central Planning Board could impose rules upon socialist managers which allocated resources and set prices as efficiently as a capitalist society of the purest stripe, and much more efficiently than the capitalist communities of experience.

Landauer (1947, p. 51) asserts:

These socialist authors, primarily Oskar Lange and H. D. Dickinson, have done an excellent job in refuting some of the arguments by which the possibility of value calculation without the institution of a market had been denied. They showed clearly that the 'real' process through which the market arrives at an equilibrium price and the calculating process which a central agency must apply for the same purpose have traits in common which make it impossible to question the practicability of advance calculation of values by a planning board.

---

[15] See, for example, Misra (1972, p. 188) and Tangri (1967, pp. vii–viii).

[16] Goldman (1971, p. 10) argues that Lange and Lerner provided "an answer acceptable to economists" when they "decided to meet von Mises on his own terms." Little (1950, p. 254) concurs: "Thus, and with some irony, the static welfare-theory armament of the supporters of laissez-faire was seized by their opponents, and effectively used against them."

Heilbroner (1970, p. 88), after summarizing the Mises-Hayek argument, concludes that

this line of attack against socialism did not fare very well. In the mid-1930s it was effectively demolished by Oscar Lange, the brilliant Polish economist then at Harvard.

Lange demonstrated . . . that a Central Planning Board could indeed plan rationally for the simple reason that it would receive exactly the same information from a socialized economic system as did entrepreneurs under a market system.

Equation solving

It is generally held that Enrico Barone's formal equilibrium argument had already established the "theoretical" possibility of socialism in 1908, long before Mises had issued his challenge, by showing that in principle the central planning board could determine prices by solving a set of simultaneous equations, much as this is done in practice by the market. Such early market socialists as Dickinson (1933) merely reiterated Barone's demonstration that the same general equilibrium logic of choice that Walras had developed to analyze capitalism could be applied to socialism.[17]

The issue of impracticability

The view is common that Hayek's and Robbins's arguments were substantially different from Mises's, constituting a retreat to the acceptance of the "theoretical possibility" but a denial of the "practicability" of socialism. The essence of their argument is taken to be that solving Barone's equations was not, in 1935, feasible as a method of central planning. Goldman (1971, p. 11) describes this "retreat":

Initially the argument focused around the feasibility of one system versus another. It was eventually accepted that both the Lange-Lerner and input-output systems could theoretically answer the economic question about the allocation of resources and manpower. Then the debate shifted to a dispute over which solution would be the most efficient one.

Misra (1972, pp. 131, 140) is unclear in his interpretation of Mises, but accepts the standard view when he says that Hayek and Robbins have pointed out that although a mathematical solution is theoretically

---

[17] The standard view of the significance of Barone's argument is contained in such works as Köhler (1966, p. 69), Lekachman (1959, pp. 394–5) Seligman (1971, pp. 107–8), Schumpeter ([1942] 1950, p. 173), and Sherman (1969b, p. 264).

correct, it does not provide a practical method of deciding how to use capital equipment. Landauer (1947, p. 57) puts the point clearly:

Hayek, relinquishing the old Mises position, conceded the formal possibility of planning, but maintained that the planning board would never finish solving the innumerable equations through which the value of individual commodities would have to be calculated.

Sherman (1969b, p. 265) agrees:

In the next stage of the debate, Hayek admits that *in theory* the planners might accumulate all the millions of pieces of necessary information and might then solve all the millions of equations necessary to make an optimal decision. *In practice*, Hayek argues, no conceivable force of planners could actually gather all of the various kinds of information from every factory and farm, and from every private and public consumer. Furthermore, *in practice*, even with all of the information, it would take hundreds of years to solve correctly all of the equations for just one year's plan.[18]

Thus, advances in mathematics and computer science since the thirties are presumed to render this Hayek-Robbins argument obsolete. Cave (1980, p. vii), for example, writes:

The potential impact of computers on economic planning is enormous. To appreciate this one only has to recall one of the arguments made in the debate in the 1930s on the feasibility of central planning. It was asserted then that an efficient allocation of resources in a centrally planned economy was inconceivable because such an allocation would require the solution of "millions of equations." At that time, of course, no electronic computers were available. Today the situation is quite different and the computational objection would have much less force.

Ames and Neuberger (1977, p. 209) take seriously the idea that "it will become possible to replace inefficient administrators by computers, to improve the knowledge of production processes by using economists, and to reallocate resources so as to improve the workings of the economy without introducing (uncontrolled) market processes."

Hayek is sometimes also credited with having raised some important issues concerning the centralization of knowledge, risk, and managerial incentives, though these are generally regarded as additional and rather ad hoc considerations to be taken into account by central planners, rather than as extensions of Mises's arguments against central planning.[19]

---

[18] See also Elliot (1973, p. 243), Harris (1949, p. 5). Köhler (1966, p. 79), Schumpeter ([1942] 1950, p. 185), and Tangri (1967, p. vi).

[19] For example, Ward (1967b, p. 25) acknowledges the seminal importance of Hayek's contributions on knowledge without recognizing either the roots of these contributions in Mises or their profound significance in support of the calculation argument. See also Chapter 6 of this study.

Trial and error

Lange and Fred M. Taylor are credited with having demonstrated not only that, as Barone had shown, a determinate equilibrium can be defined for socialism, but also, contrary to Hayek and Robbins, that the central planning board could "find" the set of prices needed for equilibrium by a process of trial and error. Thus it is claimed that socialism is practicable in principle. Although confident assertions that the Lange model is valid "in theory" or "as a model" – such as are made by Dahl and Lindblom (1953, p. 211) and by Köhler (1966, pp. 69, 71) – abound in comparative economics texts, it is frequently admitted that this model may not be workable in reality. Sikes (1940, p. 280) remarks that Lange's solution "may be a basis for economic calculation, but it is scarcely a basis for effective economic planning." Lekachman (1959, p. 397), after stating that Mises has been proven wrong, goes on to assert: "It need scarcely be said that economic planning in Russia, or anywhere else, fails rather completely to conform to Lange's model." It is taken for granted that the evident impracticability of this solution is irrelevant to its potency against Mises's "theoretical" critique.

Conclusion

The implication that is usually drawn from the debate is that economic theory per se cannot decide the great controversy between capitalism and socialism. Neither system is as praiseworthy in practice as the debators depicted them in theory. Because the standard view of the debate stresses the formal similarity of capitalism and socialism under static assumptions and believes this to have been the analytic framework of the whole controversy, the conclusion is usually expressed that both economic systems are equally valid "in theory." Thus Liebhafsky (1963) emphasizes the idea that exactly the same (static) welfare conditions apply to each, and Dalton (1974, p. 135) says that Lange, Lerner, and Taylor showed that the rules for optimization are general.

Sherman (1969b, pp. 267–8) summarizes the conclusion of the debate:

If there is pure and perfect competition under market socialism, it turns out that the resulting allocation of resources is exactly as efficient as under pure and perfect competition in private enterprise.

When we examine the pure and perfect form of each of these, we find that *in theory* they are equally capable of reaching a Pareto optimum condition.

Jesse Markham, in his "editor's introduction" to Gruchy's *Comparative Economic Systems* (1966, p. v) and in that book's only reference to the calculation debate, can find little of value in the controversy's "rather bland intellectual diet of 'theoretical' capitalism and socialism," and he summarizes the debate in these terms:

Advocates of private enterprise typically argued that, in theory, a freely functioning market economy could assure society of economic efficiency without exacting the price of bureaucratic bungling, caprice, or plain stupidity, the inevitable concomitants of socialistic central planning. Proponents of socialism with equal irrelevance, argued that the smoothly functioning blueprint of central planning boards eliminated the injustices and inefficiencies of private monopoly power and restraints on trade, the inescapable features of capitalistic economies. Since almost any system in theory can be made to appear superior to another system in practice, the debate was at best unrewarding and at worst misleading.

Suranyi-Unger (1952, p. 40) remarks that in the debate "some of the abstract results have been splendid. Yet they have been largely confined to the realm of economic theory."[20] Some critics point out that the efficiency criteria of the debate were developed under strictly static welfare assumptions, whereas under more realistic, nonstatic assumptions neither system can boast the virtues of Pareto-optimality.[21] Most economists agree that there are strengths and weaknesses in each system, some stressing that market socialism has the potential of improving upon capitalism, others emphasizing that although socialism is theoretically unassailable, it still has other major deficiencies, notably the danger of bureaucratization, that are deemed to be outside the province of economic theory and belong either to other disciplines or to empirical rather than theoretical economics.[22]

For example, Sikes (1940, p. 281) asserts that "planning . . . has

---

[20] Similar comments that pure theory is sterile can be found in the accounts of the debate by Blodgett (1979, p. 147), Dahl and Lindblom (1953, p. 20), Eidem and Viotti (1978, pp. 92–3), Elliot (1973, p. 233), and Köhler (1966, pp. 4–5).

[21] See Baran (1952, p. 386), Bliss (1972, pp. 95–9), Dahl and Lindblom (1953, p. 211), Dobb (1955, p. 60, pp. 241–3), Hunt and Schwartz (1972), Köhler (1966, p. 78), Loucks (1957, p. 263), Radner (1968), Shackle (1972, p. 270), and Sweezy (1936). See also Veblen (1919).

[22] For example, when Balassa (1965, p. 17) concludes that "economic arguments are not sufficient to make a choice between economic systems," he suggests that we study the facts instead. One can agree with the spirit of this remark, but when theoretical confusion runs as deep as it does in the calculation debate, there is not the barest analytic framework with which to begin a study of the facts. The result in practice is that empirical researchers smuggle implicit theoretical assumptions into their work.

possibilities of regularizing production not present under capitalism," and Misra (1972, p. 151) claims more specifically that the
socialist state "has greater capacity to forecast" and "control uncertainty." Neuberger and Duffy (1976, p. 96) argue that the advantage of more centralized over less centralized systems is that in
the former "the optimal solution can be reached more rapidly,
thereby avoiding a waste of resources and the possibility of disequilibrating dynamic processes leading to divergence rather than
convergence."

Landauer (1947, pp. 62–3) has a similar idea in mind when he
contends that "it is a crude method to search for an equilibrium by
experimentally varying all the determinants until they fit together,
and . . . it is infinitely more economical to carry out these variations
on paper than in reality." He argues that "in an unplanned economy
we cannot get very far by paper calculation, because we know too
little about the reactions of others to the same problems" (1947, p.
60). Only when these reactions are constrained by a preconceived,
conscious plan can such "internal uncertainties" be eliminated. Dobb
(1935b, p. 535) similarly contends that "the advantage of a planned
economy *per se* consists in removing the uncertainties inherent in a
market with diffused and autonomous decisions, or it consists in
nothing at all." Solo (1967, p. 48) makes the same point but goes on
to argue that there are other kinds of uncertainty that cannot be
eliminated under central planning.

Baldwin's summary of the debate typifies the standard view in its
statement that before the calculation debate, the controversy over
socialism versus capitalism was carried out in the fields of ethics and
politics and that it returned to these fields after the brief foray into
economics proved that from the standpoint of economic theory
there is nothing to favor one system over the other. "The blow by
Mises, Hayek, and Robbins seems to have been parried by the oppo-
sition, and once again the war rages on its original front – the political and ethical" (1942, p. 115).

Many discussions, after pronouncing economic theory incapable of
judging between capitalism and socialism, resort to ethical and psychological issues such as whether bureaucrats will be given enough
"incentives" or "motivation" to fulfill the rule-following tasks Lange
assigns them; examples of this approach are Köhler (1966, pp. 78–
9), Pickersgill and Pickersgill (1974, p. 310), and Schumpeter ([1942]
1950, pp. 205–10). Although the question of incentives is closely
connected to the calculation argument, it will be argued in Chapter 6
that it is related in a way that is quite distinct from matters of psy-

chology and more appropriately considered a matter of the theory of ownership in economics and law.

But most economists criticize theorists on both sides of the controversy for dealing on too abstract a level and for illogically comparing idealized versions of one system with the practical weaknesses of its opposite. A related reaction to the debate is the assumption that the participants focused too much on alternative isms, that the controversy was a stale quarrel over unworkable extremes (plan versus market), whereas contemporary economists agree that both institutions are indispensable and that the modern dispute is only over the proper mix of the two.[23] Eckstein (1971, p. 3) concludes that the calculation debate "led to an increasing recognition that the preoccupation with comparisons based on 'isms' were likely to yield over simple and simplistic insights into the character of economic systems. In contrast, comparisons of models and realities tended to focus on the complexity and variety of living systems and their departure from the theoretical ideal." Suranyi-Unger (1952) goes so far as to call for "A Crusade against 'Isms.' "[24]

A very diverse group of modern economists – including transition Marxists, post-Keynesians, and neoclassical welfare economists – agree that central planning should consist of a judicious mixture of centralized decision making and semiautonomous market institutions.[25] Kornai's (1959, p. 225) comment is typical:

In principle it is possible to sketch out a system in which all economic choices, including even the distribution of consumer goods to individuals and peoples' choices of occupation, are governed by instructions from the centre. It is also possible to imagine a system in which the central authorities of the State refrain completely from all interference in economic life, everything being governed by the market mechanism. In practice, some mixture of these two is the inevitable rule . . . This is also true in regard to socialist economies based on public ownership of the means of production.

Although an explicit critique of this body of contemporary market socialist theory would take us beyond the scope of this study, my

[23] The following comment by Bliss (1972, p. 92) is typical: "The protagonists on both sides were debating, without realizing it, about the Economics of Fairyland, and different Fairylands at that."

[24] This is the title of the first section of Chapter 5 in his 1952 book. See also Dahl and Lindblom (1953, p. 4), Dalton (1974, p. 112), and Golob (1954).

[25] See, for example, Beckwith (1949; 1955), Bornstein (1973), Brus (1972; 1975), Dunlop and Federenko (1969), Hall (1937), Heimann (1937), Kaser and Portes (1971), Konnik (1966), Landauer (1947, pp. 36–40; 1964), Lange (1962), Leeman (1963), Mandel (1970, p. 636), Marcuse (1961, p. 151), Meade (1976), Montias (1963), Myrdal (1960, p. 15), Porwit (1967), Sik (1967a; 1967b; 1976, pp. 193–5), Turetskii (1967), Wakar and Zielinsky (1963), and Wootton (1945, pp. 127–8).

alternative interpretation of the calculation debate contains the basis for a substantial argument against this modern view.[26]

An alternative account of the debate

Central planning theory before 1920

The standard view is not sufficiently cognizant of the extent to which the Marxian model of central planning was dominant – if not particularly explicit – in socialist economics before 1920. It is true that most Marxian socialists avoided any direct discussion of the workings of proposed socialist institutions, but a very definite idea of their concept of central planning is nonetheless evident from their critique of the "anarchy" of capitalist production. Both the dismal failure of the attempt to abolish markets and money during the War Communism period in the USSR and the arguments of Mises and Hayek make this early socialist concept of central planning very difficult to defend today. But this largely rejected early vision of central planning is the most consistent and important of any that have been developed, and therefore its abandonment marks a far more serious retreat by socialists than the standard view suggests.

Mises's critique of central planning

In my view, Mises was not denying the validity of the "pure logic of choice" for socialism; he was, on the contrary, insisting that central planners must find a way to apply this kind of logic to socialism or they will be doomed to calculational chaos and be unable to use resources efficiently. In addition, Mises was definitely not making an equilibrium argument and was aware that there is no calculation problem under static assumptions. His argument was primarily directed at proponents of Marxian socialism and thus he was primarily concerned to argue that money prices (not some objective measure

---

[26] To date, the best overall summary in English of the debate from this alternative perspective is Hoff (1949). Elements of this interpretation can be found in Armentano (1969), Bradley (1981), Buchanan (1969), Ellman (1978; 1979), Eucken (1950, pp. 333–4), Gregory (1933), Halm (1935; 1951), Hayek (1935; 1948f; 1978, pp. 232–46), Hutt (1940), Kirzner (1978), Knight (1940), Murrell (1983), Nutter (1974), O'Driscoll (1977), Ostrom (1976), Pejovich (1976), Plant ([1937] 1974), Polanyi (1951), Reese (1980), Roberts (1971), Rothbard (1962; 1976), Sirkin (1968), Steele (1978), Thirlby (1973a; 1973b;), Vaughn (1980b), and Wiseman (1973a; 1973b).

of value such as labor hours) are necessary for rational calculation. However, contrary to the standard view, I believe that Mises's argument is fully applicable to all forms of socialism that advocate common or state ownership of the means of production. Properly interpreted, his challenge has yet to be adequately answered by advocates of central planning.

Equation solving

The alternative account views Barone's argument as fully consistent with, but much less complete than, Mises's challenge. Barone simply established the formal similarity between socialism and capitalism under static conditions: If the number of (independent) equations equal the number of unknowns, the system is determinate. Mises maintained that such equations were inapplicable to the real world of continuous change. The early market socialists such as Dickinson (1933) did not merely reiterate Barone's formal argument but promoted equation solving as a practicable procedure for central planning, which Barone had argued was impossible.

The issue of impracticability

In my view, the central arguments advanced by Hayek and Robbins did not constitute a retreat from Mises's position but rather a clarification, redirecting the challenge to the later versions of central planning that had introduced the ideas of "equation solving" and "trial and error" as methods of establishing prices. Although comments by both Hayek and Robbins about the computational difficulties of the equation-solving approach were responsible for misleading interpretations of their arguments, in fact their main contributions were fully consistent with Mises's challenge and were similarly unanswered.

Trial and error

According to the alternative account, the "trial and error" response to Hayek and Robbins was based on a close analogy with the "perfect competition" model, which itself does not explain dynamic price adjustment under realistic conditions of change. Thus, contrary to the standard view, Lange's model does not constitute an answer to the Hayek-Robbins argument.

Conclusion

The usual conclusion that economic theory cannot decide any important issues in comparative economics is valid only if by "economic theory" is meant strictly static equilibrium analysis. It is possible that the broader Austrian concept of an economic theory that deals with change can shed considerable light on issues in comparative economics and can help us to understand many of the practical problems of the mixed economies of both the East and the West. The Austrians did not limit discussion to the extreme isms. They provided informative theoretical contrasts between mixed economy models and both "pure" extremes – free-market capitalism and socialism.

Rivalry and central planning

The central focus of this reinterpretation of the debate will be the notion of economic rivalry. Economic rivalry is the clash of human purposes. It is that aspect of market relations that is revealed, for example, every time one market participant bids away resources from another. When one competitor undercuts the price of a rival; when one consumer buys the last retail item in stock before another consumer gets there; when one inventor beats another to the punch on a profitable innovation – that is economic rivalry. It represents a struggle of some members of society against others, a struggle in which one person's gain in some sense represents the other's loss. Not all rivalrous struggle leads to beneficial consequences in society. The rivalry between a murderer or thief and the rest of society, for example, does harm not only to the immediate victims but to the overall social order as well. But the Austrian school contended that the specific form of rivalry that is a necessary component of the entrepreneurial market process leads to a beneficial coordinating process that makes complex capitalist production in a monetary system possible.

At the heart of the debate is a confusion between two fundamentally divergent views of "competition": (1) the rivalrous competitive process of the Austrians (similar to the classical notion), and (2) the neoclassical notion of a nonrivalrous, static, competitive equilibrium.[27] In contrast to the heavy stress in classical economics on the harmony of the market in which the pursuit of one's self-interest leads

---

[27] See Kirzner (1973; 1979), Armentano (1978), Lachmann (1977), McNulty (1967; 1968), Reekie (1979), Recktenwald (1978, p. 68), and Brozen (1975).

to the benefit of his fellows, the Austrian idea of rivalry – especially as developed by Mises's student Israel Kirzner in his theory of entrepreneurship – represents explicit acknowledgment of the rather unharmonious element in competition. Some competitors are squeezed out by their rivals, some consumers get priced out of certain markets by rival buyers: In short, some plans are necessarily disappointed by the carrying out of rival plans by others. The Austrians agree with the classical economists that the rivalrous market process leads to beneficial results in the form of a spontaneous order of plan coordination, but they do not claim that this process achieves anything like the perfect coordination that seems to be implicit in the classical "long-run" equilibrium model or more explicit in modern equilibrium models.

The original Marxian paradigm saw rivalry as an inherent aspect of a market economy and the price system, condemned capitalism for having this rivalrous attribute, and proposed central planning as a nonrivalrous remedy. This view sees rivalry as the consequence of independently devised production and consumption plans that are less than fully coordinated with each other, so that some individuals or firms discover, after the fact, that the project on which they have been working turns out to have been a mistake. Rather than permit this "antisocial" struggle among members of society for shares of the social product, a struggle in which the wealthy have an unfair advantage, Marx conceived of central planning as a way of precoordinating productive plans in society. One of the fundamental "contradictions" that Marx found in the capitalist mode of production was the fact that although on the one hand it makes members of society increasingly dependent on one another in a complex world system of production, on the other hand it leaves the crucial production decisions to independent and thus contending interests. Under capitalism, people are in perpetual "battle" with one another in an activity – social production – upon which it would seem we ought to be able to cooperate nonrivalrously. Marx believed that the natural evolution of capitalism, with a gradually increasing concentration of capital into larger and fewer separate planning entities, would pave the way for the expropriation of the means of production by "the associated workers," to then be employed cooperatively according to a single, unified plan.

Mises's challenge can be seen as an argument for the necessity of a particular kind of rivalry in order to achieve complex social production. Essentially agreeing with Marxism that markets are intrinsically rivalrous, Mises and the Austrians assert that this (or some other less

beneficial) form of rivalry is an ineradicable element of social coopera-
tion with advanced production. The nature of decision making in
economic production is complex in the Hayekian sense of being a
spontaneous order more intricate than any of its constituent minds
could possibly design. Thus numerous plans have to be made simultaneously, and, being necessarily interdependent, have to be in contention with one another to some degree. If this is true, then the fundamental question becomes not whether to permit rivalry or not but
rather what forms of rivalry can be prohibited with beneficial results,
and how. The entrepreneurial market process requires certain forms
of rivalrous activity, such as outbidding one's competitor, but yields
extremely beneficial results: It generates the continuously changing
structure of knowledge about the more effective ways of combining the
factors of production. This knowledge is created in decentralized form
and dispersed through the price system to coordinate the market's
diverse and independent decision makers. There is no way, Mises
claimed, in which this knowledge can be generated without rivalry –
that is, if all production plans are constrained in advance by being
precoordinated under a single plan. Market prices are seen as both the
consequences of this entrepreneurial rivalry and as the guides,
through economic calculation in profit/loss accounting, for decisions
that are made to achieve a more rational use of scarce resources.

The neoclassical paradigm, represented by the market socialists in
the debate, has recognized and elaborated upon this latter guiding
role of prices but has largely ignored their rivalrous underpinning.
Models of static competitive equilibrium banish economic rivalry
from the scene and employ the construct of a (centralized) Walrasian
auctioneer to adjust the prices that the actual participants passively
accept as "parametric." Within this essentially static framework it
seems quite plausible to imagine a central planning bureau fulfilling
the auctioneer's duties. But, as is being increasingly recognized today,
this neoclassical price adjustment model is inadequate for dealing
with actual market behavior, and many of the same criticisms that
present-day Austrian economists are leveling against this model can
be leveled with equal force against modern central planning theory.[28]

---

[28] For example, see High (1980), Kirzner (1973; 1979), Rizzo (1978; 1979), Shackle
(1972), and White (1978). The usual neoclassical procedure of coping with uncertainty by reducing it to risk is evident in such contributions as Eidem and Viotti
(1978, p. 47), Kornai (1974), Luch (1959), Mack (1971, pp. 30, 51), Morgan (1964),
and Sengupta (1972); in fact even risk is ignored in most planning models that
have been developed to date. See Blitzer, Clark, and Taylor (1975, pp. 35, 81, 218,
231, 304–5).

But the market socialists did not clearly discuss whether and to what extent rivalry would be permitted in their models, and indeed in places contradicted themselves on the issue. This crucial ambiguity has seriously hampered most efforts to understand and respond to their arguments. This study will try to alleviate this problem by sharply distinguishing between two fundamentally different but equally plausible interpretations of the market socialist position in the debate.

The first interpretation, the "mathematical solution" (described mainly in Chapter 4), views the market socialists as assuming away the problem of rivalry and proposing a nonrivalrous static price system in the hopes of simulating a competitive equilibrium. The second interpretation[29] (discussed in Chapter 5), views the market socialists as introducing genuinely rivalrous competition into their models without, however, being aware of the serious implications of this, particularly with respect to the question of what "common ownership of the means of production" means if rivalrous competition is permitted. Each of these alternative interpretations fails, in its own way, to appreciate the rivalrous basis of the market process.

Thus the Marxists condemned rivalry, the Austrians asserted its necessity, and the neoclassical market socialists either assumed it away or failed to recognize the consequences of its introduction into their models. The reinterpretation of the calculation debate that is offered in this study will attempt to locate the fundamental difference among these paradigms in their disparate views of rivalry and try in that way to explain what the controversy was essentially about. My overall approach in this study will be to examine the original arguments of the participants in the debate in the light of the paradigmatic differences among them that have subsequently been elaborated. Some of these underlying differences have become clarified and explicit only in more recent contributions from representatives of the various relevant schools of thought. For example, modern central planning theory in the neoclassical tradition extends Lange's argument, just as modern Aus-

---

[29] This interpretation of the market socialists may actually bear more resemblance to the liberal reformists in Soviet and Eastern European economics, associated with the name of Liberman (1966a; 1966b; 1967; 1968; 1972), than it does to any of the participants in the calculation debate. See Balassa (1959), Brus (1972; 1975), Felker (1966), Gamarnikow (1968), Gatovsky (1962), Goldman (1958; 1960), Grossman (1960b), Holesevsky (1968), Kaser (1965), Kornai (1959), Liberman and Zhitnitskii (1968), McFarlane and Gordijew (1964), Neuberger (1966), Nove (1958a; 1958b; 1966), Revesz (1968), Sharpe (1965), Sherman (1969a), Sik (1967a; 1967b; 1976), Wilczynski (1970; 1973), and Zaleski (1967).

trian analysis of the entrepreneur clarifies Mises's. My hope is to improve our understanding of the earlier arguments in the light of their subsequent evolution without doing violence to the meaning of those original arguments.

There is always, of course, the potential danger that I have illegitimately read modern Austrian notions into the earlier Austrian contributions. Could not the changes in the later Austrians' arguments that I call "improvements" be interpreted as "retreats" from indefensible positions? Perhaps. But although I contend that Hayek's later contributions have altered and indeed immeasurably improved Mises's argument, I am also convinced that this improvement should be understood as essentially an elaboration of the meaning that Mises originally attached to his own words. In any case, I will offer textual evidence from the original essays to support this view.

The history of thought has proven itself capable of attaining the goal that modern philosophers of science (from Kuhnians to Lakatosians) all agree is the mark of a progressive research program: a new theory's capacity to explain the phenomena that the older theory could not. We can understand the fruits of past controversies in ways that their participants could not possibly have understood. We can take advantage of clarifications that only emerge in the rebuttal process.

It is one of the main themes of this study that economic rivalry among competitors in the market generates knowledge that no rival on his own could have possessed in the absence of that rivalry. This, as I think Michael Polanyi has shown, is but a special case of the way that knowledge in general grows, the way that progress is attained within the "Republic of Science" (1969, pp. 49–71). Scientific discovery is a process that fundamentally depends on contention among separate rivals (paradigms or research programs, for example). This process involves a balancing between the tugs and pulls of participants, a kind of "mutual authority" that within science is based on academic qualifications and in market processes is based on money-bidding power. The outcomes of such processes are necessarily unpredictable in advance of their actual working out or living through. They are what Hayek calls *discovery processes,* processes that can reveal new knowledge that the rivals who created it could not have had.

In applying this view of discovery processes to the debate itself, I have concluded that the Austrian economists have learned much by "living through" the calculation debate. Because they have had to cope with criticisms in past debates, they now have much better, clearer ways of putting their arguments. In short, reviewing the very process of this debate may, it is hoped, shed more light on its topics than any of its individual contributors could have.

CHAPTER 2

Marx's socialism: the critique of rivalry

The standard account of the calculation debate deprecates the first stage of the controversy (Marx versus Mises) relative to the second stage (Lange versus Hayek), arguing that the two initial positions were too extreme and unsystematic and were happily abandoned by the less "dogmatic" and more "rigorous" later participants. By the alternative view of the debate, the second stage, though instructive, was marked by much confusion, inconsistency, and irrelevance, whereas the first stage was the dramatic scene of the most important confrontation of the entire debate between two of its penetrating thinkers.[1]

The aim of this chapter is to reconstruct the context of socialist theory in which the calculation argument was born. This will require a substantial excursion into the Marxian perspective, but it will be a journey with a highly restricted purpose. Clearly no claim to an exhaustive survey of Marx's complex concept of socialism can be made here. Little will be said about his psychological, sociological, or philosophical case for or description of the socialist society. I am concerned here exclusively with some particular aspects of his "extreme" view of central economic planning, a view to which few contemporary socialists would subscribe in full. Since Mises directed his challenge primarily at Marx's concept (which at the time was still the dominant concept), its main outlines will have to be clarified before the challenge to it can be appreciated.

Marx's concept of socialist central planning, however, has an importance that transcends its role in the calculation debate. In an important sense Marx's concept of central planning has never actually been abandoned by most socialists. In its broad outlines, Marx's idea of bringing social production under "conscious control," rather than leaving it to the whims of the "anarchic" forces of capitalism, is still the primary economic raison d'être of socialism. Although most contemporary socialists have forsaken Marx's particular concept of

---

[1] For a fascinating comparison of some of the economic ideas of these two thinkers, see Vorhies (1982).

planning, they have retained his critical attitude toward the unconscious mode of social production of capitalism and his goal of subsuming all of social production under a single, scientifically structured plan. It is over the implications of this conscious planning (for example, with respect to a price system and money) that contemporary socialists disagree with Marx, not over the desirability of conscious planning itself.

Beyond utopian socialism

Before beginning an examination of what Marx's concept of socialism is, we first need to establish that he had a definite idea of at least the main features of socialist society. Marx explicitly said a great deal about the capitalist society of his and earlier times and ridiculed those socialists who spent their time spinning ideal future utopias out of their heads. Both his advocates and critics have often interpreted Marx's condemnation of "utopian socialists" as a proscription of any systematic analysis of socialism and thus as a convenient device for avoiding difficult questions about its workability. "Scientific socialism," it is claimed, contents itself with a critique of historical capitalism and does not speculate about future societies. Thus Marxism is seen as exclusively a critique of capitalism, as if it said nothing about the nature of socialist society, as if Marx had left us a programmatic tabula rasa upon which the later market socialists could inscribe their schema without fear of contradicting the great critic of capitalism.

This view of Marxism fails to appreciate the essence of Marx's critique of capitalism and of his disagreement with utopian socialists. He did not blame the latter so much for discussing socialist society as for the way in which they discussed it and for the contradictions within their descriptions. Marx's scientific socialism was not merely an excuse for avoiding any examination of socialist society. It was a recommendation of a particular method for the conduct of such an examination – that is, that socialism be described through a systematic critique of capitalism.[2]

For Marx, studying capitalism and developing a positive theory of socialism are two aspects of the same endeavor. Marx conducted a critique of capitalist society from the standpoint of socialism, intending to reveal by this study the main features of the future socialist

---

[2] There is a danger, however, in examining socialism only indirectly through a study of capitalism: Potential problems of socialist organization are apt to be ignored.

society. Not only is socialism, for Marx, expected to emerge from the womb of advanced capitalism (and thus inherit many of its developmental characteristics), but many of the features of socialism can be inferred from the critique of certain inherent characteristics of capitalism. Marx said little directly about the nature of socialism, but in *Das Kapital* he described its fundamental attributes over and over again by clarifying its antithesis. In many respects, where *Das Kapital* offers us a theoretical "photograph" of capitalism, its "negative" informs us about Marx's view of socialism. Thus, contrary to the standard idea that Marx only talked about capitalism, I am arguing that there is implicit throughout Marx's writings a single, coherent, and remarkably consistent view of socialism.

Similar to the misconception that Marx had no view of socialist society is the idea that whatever view he did have, if found wanting, can be freely modified independently from his critique of capitalism. Both of these errors arise from the artificial separation of issues into two hermetically sealed theoretical topics, capitalism and socialism, as if our understanding of the one were irrelevant to our understanding of the other. On the contrary, Marx taught that implicit in his negative critique of capitalism are all the essentials of his positive theory of socialism.[3]

Marx's early writings were largely directed against "utopian socialism," the predominant form of pre-Marxian socialism. Broadly speaking, utopian socialism is the view that the socialist future can be imagined in advance in detail; that this image can be used to convert workers and capitalists alike; and that it can be achieved regardless of the current material conditions of social production. In contrast, Marx claimed that socialism was the future society that was indicated by the "laws of motion" of capitalism. Socialism becomes possible with the progression of capitalism; hence it cannot be achieved, for example, before the workers are numerous and unified enough to take common control of the means of production, or before the centralization of capital has proceeded far enough to make these means of production accessible to such centralized control.

Marx's critique of his utopian-socialist predecessors consists of three related theses: (1) that detailed speculation about the specific features of a socialist future is unscientific; (2) that the general characteristics of socialism can be scientifically established through a sys-

---

[3] An implication of this theoretical connection between the theories of capitalism and socialism is that if, as Mises's calculation argument contends, there is a fundamental flaw in Marx's socialism, this error must also be reflected somewhere in the Marxian analysis of capitalism. See n. 13 in the next chapter.

tematic critique of capitalism, and thus that utopian schemes that contradict these general characteristics are misconceived; and (3) that the likelihood and timing of the emergence of the new socialist mode of production can be gleaned from a dynamic study of the motion of capitalist development.[4]

There would be little disagreement from Mises over the first point. Details of future social life are not the province of economic science but of speculative literature. Nonetheless, both Marx and Mises treat the general characteristics of socialism (point 2), such as whether money is used or whether advanced technology is employed in production, as matters subject to systematic inquiry, that, incidentally, led the two thinkers to some interesting and substantial disagreement. But before describing Marx's view of the general characteristics of socialism, something should be said about the third point, the question of the evolutionary development of capitalism toward socialism.

If, as many Marxists contend, socialism is not merely a human goal but also an inevitable result of social evolution, then the issue raised by Mises as to whether socialism is possible seems misplaced. But one should be wary of attempts to dismiss all criticism of the socialist program in this manner. First, it should be emphasized that the Marxian theory of evolution of modes of production was never intended as a Hegelian script with which future history must invariably conform. The materialist historian uses tendencies of the past to make judgments about the present and future, but past tendencies are not necessarily future tendencies, and new "laws of motion" may today interfere with the evolutionary direction discovered yesterday. Second, the fact that the actual development of capitalism since Marx's time has not proceeded along the lines he "predicted" should

---

[4] In my view, Marx's "socialism" has definite theoretical content in itself and is not the same as "whatever comes after capitalism." Many Marxists have robbed the idea of socialism of all content by trying to make it look like whatever current economic trends suggest the future may be like. Thus we find early twentieth-century Marxists attempting to model socialism after the giant capitalist trusts. This approach to Marxism takes the notion of socialism to be crudely derivative from historical trends. Jessie Hughan (1932, p. 119), for example, seems to turn Marx's scientific socialism into a meaningless pursuit of the zeitgeist: "Scientific Socialism is clearly not synonymous with 'deduced from Marx' and Utopian with 'not deduced from Marx'; but scientific Socialism now means to use those conclusions which are drawn from the economic tendencies of the time; Utopian, those which are based upon the mere plans or preferences of the thinker. For example, the expectation that the future organization of society will be based on the trust is scientific, if arising from a present economic tendency." If present trends indicated economic collapse, a war economy, or a return to slavery, would we attribute such features to socialism?

teach us to avoid making confident pronouncements of the inevitability of socialism.[5]

For too long most Marxists have been content to develop a critique of capitalism and leave all discussions of the workings and workability of socialism to others. As Mises remarked, "They are for ever drawing up programmes of the path to Socialism and not of Socialism itself'" ([1920] 1935, p. 122). Marx's antiutopian method, whatever its legitimate purposes may have been for Marx himself, has served Marxians largely as an unscientific shield for deflecting criticisms of the practicability of the socialist economic order.

In my view, Marx did not devote his life to devising a dogma that would be immune to criticism, despite the misguided efforts of so many of his followers to do so. Marx accepted the prevailing scientific attitude of his time that all argument is susceptible to rational criticism and indeed that virtually all scientific progress occurs as a result of the rejection of dogma and the critique of earlier "knowledge" by later skeptics. Whatever one may think of the cogency of Mises's calculation argument, true followers of Marx should have welcomed this challenge and vigorously responded to it. Instead Marx's followers have almost completely ignored it, and when neoclassical theorists had to take up the defense of socialism against this challenge, the influence of Marxism in economics suffered a severe blow from which it is still trying to recover.

If Marxism is to shed its image as a rigid dogma that is immune to criticism, Marxists will have to take the initiative in specifying what would constitute a legitimate attempt to criticize Marxism. In particular it will have to be conceded that not all discussions of the practicability of socialism can be rejected out of hand as utopian. They may all turn out to be unsuccessful, but at least some of them are worthy of careful consideration. Marx's own idea of socialism should be subjected to the same scrutiny to which Marx subjected his utopian competitors.

As Mises pointed out at the beginning of his 1920 essay (quoting Kautsky, 1907, p. 1), "Investigation into the conditions of society organized upon a socialist basis is of value as something more than 'a good mental exercise and a means of promoting political clearness and consistency of thought'" ([1920] 1935, p. 88). The entire social-

---

[5] Many modern economists dismiss Marx's entire analytic framework because his "predictions" have not been very accurate. Those who do not follow the "positive" economic methodology of Friedman, however, believe that there is more to "explanation" in the sciences than the testing of predictions. See Coddington (1972) and McCloskey (1983).

ist movement to which Marx devoted his life aims at a revolution in
order to realize a socialist organization of society, yet it is at least
conceivable that such a society can never be achieved. The urgency
of a careful and honest discussion of this question among advocates
of socialism is even greater today, now that the failure of numerous
attempts to institute socialism is available for historical examination.
Every socialist revolution to date has, of course, been "premature"
from the standpoint of Marx's analysis. Nonetheless, to put the question in a Marxian way, we need to ask whether capitalist society can
ever mature in such a way as to make socialism possible.

I will, however, take a more sympathetic view of Marx's approach
than did Mises, who said, for example, that "Marxism solemnly for-
bids its adherents to concern themselves with economic problems
beyond the expropriation of the expropriators" ([1920] 1935, p.
88).[6] Indeed most neoclassical as well as Austrian critics have interpreted Marx's thesis that the law of value does not apply to socialism
as a denial that socialist society conforms to any economic laws at
all – a serious misunderstanding of Marxian theory.

For Marx, economic "laws" are not necessarily universal for all
societies but are specific to each particular mode of production. According to the Japanese economist Kōzō Uno, Marx believed that
one must distinguish between the "specific laws of a commodity
economy" and the "general norms of economic life."[7] The "law of
value," for example, represents a specific law of commodity economy, whereas the requirement that every society regulate its use of
resources in the service of economic reproduction represents a general norm of economic life. Thus the law of value is a specific mani-
festation under capitalism of a general norm to which all societies,
including socialism, must conform. Although the law of value itself
does not directly apply either to precommodity or postcommodity
modes of production, it has been only through the systematic study
of this and other features of commodity economy that the laws of
other modes of production have been revealed. Thus for Marx a
study of the laws of capitalism can yield an understanding of the
general norms of economic life from which the laws of other modes
of production can then be distilled.

The general norms of economic life limit the possibilities from

---

[6] Mises went so far as to characterize Marxism as "against logic, against Science, and
against the activity of thought itself" ([1922] 1936, p. 12).
[7] The distinction is Uno's. His careful study of Marx (mainly as explained to me
personally by Makoto Itoh) has significantly informed many parts of this chapter.
See Itoh (1980) and Uno (1980).

which visions of socialism can be devised. The limitations can be discovered by realizing that some of the features of capitalism neces-sarily imply the existence of other features of capitalism: one cannot exist without the other. The utopian socialists wanted to put to-gether various features of their ideal systems without regard to the implications from the study of economics as to whether these various features were compatible with one another. Thus Proudhon wanted an economy with exchange relations, money, and banks but without profit or interest. Marx's critique deftly revealed why abolishing capitalist forms of distribution also implies abolishing the anarchic organization of capitalist production. One cannot arbitrarily choose the attributes of capitalism that one wishes to retain and set aside the attributes that one does not like.

Surely, then, it is conceivable that among the broad features that Marx attributed to socialism are two that are incompatible with one another. In particular, the conscious central planning that will be discussed in the next section just might be incompatible with a tech-nologically advanced, world-integrated, and highly productive eco-nomic system. The latter, Marx believed, would be retained from capitalism; the former he thought would be introduced through a proletarian revolution. But if it could be shown that the unconscious organization of capitalist production is necessarily bound up with its advanced technology and high productivity, then Marx's socialism too would have to be abandoned as utopian.

At this point we need to look closely at Marx's criticisms of the utopian socialists, in order to clarify the intimate connection between his explicit analysis of capitalism and his implicit theory of socialism. The utopian socialists, according to Marx, can be divided into two major branches (corresponding to what Mises was later to refer to as *interventionism* and *syndicalism*), each of which, Marx argued, failed to appreciate the economic implications of socialism. Interventionism, which Marx generally referred to as "petty bourgeois socialism" (the approach used by Pierre-Joseph Proudhon, John Gray, and John Bray, for example), seeks to retain the fundamentally anarchic form of organization of small-scale commodity production while at the same time using the state to intervene in this order to attain socialist goals (Marx [1902] 1971, pp. 467–8; [1847]1963; [1859]1970). The syndicalist program, on the other hand (represented, for example, by the views of Louis Blanc and Michael Bakunin) would abandon the imperfect organization of anarchic production that is enforced by the profit and loss system and replace it with no social organiza-tion of production at all (Marx, Engels, and Lenin, 1972).

The syndicalists wanted workers' control of each factory and control of separate industries by democratic syndicates such as Blanc's "national workshops," but they never formulated a procedure through which these various independent factories and syndicates could have their activities coordinated and rationalized from the point of view of society as a whole. They did not realize that every society requires an ordering mechanism of some kind for economic production. Some process must ensure that society's scarce resources are used in such a manner that the means of production are reproduced and, preferably, expanded.

Now it is true that to some extent both classical long-run analysis and neoclassical general equilibrium theory have substantially exaggerated the degree of efficiency of the capitalist system's ordering mechanism, often depicting it as a smoothly operating clockwork, a fully harmonious system of perfect coordination. And surely it is a great merit of Marxian – and Austrian – analysis that capitalism is understood to be always in disequilibrium; but it must not be forgotten that capitalism does at least roughly coordinate its competing producers. Capitalism is plagued with recurrent unemployment and crises,[8] it permits waste, and it proceeds blindly in undesigned directions, sometimes yielding results that none of its participants desired, but it is, after all, capable of pushing resources toward their more highly valued uses, of expanding the total wealth of society, and of continually revolutionizing the technology of production. Syndicalism represents a step backwards from the anarchy of production to utter chaos.[9]

Marx (and Mises) understood that there is, even in the anarchic capitalist world, an element of order as well as an element of chaos. There are elements of discoordination diffused throughout any market economy. Not all entrepreneurs recoup their investments; not every realized selling price covers the entrepreneur's costs of production. Because production plans take time to complete, even if a business venture seems profitable at its inception, there is no guarantee that it will still do well by the time the products reach the market. But there are also the well-known general regularities, such as those between prices and costs of production, that are reflected in both the classical labor theory of value as well as the modern subjectivist theories of marginal utility and imputation.

[8] For Marx the trade cycle is inherent in the capitalist mode of production, but many of the Austrian economists believe that certain (fairly radical) reforms of the banking system could eliminate this problem. See White (1984).

[9] Some of what follows is revised from Lavoie (1983).

Marx saw the market as a system of partial coordination of separate decision makers and saw the alienation of these decision makers from one another as the source of the discoordination that always persists in markets. The producers' production plans are devised independently from one another and also from the consumers whose separate choices can make or break the producers' plans. Competitors struggle with one another under disequilibrium conditions to bid prices up and down in a continual flux of disappointed plans and windfall gains. But it would be a caricature to refer to Marx's "anarchy of production" as mere chaos,[10] for the law of value enforces a regularity on the market for Marx just as it does in the classical tradition from which his theories stem. Whereas such writers as Adam Smith placed greater emphasis on the long-run harmony of the market, on the eventual elimination of pure profit, on the order and regularity that market processes tend to engender, Marx stressed the continuous short-run discoordination that no market institutions can ever, by their very nature, entirely eliminate. Just from the fact that thousands of separate private-property owners independently direct their resources toward various projects through time, quite unaware *ex ante* of the many inevitable conflicts among their plans, we see that there necessarily must be disequilibrium. For Marx it is this alienation of producers from each other that makes any complete coordination inherently impossible. This does not, however, mean that there is only chaos, as would be the case with syndicalism.

Together with the development of this alienation, and on the same basis, efforts are made to overcome it: institutions emerge whereby each individual can acquire information about the activity of all others and attempt to adjust his own accordingly, e.g. lists of current prices, rates of exchange, interconnections between those active in commerce through the mails, telegraphs etc. . . . [A]lthough the total supply and demand are independent of the actions of each individual, everyone attempts to inform himself about them, and this knowledge then reacts back in practice on the total supply and demand ([1953] 1973, p. 161).

Alienation is not entirely overcome by these means, but its effects are mitigated to some degree. Market processes operating through the law of value and the equalization of profit rates guide production well enough to permit a complex network of interdependent production plans to develop. Marx does not deny this coordinating role of the market but argues that mankind can do this system one

---

[10] See, for example, Hayek, who interprets Marxism in this way (1979, pp. 169–70).

better, that central planning can enable us to adopt a much more complete coordination of productive activities. He argues not that capitalism is completely chaotic but that its coordination is crude and only operates *ex post;* plan mismatching is discovered too late in the "higgling of the market" when producers have already made their investments and are struggling, in the face of changing prices, to minimize their losses or reap their windfall gains. The question of whether there is a workable alternative to this imperfect market coordination will be explored in the next chapter; the point here is that Marx, in recognizing (and sometimes exaggerating) these imperfections, was highlighting an aspect of the real market that is often ignored in contemporary economic literature. Marx's idea of the anarchy of capitalist production does not reveal an ignorance of the coordinating function of markets but reflects a (perhaps itself utopian) desire to go beyond this undeniably imperfect system of coordination.

It has been said and may be said that this is precisely the beauty and the greatness of it, this spontaneous interconnection, this material and mental metabolism which is independent of the knowing and willing of individuals, and which presupposes their reciprocal independence and indifference. And certainly, this objective connection is preferable to the lack of any connection, or to a merely local connection resting on blood ties, or on primeval, natural or master–servant relations([1953] 1973, p. 161).

Marx condemns the market order only by contrasting this system with an ideal economic system (to this day unrealized anywhere) where individuals can "gain mastery over their own social interconnections" and subordinate their social relations "to their own communal control" ([1953] 1973, pp. 161–2). It is precisely because of the fact that the market is neither an utter chaos nor an equilibrium of complete coordination but rather what Hayek calls a "spontaneous order" (a resultant of, but not a design made by, conscious choices) that Marx criticizes it. "The totality of the process [arises] from the mutual influence of conscious individuals on one another, but neither located in their consciousness, nor subsumed under them as a whole. Their own collisions with one another produce an *alien* social power standing above them, produce their mutual interaction as a process and power independent of them" (pp. 196–7). A nonutopian socialism must be able to supplant the imperfect coordination of the law of value with some other ordering mechanism. In the case of Marxism, the conscious central plan is to function as such a mechanism.

If the syndicalists failed to understand why the ordering aspect of the market's partial ordering mechanism had to be replaced by a central planning ordering mechanism, the "interventionists" failed to understand why the features of disorder that are inherent in markets preclude their combination with central planning. The interventionist utopians never realized that certain specific historical conditions are necessary for the abolition of capitalist "exploitation."

All socialists of Marx's time shared a common desire to eradicate the "unearned incomes" that were characteristic of capitalist society. Marx, however, recognized that the appropriation of surplus value by private owners of capital is necessitated by the very nature of an exchange economy. Utopian socialists who sought to abolish interest, rent, and profit while retaining the anarchic capitalist organization of production failed to appreciate the role of these forms of distribution of wealth in the capitalist order. The interventionists who thought that they could eliminate unearned incomes by legislative edicts without first transforming at its roots the fundamental organization of capitalist society were simply ignorant of the operation of that society. Wages cannot be substantially increased relative to profits by the official decrees of a capitalist state, even if one supposes the state to sincerely wish to increase them. Private appropriation of profit is necessary for the capitalist mode of production, and legislative tinkering with prices and wages can no more alter this fact than they could repeal the law of gravity. To this extent Marx accepted the arguments against "interventionism" of the classical school from whom he adopted most of his tools of economic analysis. Under commodity production, the laws of economics that were systematically elaborated by Ricardo are unalterable.

Marx's critique of his classical predecessors begins with the observation that these laws of economics are not universal but hold only for the commodity mode of production. It was the permanence of this mode of production that he doubted. Before the appearance of a money economy, the nature of social production was subject to very different laws, and after the demise of commodity production, Marx contended, society would be subject to different laws again. But as long as economic production is organized anarchically – that is, according to the law of value – it is utopian to hope for any government policy that can achieve the aims of the socialist movement.

Those who would employ the elaborate Marxian criticism of capitalist society while trying to devise their own schemes of socialism are likely not only to contort Marx's ideas beyond recognition (a consequence, after all, with which these socialists may be quite willing to live), but they are also likely to deceive and contradict themselves.

Marx's criticism of capitalism is inextricably intertwined with his concept of central economic planning. Modern socialists need to realize that if they condemn capitalism they must either offer an alternative that eliminates this aspect of social production, or the condemnation will be empty.

Consciously ordered versus anarchic social production

For Marx, the aspect of human labor that distinguishes it from animal production is the purposive planning of human producers. Guided by instincts, bees may construct elaborate cells, but "what distinguishes the worst architect from the best of bees is this, that the architect raises his structure in imagination before he erects it in reality" ([1867]1967a, p. 178).[11]

The central idea in Marx's concept of the conscious ordering of social production is contained in the last phrase. Rational human production consists in the construction of a plan in the mind in advance, before the steps of a plan are implemented in the material world. The essence of Marx's critique of capitalism is that the capitalist mode of production does not permit all of social production to be rationally planned in advance, because capitalism involves the simultaneous design of conflicting plans by separate, "alienated" producers. The result of this anarchic clash of many conscious plans is an unplanned, unconscious mode of social production. Thus Marx's idea of central planning entails the unification of social planning into one consistent, conscious plan, one complex structure that is coherently raised in the minds of socialist "architects" before being systematically implemented.

Capitalist production has led to the construction of commodities as complex as a computer or as large as an ocean liner in the minds of

---

[11] Marx continues: "At the end of every labour-process we get a result that already existed in the imagination of the labourer at its commencement. He not only effects a change of form in the material on which he works, but he also realises a purpose of his own that gives the law to his modus operandi, and to which he must sub-ordinate his will" ([1867] 1967a, p. 178). Hayek has this "conscious planning" idea in mind when he refers, in the opening paragraph of his first major contribution to the calculation debate, to "the belief that deliberate regulation of all social affairs must necessarily be more successful than the apparently haphazard interplay of independent individuals." Indeed he even manages to evoke the motivating spirit behind this Marxian vision of advancing beyond the anarchy of capitalism when he writes: "To bring order to such a chaos, to apply reason to the organization of society, and to shape it deliberately in every detail according to human wishes and the common ideas of justice seemed the only course of action worthy of a rational being" ([1935] 1948e, p. 119).

competing capitalist architects. Marx believed that capitalist production would continue to become centralized, so that larger enterprises would subsume more and more of social production under the conscious guidance of fewer and fewer wills. Socialism, for Marx, seeks to replace those few capitalist producers with the single common will of all producers; it seeks to eliminate the last vestiges of commodity production and to build what Bukharin was to call a "new society which is consciously planned and consciously executed" ([1920] 1971, pp. 68–9).[12] Anarchic commodity production is guided, again in Bukharin's words, "not by a conscious calculation by the community but by the blind power of the social element, evidencing itself in a whole chain of social-economic phenomena, particularly in the market price" ([1917] 1972, p. 49). Capitalism is seen by Marx ([1953] 1973, p. 158) as that mode of production in which "individuals . . . produce only for society and in society" but where "production is not *directly* social, is not 'the offspring of association' which distributes labour internally. Individuals are subsumed under social production; social production exists outside them as their fate; but social production is not subsumed under individuals, manageable by them as their common wealth."

Bukharin ([1921] 1969, pp. 41–2) says that under central planning, workers "make resolutions in common and carry them out in common." No longer subject to the forces of price movements, "men control their own decisions and do not feel any pressure of blind social forces upon them, since these forces have been replaced by a national social organization."

Marx ([1871] 1974a, p. 213) expected central planning to stabilize economic activity: "United cooperative societies are to regulate national production upon a common plan, thus taking it under their own control and putting an end to the constant anarchy and periodical convulsions which are the fatality of capitalist production." In communist society, "The question then comes down to the need of society to calculate beforehand how much labour, means of production, and means of subsistence it can invest" in the planned directions. "In capitalist society however where social reason always as-

---

[12] In the following discussion, I occasionally supplement Marx's words with quotations from Nicolai Bukharin to illustrate Marx's ideas, not only because Bukharin agrees in most respects with Marx but also because he devoted a great deal of attention to the direct implications of Marx's critique of capitalism for the economics of socialism. At the time when Mises launched his critique of socialism, Bukharin was arguably the leading Marxian theoretician in the world.

serts itself only *post festum* great disturbances may and must constantly occur" ([1885] 1967b, p. 315).

In the contemporary theory of the firm, a profit-making enterprise is sometimes referred to as an island of planning in a sea of anarchy. Within the enterprise, production takes place rationally according to the single conscious will of the capitalist owner. Means of production are coordinated from a decision-making center and moved from department to department, but unfinished goods, machines, and labor within the enterprise are not exchanged. The shipping department does not buy the product from the workers of the assembly department; there is a prearranged plan by which the different complex steps required in the production process are set out and according to which organized production takes place. This distinction between the division of labor within the enterprise by conscious planning and the spontaneous and unplanned division of labor in society as a whole is central to Marx's view of planning: "Division of labor in the interior of a society, and that in the interior of a workshop, differ not only in degree, but also in kind" ([1867] 1967a, p. 354).

The fundamental difference is that the division of labor among independent producers is conditioned by their buying and selling of commodities from or to one another, whereas the division of labor within an enterprise is characterized by the fact that "the detail labourer produces no commodities. It is only the common product of all the detail labourers that becomes a commodity" ([1867] 1967a, p. 355). Marx stressed that "in every factory the labour is divided according to a system, but this division is not brought about by the operatives mutually exchanging their individual products" (p. 42).

Marx favored the deliberate ordering mechanism of the intrafirm division of labor over the rough "tendency-to-equilibrium" ordering mechanisms of the interfirm division of labor in society as a whole:

This constant tendency to equilibrium, of the various spheres of production, is exercised only in the shape of a reaction against the constant upsetting of this equilibrium. The *a priori* system on which the division of labour, within the workshop, is regularly carried out, becomes in the division of labour within the society, an *a posteriori*, nature-imposed necessity, controlling the lawless caprice of the producers, and perceptible in the barometrical fluctuations of the market-prices (p. 356).

Thus Marx could remark that

the enthusiastic apologists of the factory system have nothing more damning to urge against a general organization of the labour of society, than that it would turn all society into one immense factory (p. 356).

As contrasted with the "undisputed authority" of the capitalist over his deliberately organized division of labor, "The division of labour within the society brings into contact independent commodity-producers, who acknowledge no other authority but that of competition, of the coercion exerted by the pressure of their mutual interest." (p. 356).[13]

Individual capitalists set out on their own initiative, at their own risk, with their own means of production, secured in exchange relations with other capitalists, and with their own individual conscious plans for making profits. Production is integrated through markets over a vast geographic area, and all individuals become interdependent while maintaining independence in production decisions. Individual capitalists compete with one another, clash in a race for profit, and are in this respect in an antagonistic relationship with one another. Yet although they are rivals in profit making, or in the struggle to make a living, producers come to depend more and more on one another's efforts.[14]

Capitalism thus expresses what Marx refers to as an internal contradiction between, on the one hand, the widening and deepening interdependence of producers upon one another and, on the other, their antagonistic struggle in the market. As Bukharin put it, commodity production is "an unorganized unity" in which "capitalist enterprises, which are 'independent' from each other, must nevertheless rely on each other because one branch of production supplies raw materials, parts, etc., for the other" ([1920] 1971, pp. 13–15).

In every mode of production social phenomena are the consequences of human action, but in commodity production – that is, in unorganized production – the end result is not the conscious aim of the producer. Market phenomena are what Bukharin called a "resultant of the individual wills in unorganized society":

Prices are an excellent example. Buyers and sellers go to the market. The sellers have the goods, the buyers have the money. Each of the sellers and buyers is aiming at a certain object: each of them makes a certain estimate of goods and money, ponders, calculates, scratches and bites. The result of all this commotion in the market is the market price. This price may not repre-

---

[13] It will be argued in the next chapter that the specific "pressures of their mutual interest" that "coerces" independent producers to adopt some methods of production and abandon others is the very element of rivalry whose absence makes central planning unworkable.

[14] In their influential "textbook" of communism, Bukharin and Preobrazhensky ([1919] 1966, p. 13) wrote that "the turmoil of the market place conceals from people that in actual fact they work for one another and cannot live without one another."

sent the idea of any individual buyer or seller; it is a social phenomenon arising as a result of a struggle of the various wills.[15]

It is seen as an essential characteristic of the capitalist mode of production that men are independent rivals in an anarchy of production and are thereby subject to the "blind forces" of the market.

Thus, the rapidly increasing material productive capacity of the expanding capitalist system is accompanied by a definite disadvantage. Individuals throw their fate onto the impersonal market and have to succumb to these "blind forces" just as if they were laws imposed by nature.

Individuals in a market economy take actions that lead to (but are not designed to lead to) a particular constellation of prices, which in turn influence the choices made. A price is a reflection of what is to Marx a contradiction of capitalism: It is both the organizing and rationalizing guide for production decisions and at the same time a reflection of the antagonistic social relations among buyers and sellers. On the one hand, prices guide calculations and determine the profits of producers in their expansion of the productive powers of society, and on the other hand prices are the stark reflection of competition among independent producers, of their unending struggle with one another for profits.

In the act of bidding up or bickering down a price on a market is contained the essentially rivalrous character of the capitalist order. The movement of any price by such an act reflects the gain to one competitor and the loss to another. Thus the planned production that takes place by firms (or governments) under capitalism is the conscious planning of necessarily only a portion of social production, because they must buy from or sell to other independent "islands" of planning. The portion in which market rivalry prevails (and that thus remains unplanned) leaves the possibility of overproduction of some commodities and underproduction of others. Production is guided by profit opportunities that can either be simultaneously perceived by numerous producers (leading to overproduction of that product) or can be unnoticed by any producers (leading to underproduction). Thus unconscious production can result in duplication and squandering of resources, relative to that which could conceivably be attained by complete central planning (if this is workable).

---

[15] Bukharin ([1921] 1969, pp. 37–8). See also his comment that: "social phenomena do not express the will of individual persons but frequently are a direct contradiction of this will; they prevail over it by force, with the result that the individual often feels the pressure of social forces on his actions" (p. 40). This Marxian idea bears remarkable similarity to the Hayekian notion of "spontaneous order," and both can be traced to Thomas Hobbes, Bernard Mandeville, and Adam Smith.

In the productive process that Marx designates by

$$M - C \dots P \dots C' - M',$$

he distinguishes between *production time (C ... P ... C'*: the transformation of inputs into outputs) and *circulation time (M − C* [buying inputs] and *C' − M'* [selling outputs]). Production time represents actual time spent producing the commodity that the capitalist intends to make from the inputs he bought. Circulation time represents the time spent transforming money into commodities (buying) and commodities into money (selling). Production time can, for the most part, be consciously planned in advance by the capitalist, since he controls all the factors necessary for its completion. The circulation activity, however, cannot be consciously planned in advance, since the capitalist cannot know for sure either how many of his desired inputs he can buy and at what price or how much of his own outputs he can sell and at what price. These uncertain quantities and prices depend on the plans of other independent capitalists. In the competitive battles that are fought every day on the market, prices of commodities are the unplanned results of their clashing at any moment of time. The outcome of these confrontations of offers and bids is a resultant, not a design, of these independent decision makers and thus cannot be predicted by any of them in advance. In the sphere of circulation – that is, in the acts of buying and selling in a monetary economy, is to be found the unorganized or anarchic character of commodity production. For Marx, and, as we shall see, for Mises as well, the use of money as such precludes the world of perfect coordination depicted in neoclassical equilibrium constructions.

It is also precisely this aspect of the production process – circulation time – that is claimed to be unnecessary under Marxian socialism. From the point of view of society, resources in the sphere of circulation appear to Marx as a deduction from the social product, to be subtracted from the capitalist's surplus value. "Time of circulation and time of production mutually exclude each other. During its time of circulation capital does not perform the functions of productive capital and therefore produces neither commodities nor surplus-value" ([1885] 1967b, p. 124). Marx distinguishes between those circulation costs that are specific to commodity production (buying and selling, and much of capitalist accounting) and those that are necessary, though changed, under planned production. "Bookkeeping, as the control and ideal synthesis of process, becomes the more necessary the more the process assumes a social scale and loses its purely individual character" (p. 135).

The costs spent in circulation, such as expenses, for sales, advertising, a large part of inventories, and purchasing, can be avoided only if Marx's concept of central planning can be implemented. If all of society can be organized as "one immense factory," with the movement and processing of intermediate products performed according to a single conscious plan, then buying and selling are superfluous. But if, as many contemporary socialists contend, planning cannot do without and can only proceed by means of the market, then they are in fact advocating a form of commodity production within which, Marx explicitly argued, costs of circulation are absolutely necessary. "In the production of commodities, circulation is as necessary as production itself" (p. 126). It is only from the specific perspective of contrasting the anarchy of commodity production with complete central planning that competitive efforts can be called "wasteful." "The capitalist mode of production, while on the one hand, enforcing economy in each individual business, on the other hand, begets by its anarchical system of competition, the most outrageous squandering of labour-power and of the social means of production, not to mention the creation of a vast number of employments, at present indispensable, but in themselves superfluous" ([1867] 1967a, p. 530).

Despite its increasingly rational organization of production according to a set plan within a capitalist enterprise, the antagonistic relationship among competing enterprises under capitalism seemed to Marx an unnecessary waste. If it is possible to direct all social production according to a single precoordinated plan, then innumerable features of capitalist production can, from this point of view, be seen as wasteful.

But if this complete central planning must be discarded as impossible, as the calculation argument claims, then the criticism of capitalist anarchy must be reexamined in this light. Thus he who would disparage the wastes of circulation under capitalism cannot also advocate a "socialism" that retains market relations. Where there are markets, there are unplannable exchanges of commodities for money, and of money for commodities. Where these persist, there is every bit as much need for producers to spend resources searching for a good price, informing potential buyers of their commodities and prices through advertising, stocking up extra inventories for possible variations in demand, and so forth, as there is under the form of commodity production that Marx analyzed.

Marx explicitly said that his view of central planning as "directly associated labour" is "a form of production that is entirely inconsistent with the production of commodities" ([1867] 1967a, p. 94). For Marx, socialism means first and foremost the abolition of all market relations, the relegation of the entire social production process to the conscious design of the workers in common. By expropriating the expropriators, the proletariat is supposed simultaneously to terminate the anarchic and rivalrous aspects of private production and to reestablish the bond between the producers and their means of production.

It should be clear by now that in my view Marx's concept of central planning constitutes an extreme among socialists. But there is a common belief among many Marxists that this extreme description applies only to the "second phase" of communism discussed by Marx ([1891] 1974b) in which scarcity has been vanquished. The extreme view of central planning is relegated to the distant future, whereas the "first phase" of communist society, or in many cases an intermediate "transitional" stage following capitalism and preceding the first phase, is depicted as a more moderate form of "central planning" in which market forms are allowed to coexist with a planning apparatus. Marx's mention of the possible use of labor coupons is often cited as an admission that a form of money may be compatible with central planning.

This interpretation of Marx, cannot, however, be sustained. Marx repeatedly and explicitly rejected what he called "the Utopian idea of 'labour money' in a society founded on the production of commodities" ([1867] 1967a, p. 94; see also [1847] 1963 and [1859] 1970). The idea of labor coupons that Marx referred to in 1891 was borrowed from Owen, and, he said, "is no more 'money' than a ticket for the theater" ([1867] 1967a, p. 94). See also Marx ([1885] 1967b, p. 358): "In the case of socialised production the money capital is eliminated. Society distributes labour-power and means of production to the different branches of production. The producers may, for all it matters, receive paper vouchers entitling them to withdraw from the social supplies of consumer goods a quantity corresponding to their labour-time. These vouchers are not money. They do not circulate."

The interpretation of Marxian central planning as employing money has by now been so conclusively refuted by others, especially Buick (1975), Reese (1980), Roberts (1971), Roberts and Stephenson (1973), and Steele (1978), that a further meticulous exegetical study of this issue is no longer required. From what has already been said it should be clear that the notion of a centrally planned society that retains the anarchic market institutions from capitalism renders the entire corpus of Marx's critique of capitalism nonsensical. As Buick (1975, p. 68) has noted, the contemporary Marxists' notion of a "transitional society" that reconciles central planning with commodity production not only will not be found anywere in Marx's voluminous writings but furthermore "is based on a complete misunderstanding of the Marxian theory of money."

It is in monetary theory that the limitations of neoclassical equilibrium theorizing are most evident, and it is here that the strengths of the Marxian (and Austrian) disequilibrium approaches are the most apparent. Once Marx's theory of money is clearly understood, the absurdity of the notion of a centrally planned monetary economy is plain. Money economy, depicted as $C - M - C$, the exchange of commodities necessarily through the intermediary of the medium of exchange, was being criticized precisely because it separates those acts of purchase and sale. These separate, rivalrous acts of buying and selling lie at the root of Marx's disequilibrium critique of capitalism and thus cannot be sensibly joined to his concept of conscious planning.

HI

CHAPTER 3

Mises's challenge: the informational function of rivalry

Against the analytic background provided in Chapter 2, my purpose in this chapter is to show that Mises's argument against Marx's socialism is not a utopian exercise in speculation about the unknowable future but rather a legitimate contribution to economic science, rooted in a sound theoretical understanding of the economics of capitalist society. I will offer a detailed exposition of the argument as it appeared in the 1920 essay, "Die Wirtschaftsrechnung im sozialistischen Gemeinwesen" ("Economic calculation in the socialist commonwealth") ([1920] 1935) and reappeared almost verbatim as the central argument of his book *Die Gemeinwirtschaft* ([1922] 1936, pp. 114–22, 131–5). The discussion will examine (1) Mises's analysis of the function of economic calculation under capitalism; (2) his claim that this function cannot be performed under a centrally planned economy and that without it rational economic planning is impossible; (3) his case against the feasibility of using labor time as a unit for economic calculation under socialism; and (4) his brief anticipatory remarks criticizing market socialism.

The nature of economic calculation under capitalism

Mises is typically understood to have put forward in 1920 an abstract argument about the detached "logic" of the theory of socialism, and it is on this level that virtually all of the English-language responses in the 1930s were formulated. Mises is thought to have denied the determinateness of equilibrium for a socialist organization of production, to which the market socialists retorted that as Pareto, Barone, and Wieser had shown there is a "formal similarity" in the general logic of choice that applies to either capitalism or socialism (see Chapter 4). It is only with Hayek's rejoinders that the debate is believed to have shifted to more practical questions, and even then the emphasis is said to have been on "practicability in principle" – whatever that may be.

In my view, the challenge by Mises was an eminently practical issue from the outset, concerned with the workability of widely proposed socialist programs and with the attempts prior to and during 1920 to actually implement such proposals. Mises was taking as his cue not the abstract controversies of theoretical economics but the attempts at "war planning" in Austria and Germany through which he had just lived and, even more directly, the ongoing collapse of the Russian economy of the Bolsheviks. In particular, Mises's argument can be seen as a theoretical explanation of why Lenin's attempt to abolish markets and money during the so-called War Communism period resulted in such unmitigated disaster.[1]

This is not to say that the essay contained any specific historical analysis of these programs. Instead Mises offered a theoretical framework that could explain the varying degrees of failure of the socialist programs being implemented around him. His essay is "theoretical" in the broad sense; it is a general analysis of the implications of centralized ownership of the means of production for a modern economy. It was not theoretical in the narrower, neoclassical sense of an abstract exercise in the pure logic of choice.

In what follows, Mises's specific argument for the necessity of money prices will be explained in some detail, despite the fact that it bears superficial similarity to the familiar neoclassical thesis that "prices" are required for the efficient allocation of resources; my purpose is to show that these two arguments for the necessity of "prices" differ. When, in his response to Mises, Oskar Lange conceded that "prices" are necessary, he was not discussing genuine money prices emerging from the competitive process but simply numerical "terms on which alternatives are offered."

It is also important to note that Mises's use of the word *competition* has virtually the opposite meaning of the term as it is used by the neoclassical participants in the debate. Whereas for the latter "competition" refers to a certain kind of optimal state in which all participants are viewed as passive "price takers," for Mises the term describes a dynamic struggle among active entrepreneurs seen as "price makers."

Such differences between the neoclassical and Austrian arguments for the "price system" are stressed for two reasons. First, many critics of the price system (for example, Maurice Dobb) reject the neoclassical argument for the importance of prices because of the aspects of this argument (such as its emphasis on static conditions) that cannot

---

[1] Mises describes "what is happening under the rule of Lenin and Trotsky" as "merely destruction and annihilation" in which "all branches of production depending on social division of labour are in a state of entire dissolution" ([1920] 1935, p. 125).

be attributed to its Mises-Hayek version. Second, many advocates of the "price system" (Lange, for example), who concur with the neo-classical argument have failed to grasp the way in which prices convey the information that, they agree, is indispensable for rational planning.

In my view the calculation argument as explained by Mises is substantially the same as that subsequently argued by Hayek, in contrast to the standard view, which, we have seen, holds that Hayek retreated from a more extreme Misesian position. The similarity of their positions is somewhat hidden by the fact that Mises focused his challenge on the Marxian view of central planning, whereas Hayek redirected the argument to market socialism. Since Marxian socialism specifically denies itself any use of money prices, Mises naturally placed greater emphasis on the (now generally acknowledged) need for price information per se than on the related argument, later stressed by Hayek, that prices presuppose competitive markets and private ownership if they are to be able to serve their informational function. Nonetheless, many elements of Hayek's later contributions on knowledge and competition can be found in embryonic state in Mises's original statement of the problem of calculation under socialism.

Mises begins Section 2, entitled "The Nature of Economic Calculation," by distinguishing among three kinds of judgments of value. These will be referred to here as *primary evaluations, consumer evaluations,* and *producer evaluations,* each of which pertains to a particular category of ends/means framework.

Primary evaluations refer to subjective rankings of wants in utility space and neither require nor permit any form of numerical calculation.

Consumer evaluations are the judgments of the efficacy of certain means – consumption goods (the end products of social production) – for facilitating the pursuit of primary wants (the ends). Like the primary evaluations from which they derive, the consumer evaluations of an individual need not be reduced to numerical terms to be made intelligently. Whether the cost of a consumer good is reckoned in terms of dollars, a collection of bartered commodities, or labor hour coupons, the consumer merely has to directly compare the relative merits to him of the thing to be gotten with those of the thing to be given up. For "the man who knows his own mind" ([1920] 1935, p. 96) it is a simple matter to judge the relative satisfaction he can expect to derive from the immediate use of consumption goods. Neither an individual's primary evaluations nor his consumer evaluations contain even the potential of a "calculation problem" under any mode of production, because they are made in ordinal terms and depend only on the subjectively perceived use value of the evaluated items, which can be directly assessed by the evaluator. For consumer evaluations, Mises wrote, "calculation *in natura*" — that is, calculation in kind, without a standard of value — is sufficient, for here the "apples and oranges" can be compared ordinally by the individual human mind, even if the mind cannot add quantities of one to the other (p. 104).

Mises points out that "it is impossible that there should ever be a unit of subjective use-value for goods. Marginal utility does not posit any unit of value . . . Judgments of value do not measure; they merely establish grades and scales" (pp. 96–7).

Producer evaluations pertain to the judgment of the efficacy of "higher order" goods as means for the production of consumption goods. Just as consumer evaluations, being based directly on a judgment of the efficacy of consumption goods to facilitate the satisfying of primary wants, are derived from primary evaluations, so producer evaluations are derived, although sometimes only remotely, from consumer evaluations. In a complex, multistage production structure, these evaluations of higher order goods are "derived" or "imputed" from the producer evaluations at the next lower stage of producer goods and ultimately from the consumers' demands for the lowest order of goods.[2] Were anything to sever this connection of value imputation between lower and higher stages of production, a potential "calculation problem" — that is, a difficulty in making a rational producer evaluation — could emerge.

Any particular consumer or producer evaluation can be meaningfully criticized as an inaccurate reflection of the "true" efficacy of a particular means for the attainment of the ends sought. Consumer evaluations may be inaccurate in the sense that consumption goods may fail to meet expectations, but producer evaluations that combine complex technological questions with value questions are far more susceptible to error, and the error that results is more likely to have serious social consequences. Mises's calculation argument concerns the question of whether accurate producer evaluations will be possible under common ownership of the means of production.

---

[2] The idea of such "imputation" as a link between consumer and producer evaluations is seen very differently by the Austrians from the way it is described by some neoclassical theorists. Imputation is seen by the Austrians as a dynamic process, not as a static, logical derivation as Schumpeter treats it. (Note that for our purposes "imputation" is understood in the later-Austrian and Clarkian sense of estimates of marginal value products, not in the early-Austrian sense of the "imputation problem" as in Wieser.)

Mises admits that "under simple conditions" it is possible for a decision maker to directly "form judgments of the significance to him of goods of a higher order" without numerical calculation. Thus "a farmer in economic isolation" or Robinson Crusoe may be able to judge how to allocate the hours of each day to the "relatively short" production processes with which he is concerned. Crusoe's "expense and income" can be "easily gauged" (p. 96) – that is, it can be judged qualitatively, without the use of quantitative calculation.

But as both Marx and Mises repeatedly warned, it is often hazardous to equate the economics of advanced capitalist production to the simple economics of the imaginary world of Robinson Crusoe. Although Crusoe economics may be heuristically useful at an introductory stage of analysis, conclusions that might be valid for the Crusoe world may not be for the modern capitalist world.[3]

Speaking of the primitive economies of the ancient world, Marx ([1867] 1967a, p. 79) points out that "those ancient social organisms of production are, as compared with bourgeois society, extremely simple and transparent." Similarly with Crusoe and his elementary means of production: "All the relations between Robinson and the objects that form [the] wealth of his own creation, are here so simple and clear as to be intelligible without exertion . . . And yet those relations contain all that is essential to the determination of value" (p. 77). The producer evaluation for Crusoe, Marx argues, is straightforward and direct. "In spite of the variety of his work, he knows that his labour, whatever its form, is but the activity of one and the same Robinson, and consequently, that it consists of nothing but different modes of human labour. Necessity itself compels him to apportion his time accurately between his different kinds of work. Whether one kind occupies a greater space in his general activity

---

[3] Marx's strictures against applying "bourgeois" categories such as capital to noncapitalist modes of production are well known. The following statement by Mises indicates a measure of agreement with Marx on this point: "Looking backward from the cognition provided by modern accountancy to the conditions of the savage ancestors of the human race, we may say metaphorically that they too used "capital." A contemporary accountant could apply all the methods of his profession to their primitive tools of hunting and fishing, to their cattle breeding and their tilling of the soil, if he knew what prices to assign to the various items concerned. Some economists concluded therefrom that 'capital' is a category of all human production, that it is present in every thinkable system of the conduct of production processes – i.e., no less in Robinson Crusoe's involuntary hermitage than in a socialist society – and that it does not depend upon the practice of monetary calculation. This is, however, a confusion. The concept of capital cannot be separated from the context of monetary calculation and from the social structure of a market economy in which alone monetary calculation is possible" (1949, pp. 261–2).

than another, depends on the difficulties, greater or less as the case may be, to overcome in attaining the useful effect aimed at. This our friend Robinson soon learns by experience" (pp. 76–7).

Capitalist relations of production considerably complicate this situation. Unlike Crusoe, who directly assesses his means of production in relation to the consumption goods he subjectively wants to have produced, the capitalist decides what to produce largely on the basis of what his profit/loss calculations tell him. Before choosing a plan of action he must first calculate the revenue expected from the sale of the commodity whose production he is contemplating and compare this with an estimate of the costs expected to be expended in this production. A numerical calculation of expected profit or loss precedes his decisions over what to produce as well as how to produce it.

Marx and Mises agree that it has always been this accounting practice of calculating profit and loss that has guided capitalist production and that this capitalist form of production has made possible an unprecedented revolution in technology. To be sure, important differences arise between them over whether there might be a necessary and not just a historical connection between economic calculation and technological advance[4] and whether the "complication" introduced by capitalism is genuine or essentially a "mystical veil" that makes things appear more complex than they really are.[5] But Marx and Mises both would insist that under the commodity mode of production, economic calculation of profit and loss is absolutely indispensable. A further examination of Mises's description of the positive function that economic calculation performs under capitalism should help to elucidate his contention that rational economic calculation would be both necessary to, and yet impossible for, Marx's socialism.

Mises cites three advantages of economic calculation under capitalism. First, calculation in terms of prices makes it possible "to base the

---

[4] Marx believed that it would one day be possible to sever this connection, to continue the technological progress while abandoning the anarchic mode of production from which modern technology was born. Mises argued that these advanced production processes depend on that very anarchic organization that Marx had sought to replace with central planning.

[5] See Marx ([1867] 1967a, p. 80). The main point of Marx's idea of the "fetishism of commodities" is that capitalism disguises relations among people as relations among things, that it "conceals, instead of disclosing, the social character of private labour and the social relations between the individual producers" (p. 76). Mises, on the other hand, sees the complex price system as a genuine reflection of an even more complex network of production processes.

calculation upon the valuations of all participants in trade," whereas such interpersonal valuation comparisons would not be possible on the level of subjective assessments of use value. Thus "exchange-value, which arises out of the interplay of the subjective valuations of all who take part in exchange" (p. 97) represents a social institution that reflects in some way the valuations of the various individuals engaged in exchange relations.

Where production decisions are not precoordinated but are made independently by contending private owners of resources, some mechanism is required by which each individual's plans can be at least roughly meshed with the needs of society as a whole. Prices thus act as guide posts in the imperfect coordination of anarchic production, permitting the integration of separately made decisions across the entire society. When any one decision maker uses a price in his accounting calculations, he is unconsciously taking into account the entire complex of consumer and producer evaluations that resulted in that price being what it is. Without some social institution such as prices to connect the separate production decisions, the partially coordinated anarchy of production would degenerate into total chaos.

The second advantage of calculation, according to Mises, is that since prices reflect the economic activities of all market participants, "calculation by exchange-value furnishes a control over the appropriate employment of goods." That is, accounting practices can reveal whether a particular expenditure of money has been profitable, and this profit/loss signal can guide resources toward more valuable uses.

No claim need be made here either for an ethical justification of the manner in which distribution of social wealth takes place through the price system or for the optimal efficiency of this system. Mises is not arguing that the price system offers the best among a variety of possible methods of allocating the scarce goods of an advanced technological society. He is saying that the price system is the only possible way. Contrary to many accounts of the calculation debate, Mises never claimed that a free competitive market achieves that Pareto-optimal level of efficiency that is discussed by neoclassical theorists.[6]

In Mises's view, economic calculation does, however, promote efficiency, since it eliminates from consideration a plethora of technologically feasible but economically infeasible ways of combining soci-

[6] See Chapter 4 on this point.

ety's means of production.[7] The economic problem is not merely the technological one of applying given means to the pursuit of given ends.

Mises points out that "technical calculation is not enough to realize the 'degree of general and teleological expediency' of an event; . . . it can only grade individual events according to their significance; but . . . it can never guide us in those judgments which are demanded by the economic complex as a whole" (p. 129).[8]

The choice of which ends to pursue and of which means to employ for the various ends is not simply a problem of engineering but is a problem of valuation. When deciding what industrial use to make of, say, a gasoline engine, it is not enough to learn that the engine yields so many ergs of physical energy from the burning of so many liters of gasoline. We also have to know whether to use the engine to pump water from a well or to propel a car that can transport workers to a coal mine. This decision depends on our prior assessment of the value of coal and water, which in turn depends on our need for each of these for other productive purposes.[9] Consumer evaluations are imputed, via the price system, through a complex and continually changing structure of production, to producer evaluations of each higher order good. This extension of consumer evaluation into the capital structure is per-

---

[7] The word *efficiency* has, since 1920, come to imply the neoclassical notion of a static, Pareto-optimal allocation of "given" resources according to "given" technology and tastes and it would therefore probably be best to avoid it altogether in discussing Mises's argument. Since Mises is concerned to show the very process by which these "givens" come to be "known" by decentralized decision makers, the neoclassical efficiency criterion really begs the important question. Today, Hayek's terminology, by which the market promotes "plan coordination" rather than "efficiency," is preferable.

[8] Mises refers to a discussion by Gottl-Ottlilienfeld (1914, p. 219), whose phrase is quoted. Hayek's concise discussion of the difference between technological feasibility and economic feasibility ([1935] 1948e, pp. 120–4) remains among the best in economic literature. Technological problems assume a given end and permit the use of any means to achieve that end, whereas "the economic problem arises . . . as soon as different purposes compete for the available resources." The engineer, in practice, must work within a budget, and the costs of the factors of production that he can design into a project are outside of his control. But Hayek argues that "the spontaneous forces which limit the ambitions of the engineer themselves provide a way of solving a problem which otherwise would have to be solved deliberately" (p. 124).

[9] When we consider that some higher order goods are used in virtually every stage of production – that steel is used to produce steel and that, as Leontief's work (1966) has shown, it is extremely difficult to master the interrelationships of even broad industry aggregates – the enormous complexity of a modern economy can be appreciated. It is important to recognize that the interconnections among the factors of production make it impossible to delegate authority in the central plan to subordinate departments. See Plant ([1937] 1974).

formed adequately – though certainly not perfectly – by the price system and with the guidance of profit and loss calculations: "Anyone who wishes to make calculations in regard to a complicated process of production will immediately notice whether he has worked more economically than others or not; if he finds, from reference to the exchange-relations obtaining in the market, that he will not be able to produce profitably, this shows that others understand how to make a better use of the goods of a higher order in question" (pp. 97–8).

It should be noticed that Mises is not claiming that money prices under capitalism are *at* equilibrium values, as he has often been interpreted as saying. On the contrary, Mises argued that a complete equilibrium configuration of prices is in principle unattainable by any real, changing economic system and that if the static assumptions necessary for such an equilibrium did ever obtain, there would be no calculation problem requiring a solution in the first place.

Thus, in contrast to the neoclassical emphasis on the state of competitive equilibrium in which the correct substitution relations among commodities are already established, Mises is concerned with the competitive process by which these relations *tend* to be realized. As subsequent contributions in the Austrian tradition have emphasized, prices can provide a framework for the rational guiding of those who calculate with them only because of the rivalrous struggle among competitors under disequilibrium conditions to bid prices up when the demand exceeds the supply or down when the supply exceeds the demand. An entrepreneur who notices a better use of the gasoline engine than his rivals have noticed bids its price above what existing users have been willing to pay, thereby tending to draw resources toward their more highly valued uses. Profits are continually made from noticing particular "gaps" in the price system (as seen, for example, in buying low and selling high) and by tending to eliminate these gaps through such activity. As Mises expressed it, "The higgling of the market establishes substitution relations between commodities" ([1922] 1936, p. 115). It is this equilibrating or coordinating tendency, not any alleged achievement of an equilibrium state, that is being claimed as the indispensable advantage of the price system.

The rivalrous "higgling" among entrepreneurs supplies the equilibrating pressures on the network of relative prices, and it is this constantly changing configuration of relative prices that in turn enables economic calculation to perform its control function. Each particular configuration of prices permits some potential production plans (that are calculated to "promise" profitability) but eliminates from consideration the infinite variety of uneconomic though technologically feasible production plans.

Neither calculations of past profit nor estimates of future profit are guarantees of future realized profit. Many aspects of accounting calculation are necessarily formulated on the basis of particular expectations about the future, rather than on the basis of any "rigorously ascertainable data." Aside from the obvious possibility that the prices used in the calculation may change during the production process, Mises offers the example of the practice of estimating the amortization of machines by assuming a certain durability for the machines. Such elements of uncertain expectations of the future can never be eradicated from profit/loss calculations. Since all human action is directed at improving future states of affairs, an element of uncertainty is for Mises a permanent and necessary attribute of every decision, including those based on cardinal calculations of profitability. The apparant exactness of accounting practices disguises an inherent element of guesswork ([1920] 1935, p. 111).

Mistakes will be made, but "all such mistakes can be confined within certain narrow limits, so that they do not disturb the net result of the calculation" (p. 111). The inevitable uncertainty can be reduced or "confined" by the knowledge generated by economic calculation, until "what remains of uncertainty comes into the calculation of the uncertainty of future conditions, which is an inevitable concomitant of the dynamic nature of economic life" (p. 111). Again this statement makes clear the gulf between Mises's argument for the necessity of prices to reduce uncertainty and the neoclassical argument in which uncertainty is simply assumed away.

The fact that estimates of prospective profit do not ensure either optimal social use of resources or profit for the individual does not mean that such estimates serve no purpose. Economic calculation, despite its imperfect configuration of disequilibrium relative prices, still, as we have seen, enables entrepreneurs to eliminate from consideration the innumerable possibilities of technologically feasible but uneconomic production processes. By reducing the possibilities under consideration to the handful that appear in advance to be profitable, economic calculation greatly simplifies decision making in the production process (pp. 103, 110).

The third advantage of economic calculation is that it permits production evaluations to be reduced to a common denominator. To arrive at a quantitative profit/loss assessment of any particular project, it is of course necessary to reduce the exchange value of the list of inputs to a single value whose arithmetic subtraction from the estimated exchange value of the output can serve the control function referred to previously. Under capitalism, it is money that serves as the common denominator of economic calculation.

Mises admits that money is not perfect, but only serviceable, in its function as the unit for economic calculation.[10] The value of the money unit itself is unstable, as Mises had argued at length in 1912 ([1912] 1980), and is "subjected to constant, if (as a rule) not too violent fluctuations originating not only from the side of other economic goods, but also from the side of money" ([1920] 1935, p. 89). However, such fluctuations normally do not seriously disturb value calculations. The more fundamental shortcoming of monetary calculation is that it takes into account only those elements that are within the domain of exchange transactions. Such "ideal goods" as "honour" or "the beauty of a waterfall" (pp. 99–100) that are the object of no exchange transactions have no market price associated with them and thus cannot enter directly into monetary calculation, even though such considerations "can scarcely be termed irrational" and are "just as much motive-forces of rational conduct" as are commodities that are exchanged. Yet "this does not detract from the significance of monetary calculation," which is needed to facilitate producer evaluations because all such ideal goods are *consumption goods* and thus lie directly "within the ambit of our judgment of values" (p. 99, emphasis added). Mises concludes, "Admittedly monetary calculation has its inconveniences and serious defects, but we have certainly nothing better to put in its place, and for the practical purposes of life monetary calculation as it exists under a sound monetary system always suffices" (p. 109).

Within its limits, "monetary calculation . . . affords us a guide through the oppressive plenitude of economic potentialities" by enabling us "to extend to all goods of a higher order the judgment of value, which is bound up with and clearly evident in, the case of goods ready for consumption." The exchange value that is attached to higher order goods gives us "the primary basis for all economic operations" with these goods, without which, he says, complex production processes would be mere "gropings in the dark" (p. 101).

Mises mentions two related conditions as necessary for the successful functioning of money as the unit of economic calculation. First,

---

[10] In times of rampant inflation, this variation in the value of money will seriously interfere with the informational function of money prices.

the higher order goods, as well as consumption goods, must all "come within the ambit of exchange." Second, there must be "a universally employed medium of exchange . . . which plays the same part as a medium, in the exchange of production-goods also" (pp. 101–2). That is, the common denominator that is to serve as the unit for calculating the value of higher order goods must in fact be regularly used in exchange with those goods as well as with consumption goods. It is the myriad underlying subjective judgments of value that apply differential pressure on each price to rise and fall and thus to reflect increasing or decreasing scarcity relative to other goods. The money price is functional as a guide to the valuation of any one good only to the extent that money can serve as a genuine common denominator for the exchange transactions of all goods.[11]

It must be emphasized that Mises is explicitly and consciously talking about money prices as resultants of the bidding activities of competitive private owners, not about abstract accounting prices that could conceivably be set by a central planning board and expressed in terms of a *numeraire*. Mises viewed such abstract accounting prices as imaginary constructs for the equilibrium world of an "evenly rotating economy," not to be confused with money prices that pertain to the real world of continuous change. For Mises, as his other writings made more explicit, "money is necessarily a 'dynamic factor'; there is no room left for money in a 'static' system" (1949, p. 249), or again,

Where there is no uncertainty concerning the future, there is no need for any cash holding. As money must necessarily be kept by people in their cash holdings, there cannot be any money. The use of media of exchange and the keeping of cash holdings are conditioned by the changeability of economic data. Money in itself is an element of change; its existence is incompatible with the idea of a regular flow of events in an evenly rotating economy (1949, p. 417).

All market participants play a role in the emergence of monetary calculation in a twofold way – as consumers evaluating the end products and as producers putting higher order goods to the uses that yield the greatest return. "Through the interplay of these two processes of valuation, means will be afforded for governing both consumption and production by the economic principle throughout"

---

[11] This point bears more on models of market socialism than it does on Marx's socialism.

([1920] 1935, p. 107).[12] This "interplay" consists of rivalrous competition among entrepreneurs to direct production activities in accordance with consumer evaluations by struggling to bid away from one another the means of production necessary for such production. Given the anarchic organization of capitalism, posted market prices of capital goods are a necessary means of orientation for making such producer evaluations.

Economic calculation under socialism

My main purpose in this section is to examine Mises's argument that Marx's concept of central planning is "utopian" in Marx's own sense of the word – that is, is demonstrably unworkable, as is revealed through an analysis of the way the existing capitalist economy works. Mises contends that advanced technological production is too complex to be subsumed under a conscious plan and therefore must be broken up into subplans that require coordination. But since Marxian socialism eschews the use of money, there is no suitable common denominator for the quantitative calculations that decentralized coordination requires.

What has been said about the functioning of monetary calculation under capitalism does not necessarily preclude the possibility that the nonanarchic, moneyless central planning advocated by Marx could consciously allocate society's means of production directly, as Mises admits can be done under primitive conditions. It might be argued that the necessity of prices for orienting separate decision makers under capitalism does not imply the necessity of any such orientation when all of social production is consciously planned.

The basis of Mises's contention that moneyless central planning would not be possible rests on a fundamental distinction between simple producer evaluations and complex producer evaluations. Marx, in a passage that immediately follows his discussion of the

[12] Mises offers little explanation of this "economic principle," though he must, of course, have had in mind the value theory of the marginalist/subjectivist economics rather than the objective value theory of Marx. This might be thought to be an underlying difference about which there is little likelihood of resolution and upon which the whole force of the calculation argument rests. Contemporary Marxists are divided on the question of whether the labor theory of value can only be justified as an analytic framework for understanding capitalism or whether it can also be justified as a practical basis for planning a socialist economy. See, e.g., Becker (1977, pp. 111–29) and Bettelheim (1975). But I will argue that the labor theory of value, whatever its "value" for economic theory, cannot answer the practical objection that Mises was raising to socialism.

simplicity of Robinson Crusoe's productive evaluation, asserts that in a socialist society "all the characteristics of Robinson's labour are ... repeated, but with this difference, that they are social, instead of individual" ([1867] 1967a, p. 78). Mises, however, argues that another difference, the complexity of the decision being made, sharply distinguishes Crusoe's problem from that which would be before the central planning board. Marx's assertion that "the social relations of the individual producers, with regard both to their labour and to its products, are [under socialism] perfectly simple and intelligible" (p. 79), Mises asserts, is not supported by any specific argument.

Whereas Crusoe can easily survey the whole production process, Mises argues that no single person could survey the production process of the modern economy. "Within the narrow confines of household economy ... where the father can supervise the entire economic management, it is possible to determine the significance of changes in the process of production," and "it is possible throughout to review the process of production from beginning to end, and to judge all the time whether one or another mode of procedure yields more consumable goods" ([1920] 1935, pp. 102–3).

So long as the division of labor is in its "rudimentary stages," so that the whole production process can be surveyed by a single decision maker, the immediate evaluation of consumption goods can be extended, in the mind of this decision maker, to each stage of the production process. In this way the higher order goods can receive their "derived demand" from the direct, subjective valuation of the consumption goods to the production of which they contribute.

But the evolution of commodity production has led to the adoption of increasingly complex and time-consuming processes of production that integrate the whole world into a giant system of advanced technological production. As these complex production processes are undertaken with an increasingly intricate division of labor, no such survey by a single person of the entire production process from beginning to end takes place any longer. Instead the separate decision makers of an exchange economy have come to rely on prices to help them evaluate the numerous components of the production process. Mises argued that the use of the unconscious ordering mechanism of the price system and money calculations has led to such an advance in the complexity of the social production process as a whole that it is no longer possible for the human mind to directly subsume this process under conscious control.

It is no longer possible to make rational decisions without the intervention of more exact cardinal calculations.[13]

Those economically feasible production processes that survive the rivalrous struggle for profit could never have been discovered if economic calculations did not first eliminate from consideration innumerable infeasible processes that need never be attempted. Without such aid from profit/loss calculations, "The human mind cannot orientate itself properly among the bewildering mass of intermediate products and potentialities of production" and thus "would simply stand perplexed before the problems of management and location" (p. 103).

The problem that Mises was addressing was not the neoclassical one of how to best allocate "given" resources to the ends that are implicit in consumer demand according to a "given" technology of production. The basic issue is rather the question that Hayek was later to call the "central question of all social sciences: How can the combination of fragments of knowledge existing in different minds bring about results which, if they were to be brought about deliberately, would require a knowledge on the part of the directing mind which no single person can possess?" ([1937] 1948b, p. 54).

As Mises put it, "The mind of one man alone . . . is too weak to grasp the importance of any single one among the countlessly many goods of a higher order." There are limits to the knowledge of each member of society, but prices serve as "aids to the mind" that enable society as a whole to engage in production processes that would be

---

[13] Mises's argument, if valid, implies that the tendencies toward concentration and centralization that Marx believed would proceed until it was possible to subsume all of production under a central plan have in fact a logical limit. Centralization of any given firm cannot continue beyond the point where the knowledge generated by the rivalrous bidding of its competitors is sufficient to rationally guide its economic calculation. Were the firm to centralize any further it would increasingly find itself "in the dark" concerning the proper productive evaluations it should attach to the factors of production under its control. Unaided by the knowledge generated by its rivals, it would begin to lose to those less centralized rivals who could still benefit from such knowledge. Thus a possible flaw may be identified in the Marxian critique of capitalism that reflects Marx's failure to anticipate the calculation problem for socialism. Marx sought to bring the division of labor of society as a whole under what he called the "pre-determining control of society" ([1894] 1967c, p. 187), analogous to the conscious direction of production within a capitalist firm. What he seems to have failed to notice is that the technologically advanced planning of production that takes place within a profit-making firm fundamentally depends on the firm's position in an anarchic, rivalrous price system. The evolutionary implication of this argument is that central planning cannot be the future product of capitalist development because capitalist firms have a necessary limit to their possible centralization. See Rothbard (1962, pp. 544–9) and Machlup (1976, p. 114).

beyond our mental capacities were any of us to have to consciously plan them in their entirety (p. 102). Each participant can focus his or her limited mental powers on particular portions of a larger production process that is coordinated as a whole unconsciously through the price system, thus enabling society to be more productive than the sum of its parts.

No single man can ever master all the possibilities of production, innumerable as they are, as to be in a position to make straightway evident judgments of value without the aid of some system of computation. The distribution among a number of individuals of administrative control over economic goods in a community of men who take part in the labour of producing them . . . entails a kind of intellectual division of labour, which would not be possible without some system of calculating production and without economy (p. 102).

The "intellectual division of labour" that the unconscious ordering mechanism of the price system makes possible frees market participants from having to concern themselves with tracing out the complex social implications of their productive activities. Instead each can simply orient himself to others anarchically through the price system and concentrate on the development of better production processes within his own field of expertise.

Suppose, for example, that the minister of transportation in a Marxian socialist society is trying to decide the value of a proposed project to construct a railroad line between two cities. To know whether the anticipated benefits of this plan exceed the costs, the minister will have to take into account the multitude of alternative uses for each of the factors of production that the plan calls for. The iron, for example, could have gone for cars, whose production is supervised by his own ministry, or for factories and tools that are supervised by other ministries. And the value of each of these factories and tools depends on the value of the products it produces. Unless one could make a numerical calculation of the costs and benefits of this particular plan to build a railroad, one would need to have knowledge of all the other plans that "compete" in any way for the required resources. "Where one cannot express hours of labour, iron, coal, all kinds of building materials, machines and other things necessary for the construction and upkeep of the railroad in a common unit it is not possible to make calculations at all" (p. 108).

To grasp what Mises meant by the "complexity" of production processes (about which he had very little to say in the 1920 essay), it is necessary to refer to the wider intellectual tradition from which Mises's ideas emerged, and in particular to Austrian capital theory.

Indeed one could almost say that the major theme of Austrian capital theory, both before and since 1920, has been the idea that the capital structure is intricate and composed of innumerable relations among heterogeneous capital goods.[14] Each relation may be one of substitutability, or of complementarity,[15] or some mix of these, and in each case not only the presence of each attribute but also the degree of substitutability or complementarity has to be taken into account.

We can again see a sharp difference between the Austrian and neoclassical approaches in their respective analyses of the way in which the producer evaluations are ultimately "derived" from consumer evaluations. For the neoclassical theorist who takes the technology as "given," once the central planning board learns the supplies and demands of all relevant consumption goods, the value of capital goods can be directly solved for. Producer evaluations are treated as logically implicit in the consumer evaluations. The Austrian, however, views the derivation of producer evaluations from consumer evaluations as a complex practical problem continuously facing entrepreneurs, which is solved only by approximation and largely unconsciously by a competitive process. The neoclassical theorist treats this as a mathematical solution to a maximization problem in which all of the necessary knowledge is given and which therefore has a determinate solution. The Austrian views it as an "imputation process" in which no evident solution is given to the entrepreneurs who must nonetheless make reasonable judgments and who vie with one another to make more accurate guesses about the "true" value of each capital good. To the Austrian it is only through a competitive clash of many divergent estimates of producer evaluations that those entrepreneurs that survive can approximate the "correct" imputed value that the neoclassical economist assumes is known by each market participant.

The price knowledge generated by rivals in this competitive process is what enables any particular entrepreneur to assign roughly appropriate values to the factors of production under his control. Removed from this competitive environment, the entrepreneur would not be able to intelligently attach value to his factors.

[14] Böhm-Bawerk ([1888] 1959), although in some passages he evokes the image of capital heterogeneity as eloquently as anyone in this tradition, has been criticized by other Austrians for sometimes oversimplifying capital. Menger, Mises (1949, chap. 18), Hayek (1941), Lachmann ([1956] 1978), and Kirzner (1966) have all stressed the complexity of the capital structure.

[15] Menger has been credited (by Böhm-Bawerk, [1888] 1959, p. 161) with having coined the term *complementary goods*.

Another important feature of the Austrian paradigm that under-lies Mises's argument is the particular stress of these writers on the importance of time and change in economics. Competition is seen as a dynamic process, relative prices are seen as continually in motion, plans as repeatedly in need of revision, and the future as imaginable but not knowable. In the 1920 essay, unfortunately, Mises had very little to say explicitly about the Austrian theory of capital and time upon which much of the force of his argument rested.[16]

The underlying notion that the economy is never static but con-tinuously changing is central to Mises's whole argument. Were the entire network of capitalist production processes, however complex, to cease its turbulent movement it might seem entirely plausible that the multitude of activities could be set to memory or laboriously documented and, after the revolution, continued by decree of the socialist planning board. Mises apparently did not take seriously the notion of an unchanging world with an economy in general equilib-rium and in which the structure of technological knowledge, con-sumer desires, relative scarcities of labor, and all other factors are constant; to Mises this was only a "theoretical assumption" that may be necessary "for our thinking and for the perfection of our knowledge of economics" but is simply "impossible in real life" (p. 109).

The neoclassical participants in and the early commentators on the debate seemed to presume that the economy is normally in general equilibrium, from which it is occasionally disturbed by changes and to which it rapidly returns by "adjusting supplies to equal demands." To Mises and Hayek, any sensible meaning of "equilibrium" suggests that it is a totally fictitious state of affairs that is never attained. To the neoclassical theorists it seems that one merely has to observe current markets to see if they have "cleared" – that is, whether they have matched quantitative "demands" to "supplies" – in order to es-tablish whether the economy is in equilibrium. To the Austrians, equilibrium implies the complete compatibility of separately made plans with one another through time, evidently a situation that would be a miraculous coincidence in the real world.

If society's production processes, as seen from the Austrian per-spective, are understood to be both extremely complex and in con-tinuous motion, the enormous difficulty facing the central planning

---

[16] That neither of these two themes of the Austrian school have been well preserved in the subsequent evolution of mainstream economic theory may help to explain why Mises's argument was so widely misunderstood.

board can be appreciated. Under such conditions of complexity, Mises points out, "the roundabout processes of production are many and each is very lengthy; here the conditions necessary for the success of the enterprises which are to be initiated are diverse, so that one cannot apply merely vague valuations, but requires rather more exact estimates and some judgment of the economic issues actually involved" (p. 96).

How, Mises was asking, under such complex conditions could the consumer evaluations – whether originating from a competitive consumer market or from the government – be passed on appropriately to the producer evaluations of the various factors of production? The whole of a static complex production process could conceivably be surveyed "from beginning to end" because the time and effort necessary for the survey would not render the gathered information obsolete. In such a world, producer evaluations – indeed genuine choice of any kind – would no longer be necessary. But in order for conscious central planning of a real economy to be rationally based on the "economic imputation of the yield to the particular factors of production," the planners would have to grasp the whole of a complex and changing production process. This, Mises argued, is a task far more complicated than the human mind is capable of consciously undertaking. Instead of the rationalization of anarchic production, central planning would offer "the spectacle of a socialist economic order floundering in the ocean of possible and conceivable economic combinations without the compass of economic calculation" (p. 110).

But could not such a conscious grasp of the entire production process of a modern society, even though beyond human capacities, be within reach of sophisticated electronic computers? Although we have seen Mises refer to the limits of the human mind – limits that evidently have been extended by computers – the calculation difficulty he described is even more difficult a hurdle in our computerized era than it was in his day.[17] To preserve the advanced level of modern technology, the central planning board's computers would have to consciously control the detailed operation of the hundreds of thousands of computers that are already employed in production processes.

Whether the mind's power is extended by having access to computers or not, the advantage of concentrating on various production

---

[17] To date, the "mental capacity" of computers in some ways exceeds that of the human mind (e.g., computational speed) and in some ways still falls far short of it (e.g., concept formation and manipulation).

problems rather than being saddled with the task of consciously coordinating all production still holds. Were society to try to subsume all production under the guidance of a computer, social production would be constrained by the limits of that computer's capabilities (which, it is assumed, are finite). If, on the other hand, social production is anarchically organized, each computer can be employed in competing ways to expand the productivity of society. Thus it appears that whether the intelligence that consciously controls production is human or artificial, it is aided in its task by the coordination function performed by economic calculation and would handicap itself if it were to abandon this aid.

Difficulties with the labor time solution

The usefulness of the labor theory of value as an analytic tool for examining capitalism has to be distinguished from the usefulness of labor hours as units for economic calculation under socialism. The former is a methodological question for economic theory; the latter is a practical question of the administration of a socialist economy. One may believe the objective labor theory of value to be helpful in explaining the operation of capitalism without believing that labor hours can ever serve as the unit of account for economic calculation under socialism. It is only the second question that will be addressed here.

Although Mises states that for those who adopt the labor theory of value his calculation problem seems to admit of a "simple" solution, he raises two objections to the practicability of such a solution – the heterogeneity of labor, and its unsuitability in accounting for nonreproducible, nature-given factors of production – objections that do not in themselves depend on deciding between the subjective and objective theories of value ([1920] 1935, pp. 35, 112).

Each of these objections has its counterpart in the subjective value theory's critique of the labor theory of value (as in the famous transformation problem controversy between the Austrian Böhm-Bawerk and the Marxian Hilferding; see Böhm-Bawerk [1896] 1973). But what might have sufficed in the value theory debates as an answer to these two objections will not necessarily suffice in the context of the calculation debate. Thus although Mises's objections may look to Marxists like familiar arguments that have already been answered and may look to neoclassical theorists like elementary principles of value theory that are now accepted by most of the economics profession, they should be reexamined within the specific context of the calculation debate.

Mises considers a socialist society that keeps track of the labor hours expended by each worker under centrally planned production and that issues labor coupons, corresponding to hours worked, that are redeemable for a certain proportion of consumer goods. This procedure would try to regulate distribution of the social product by determining the labor hour content of each product and by allocating products to those workers who redeem coupons for them. "In that way every hour of work put in would carry with it the right of taking for oneself such amount of goods as entailed an hour's work" (p. 94).

This is essentially the scheme that Marx, in his "Critique of the Gotha Programme" ([1891] 1974b) somewhat tentatively suggested as a possible planning procedure for the first phase of communism. It should be noted that this coupon scheme is consistent with Marx's critique of the anarchy of capitalist production. The coupons are not money. They do not bid up or down "prices" of goods, since these so-called prices are fixed in advance by their labor content rather than by the anarchic fluctuations of supply and demand. Marx described the same idea in *Das Kapital*:

We will assume, but merely for the sake of a parallel with the production of commodities, that the share of each individual producer in the means of subsistence is determined by his labour-time. Labour-time would, in that case, play a double part. Its apportionment in accordance with a definite social plan maintains the proper proportion between the different kinds of work to be done and the various wants of the community. On the other hand, it serves as a measure of the portion of the common labour borne by each individual, and of his share in the part of the total product destined for individual consumption ([1867] 1967a, pp. 78–9).

Mises argues that this procedure would be unworkable both because "labour is not a uniform and homogeneous quantity" (p. 94) and because calculating in terms of labor does not properly account for "the cost of materials" (p. 95).

Mises admits that labor calculations seem to explicitly take into account the natural nonhuman conditions of production:

The law of diminishing returns is already allowed for in the concept of the socially necessary average labour-time to the extent that its operation is due to the variety of the natural conditions of production. If the demand for a commodity increases and worse natural resources must be exploited, then the average socially necessary labour-time required for the production of a unit increases too. If more favorable natural resources are discovered the amount of socially necessary labour diminishes (p. 113).

Thus when some material resources become more scarce, this is taken into account in the labor calculation theory by the fact that more labor will have to be expended in replenishing those resources. Yet Mises insists that "valuation in terms of labour . . . leaves the employment of material factors of production out of account" (p. 113). He illustrates this point by contrasting two production processes that would be assessed differently by labor accounting than he thinks they ought to be:

2 hours <---> nature   1 hour <---> nature

    2a <---> 8 hours   a <---> 9 hours

       P   *Q*   end product

Here Mises is contrasting two production processes, both of which employ the raw material *a* in the production of final products *P* and *Q*. For example, we could imagine *P* to represent a table and *Q* a chair, where to produce either requires first producing intermediate goods, say, logs (*a*). The production of the table requires 2 logs combined with 8 hours of carving, whereas the production of the chair requires 1 log and an extra hour of carving. Assuming that it takes 1 hour of cutting to produce a log, is it more costly to produce the chair or the table? Since each process uses up a total of 10 hours of socially necessary labor time, labor calculation would treat them as equivalent, but Mises shows that in fact *P* is more costly than *Q* (p. 113). Mises argues that what is missing from labor calculations is a "material substratum," by which he means those nonreproducible resources that, although given by nature, are only present in such quantities that they become subject to "economizing" and therefore "must be taken into account in some form or other in value-calculation" (p. 114). In our example, the table uses up more wood and thus must be judged more costly.

Although labor calculation can try to account for the scarcity of some "raw materials" such as trees by reducing them to the labor time necessary for their production,[18] there is no direct way such calculation can cope with nonreproducible natural conditions of production. If coal cannot be manufactured, then the gradual depletion of coal reserves clearly cannot be properly accounted for by a calculation of the labor that would be necessary for reproducing coal.

In the value theory debates, it may have sufficed for Marxists to

---

[18] It is legitimate to refer to the reproduction cost of trees only if the time horizon of the decision makers in question is such as to include replanting as a viable option. The scarcity of trees today may so impinge on one's options that the possibility of future trees may be, practically speaking, completely irrelevant. This, of course, brings up the significance of time for valuation, which is discussed below.

respond that their theory is not intended to analyze the "value" of nonreproducible goods such as coal (or, one might add, paintings by Rembrandt). Marxian theory is only postulated as an explanation of the value of produced commodities, which, it can be admitted, comprise the bulk of traded goods under capitalism. In this context Marxists could contend that they are not trying to explain the prices of the "material substratum" that is furnished by nature.

But such a response does not answer Mises's criticism. The labor theory approach essentially reduces all scarcities to scarcity of labor time, but the practical task before the central planners is to husband all scarce goods. As Mises put it in his book *Socialism*, "Computation of changes in marginal labour costs only take account of natural conditions in so far as they influence labour costs" ([1922] 1936, p. 133). One can, for example, imagine a situation in which a natural resource is being exhausted while the labor costs for its extraction are diminishing. Labor calculation under such circumstances would undervalue, and thus overuse, the scarce resource in question.

Thus the central planners presumably would have to develop some kind of proxy for the value of nonreproducible goods in units of labor hours. It is difficult to imagine how this could be done in a way that would not be completely arbitrary.

The other and equally serious defect of the labor hour as a unit for economic calculation is that it "is not a uniform and homogeneous quantity." There are qualitative differences among hours of labor that, Mises contends, render it "utterly impossible in any socialist community to posit a connection between the significance to the community of any type of labour and the apportionment of the yield of the communal process of production" (p. 94).

Among the important factors that render labor inputs heterogeneous but that Mises fails to mention is the time that elapses between their insertion into the production process and the moment when they bear fruit in useful products. The "waiting time"—that is, the extent of time separating a consumer evaluation from a producer evaluation that "derives" from it—is often economically significant. If we take the example of the chair and table, the cost of producing the table could easily be greater than the cost of producing the chair, even if we disregard the missing "material substratum," since the table requires 2 hours of initial investment compared with 1 hour for the chair, and the table thus requires longer average waiting time.[19] Undated labor hours cannot account for a "temporal substratum" reflected in the fact that, even for socialist planners, there is disutility in waiting. The extent to which the value of future goods is to be discounted with respect to present goods (that is, the interest rate) has to be taken into consideration. Thus the value (in the sense of the producer evaluation) of an already produced capital good is not equivalent to the value of the total labor hours necessary to reproduce it, since the former can more quickly yield its product and thus contains a "time premium" of value.

Again, in the debates over value theory the Marxist could admit that his theoretical apparatus is readily applicable only to cases where labor is relatively homogeneous and could deny that he is trying to account for the "value" of time. But the central planner who is trying to make a producer evaluation of a particular factor of production cannot let his fundamental unit of account be limited to cases where labor homogeneity can be assumed, nor can he dispense with considerations of waiting time.

The major difficulty with using labor time as a calculating unit is the fact that qualitatively and temporally heterogeneous labor hours are incommensurable. Clearly, in order for this claim to be sustained it will have to be shown that "advanced" types of labor cannot be reduced to "simple" labor and that separately dated hours cannot be weighted according to waiting time in order to reduce this great variety of labor to a common denominator. Most advocates of labor calculation have been aware of the fact that labor hours are not all identical, but they have claimed that labor hours could be reduced to a homogeneous unit. Mises (p. 114) quotes Marx's argument that

skilled labour counts only as intensified, or rather multiplied, simple labour, so that a smaller quantity of skilled labour is equal to a larger quantity of simple labour. Experience shows that skilled labour can always be reduced in this way to the terms of simple labour. No matter that a commodity be the product of the most highly skilled labour, its value can be equated with that of the product of simple labour, so that it represents merely a definite amount of simple labour ([1867] 1967a, p. 44).

Marx was not explicitly aiming here at establishing the possibility of using labor hours for economic calculation under socialism. He was

---

[19] For example, if we assume that the two production processes take place in two stages, on day 1 and day 2, and apply a rate of time discount per day (r), then the value of P (the table) would be $8 \ (1+r) + 2 \ (1+r)^2$, whereas the value of Q, the chair, would be $9 \ (1+r) + (1 + r)^2$. Simple algebra shows that the table would be more costly than the chair for any positive rate of time discount.

only setting up a framework, by means of certain simplifying abstractions, for using the labor theory of value in his analysis of capitalism. For that purpose Marx's argument may be acceptable.

However, Mises argues that there is no way in practice to translate labor hours contributed by electrical engineers, janitors, and professional athletes into a common unit called a simple labor hour. It is not just that some laborers are better educated or more skilled, energetic, dexterous, or physically strong than others. If the problem were merely one of physical productivity, then in many cases, at least, tests could be conducted to determine degrees of ability. But, as has been argued, the serious difficulty in making producer evaluations is not in determining technical productivity but in determining value productivity. The question of whether electrical engineering labor hours are more valuable than janitorial ones, and, if so, how much more valuable they are, can be answered only by imputing consumer evaluations through many stages of the structure of production in order to attribute to each factor its part in producing the final product.

No doubt, as Marx says, "experience" under capitalism shows how this reduction of skilled to simple labor should proceed. But this is done within the context of a price system in which relative wage rates are unconsciously (competitively) determined. In the very next sentence after the ones that Mises quotes, Marx says that "the different proportions in which different sorts of labour are reduced to unskilled labour as their standard, are established by a social process that goes on behind the backs of the producers, and, consequently, appear to be fixed by custom" (p. 44). This process that goes on unconsciously "behind the backs" of producers, Mises argues, is "a result of market transactions and not its antecedent" ([1920] 1935, p. 115). As with material factors of production, without the guide of prices (wages) there is no way of selecting, from among the myriad alternatives presented by a complex economy, those that are economically more efficient. The relative value of different grades of labor would have to be assessed without the aid of this market process. Thus Mises concludes that "calculation in terms of labour would have to set up an arbitrary proportion for the substitution of complex by simple labour," and this would render labor units useless "for purposes of economic administration" (p. 115).

In fact for Mises the problem of reducing heterogeneous labor hours to a common labor unit is only a subset, and a particularly large subset, of the general problem discussed in the last section of reducing heterogeneous factors of production to a common unit. The two main conditions of a calculating unit are that it be universal in the entire production process and that it be homogeneous. Labor hours satisfy the first condition reasonably well, being ubiquitous throughout the complex structure of production, but the diversity of labor makes the second condition – finding a common unit for labor – virtually as difficult as the original and more general problem was. Since labor participates in production in so many ways, at so many stages of production, and varies in its relations to other labor in both substitutability and complementarity in such a plethora of possible combinations, labor "hours" are scarcely any better a measuring rod for calculation than "pounds" of material factors of production would be.

Yet perhaps the most serious difficulty with using labor hours as the unit for economic calculation is the fact that the relevant unit for rational producer evaluations is not historical labor time, which could at least conceivably be recorded. Rather the relevant unit is average, forward-looking, socially necessary labor time, a much more abstract and ephemeral concept. Under capitalism, competition for profit regulates the labor time that is employed in various projects, eliminating wasteful techniques and encouraging innovations. Without this selection process, would the socialist plant manager even know whether his factory's performance in labor time is above the average that is socially necessary? The central planners would have to provide projections of the labor time necessary to reproduce each capital good currently in use in the economy, many of which are no longer being reproduced at all. And each such estimate itself depends on a consideration of a long sequence of stages of production, at each stage of which a whole set of socially necessary labor times have to be estimated and factored into the computation. From the Austrian's view of a continuously changing and complex structure of production, such estimates of necessary labor time would appear to be little more than guesses.

Similarly, the possibility of using dated labor hours (continuously adjusted for changing plans) to keep track of the time component of labor inputs is no simple matter in a complex and continuously changing capital structure.[20] How would one date the labor hour of a steelworker when the steel is dispersed to every stage of production and the proportions dispersed in different stages vary over time?

---

[20] In examples more complicated than our simple table and chair example, it is not always so evident which of two processes requires more waiting time. The recent debates on "reswitching" have shown that for certain technologies that have three or more stages, the cheaper process depends on the rate of interest and cannot be solved for algebraically in the abstract, as was done with the example in n. 19.

Of course the method by which waiting time is accounted for under capitalism is imperfect. But the advantage is that no one has to consciously place any factor into the time structure of production. The interest rate is reflected in all factor prices and is bid up and down through entrepreneurial adjustments. Time is unconsciously factored into monetary calculation in a way that tends to coordinate consumption, saving, and investment without the necessity that anyone grasp the intricate network of social relations that comprise the time structure of production.

The Marxian scheme for abolishing the rivalry of capitalist production appears, then, to be subject to serious objections. The complexity of advanced technological production seems to be too great to permit vague *in natura* calculation and so demands quantitative economic calculation. But without money, and with labor units unworkable, no suitable unit for such calculation is readily available for the central planners to use.

Mises's anticipatory critique of market socialism

Most contemporary advocates of central planning have reverted to a less extreme model of socialism that permits monetary calculation. But even in Mises's initial challenge, this market socialism was addressed, if only very briefly. Although the challenge was directed at Marxism, its potency is not limited to this original view of planning but poses a problem for all proposals for economic planning.

Mises's socialism is a more inclusive classification than Marx's socialism, but the former includes the latter as a special case. The essential distinguishing characteristic of a socialist economy, for Mises, is that "production goods . . . are exclusively communal; they are an inalienable property of the community, and thus *res extra commercium* ([1920] 1935, p. 91; see also p. 89). Higher order goods are not subject to competitive exchange relations but are the common property of the associated producers. Whether there are exchange relations for consumer goods or whether there are markets for labor is, however, a "consideration of more or less secondary importance" (p. 90). Marx's view of socialism would abolish exchange relations per se, including consumer and wage markets, but Mises's argument can be applied to any "socialism" that eliminates exchange relations for the means of production.

Mises's brief discussion of the possibility of salvaging money under less extreme, non-Marxian concepts of socialism anticipated the subsequent evolution of socialist economics. Certainly a socialism that retains some exchange relations – for consumer goods and labor, for example – while taking conscious control of the means of production is conceivable. Although this hybrid "market socialism" was not yet popular in 1920, it was to become the dominant view in the calculation debate; thus Mises's comments on this are of particular interest. Since this scheme would have money and prices from genuinely competitive markets in consumption goods, and wages from labor markets, could not the central planning board use the money, prices, and wages from the competitive spheres as the basis for economic calculation within the centrally planned sphere of production goods?

Mises argued that a money whose circulation is limited to the sale and purchase of consumption goods would not be suitable as the unit for economic calculation in producer evaluations, even though its role "as the universal medium of exchange" would be "fundamentally the same in a socialist as in a competitive society" (p. 92). The "significance" of such a money would be "incomparably narrower." Since no rivalrous competition over alternative uses of production goods would take place, the knowledge dispersal function of money prices would aid only consumer evaluations and would do little for the crucial producer evaluations upon which any rational use of higher order goods depends. Prices are guides for productive coordination only to the extent that rivalrous entrepreneurs actively bid them in equilibrating directions; thus, "Just because no production-good will ever become the object of exchange, it will be impossible to determine its monetary value" (p. 92).

Establishing competitive prices for consumer goods is "but one of the two necessary prerequisites for economic calculation." Without markets in production goods there would be no way to ascertain the relative value of the individual means of production. The central planning board "may establish the value attained by the totality of the means of production; this is obviously identical with that of all the needs thereby satisfied." But the board could not "reduce this value to the uniform expression of a money price" for each factor of production (pp. 107–8). The board would have no way of estimating the marginal value of productivity of the various components of the commonly owned means of production.

But if relaxing the Marxian prohibition of exchange relations for consumer goods and labor does not necessarily circumvent the calculation problem, perhaps we might imagine what later came to be called a "competitive" socialism in which "exchange between particular branches of business is permitted, so as to obtain the mechanism of exchange relations (prices) and thus create a basis for economic calculation" (p. 111). Thus we could imagine "independent and authoritative" labor collectives that "assign each other material goods and services only against a payment" made in money, while still behaving "in accordance with the directions of the supreme economic council" that owns the means of production. Mises's response to this is that genuine exchange relations can take place only among separate private owners of the objects being traded. "When the 'coal syndicate' provides the 'iron syndicate' with coal, no price can be formed, except when both syndicates are the owners of the means of production employed in their business" (p. 112).

To Mises, the standpoint of a manager of a privately owned concern and that of a plant manager under socialism are fundamentally different. It is not a question of training plant managers to "think less bureaucratically and more commercially," because "commercial-mindedness is not something external, which can be arbitrarily transferred" (p. 120). "It is not a knowledge of bookkeeping, of business organization, or of the style of commercial correspondence, or even a dispensation from a commercial highschool, which makes the merchant, but his characteristic position in the production process, which allows of the identification of the firm's and his own interests" (p. 121).

The plant manager's attitude with respect to the socially owned means of production cannot be made identical to the attitude of a private owner because "in practice the propertyless manager can only be held morally responsible for losses incurred" (p. 122). Thus Mises contends that "the entrepreneur's commercial attitude and activity arises from his position in the economic process and is lost with its disappearance" (p. 120).

Allowing separate syndicates to actually own their means of production, however, would abandon the distinguishing feature of socialism – common ownership of higher order goods – and constitute a retreat to a workers' capitalism or a syndicalist position. As such it can hardly serve as an answer to Mises's critique of socialism.

Among modern socialists today, many in fact no longer advocate collective ownership of the means of production but merely advocate nationalizing a few key industries. Mises had made it clear that his argument was strictly applicable only to a socialist economy – that is, one in which there is common ownership of the means of production.[21] It is evidently possible for a few nationalized indus-

---

[21] However, Mises's argument will be reformulated in Chapter 6 in such a way as to represent a direct argument against what he called "interventionist policies."

tries to calculate on the basis of the prices generated by the capitalist market in which they are imbedded, since they "operate within the sphere of a society based upon . . . the system of monetary exchange, being thus capable of computation and account" (pp. 104–5). Thus Mises agrees with the more extreme (e.g., Marxian) socialists that "the nationalization and municipalization of enterprise is not really socialism, since these concerns in their business organizations are so much dependent upon the environing economic system with its free commerce that they cannot be said to partake . . . of the really essential nature of a socialist economy" (p. 104). A bureau of government in a commodity economy is not "socialism" but "only a socialistic oasis in a society with monetary exchange": "In state and municipal undertakings technical improvements are introduced because their effect in similar private enterprises, domestic or foreign, can be noticed, and because those private industries which produce the materials for these improvements give the impulse for their introduction" (p. 104).[22]

Mises's comments on these hybrid socialisms seem extremely terse in the context of today's socialist theory. Elaborate methods of imputing value from consumer goods to producer goods, as well as schemes of "socialist competition," have subsequently been devised that require more careful analysis than has been offered here. But, as the next three chapters will show, the essential arguments that Mises briefly sketched in 1920 anticipate those later developments and, when complemented by his, Robbins's and Hayek's more detailed rejoinders, constitute a powerful critique of "market socialism" even today.

---

[22] Mises does not say when a mere "oasis" turns into a large enough unit to constitute socialism. Presumably an economy that was 80-percent government run and that had little foreign trade would not be considered an oasis. Mises merely says the society must be "free . . . to a certain degree" (p. 104).

CHAPTER 4

The diversion of the debate into statics: rivalry assumed away

This chapter represents a detour from the central issue raised in the previous chapter of how the relevant knowledge necessary for modern technological production can be conveyed without rivalrous competition among private owners. Most of the contributions to the debate that are considered here either explicitly or implicitly assumed this knowledge to be available by restricting the analysis to a world of unchanging equilibrium. Although the standard account of the debate contends that the entire controversy suffered from an inordinate attention to such "static" issues, in my view the controversy began with "dynamic" issues and was diverted to "statics" by the market socialists. The use of two such commonly abused words as these undoubtedly invites some confusion; however, there appears to be no readily available pair of words that can as naturally contrast an approach that is essentially timeless with one in which time and change are of the essence. Of the dozens of distinctions between statics and dynamics enumerated by Machlup (1959), perhaps the one attributed to Shackle comes closest to the sense in which I will use the terms. Shackle (1955, p. 218) describes "statics" as "economics of perfect adjustment" in which "time has no significant place, and uncertainty no place," and his "expectational dynamics" in which time and uncertainty are vital comes closest to the meaning of "dynamic" as used in this study. I agree with Shackle in regarding the mere dating of commodities without the introduction of true uncertainty (as occurs in Hicksian dynamics) as a species of statics.[1]

The significance of static analysis for Mises's calculation argument has been assessed quite differently by various participants in the debate: For example, to Lange a static demonstration (such as those

---

[1] For the purposes of this study, the adjective *static* will be used to describe (1) all analyses of the formal properties or conditions of the state of general equilibrium, and (2) any analyses that seem to treat the real world as if it were usually in or very near such an equilibrium. The static analyses of the first type are legitimate in principle, but, it will be argued, are largely irrelevant to the calculation argument, whereas those of the second type are erroneous and a perversion of the legitimate uses of static analysis.

of Wieser and Barone) answered Mises's challenge whereas to Hayek it comprised a necessary part of Mises's challenge. Further confusion arises from the fact that several different static arguments that have been associated with the debate have often been conflated. Hence, although this chapter is a detour from the original theme of the calculation argument, it is a necessary route to take if we hope to mitigate the confusions of the debate.

From "formal similarity" to "theoretical possibility"

Five distinct static issues will be examined in this section in roughly chronological order. These include a "formal similarity" argument (in two different variants: Wieser's and Barone's); a "mathematical solution" (also in two different variants: "equation solving" and "trial and error"); and a "computation" argument. Some of these are neutral with respect to the practicability of socialism, some are prosocialist, and some are con, but all of them assume that the dynamic problem of knowledge dispersal can be solved. The latter part of this chapter will explore some underlying differences between the neoclassical and Austrian paradigms that help to explain why the various participants had such completely divergent views of the significance of these static issues. Discussion here of these paradigmatic differences is intended not only to help to clarify the significance of the static issues themselves but also to serve as an analytic preface for our return to dynamics in the next chapter by indicating what the introduction of continuous change entails.

The standard view of the debate as the reader may recall from Chapter 1, contends that Mises (in 1920) denied the "theoretical possibility" of socialism even under static assumptions; this was a position that Barone (in 1908) and, some argue, Wieser (in 1889 or 1914) had already refuted and that the early market socialists such as Taylor (in 1929) and Dickinson (in 1933) merely reiterated by showing the formal similarity of socialism to capitalism; whereupon Robbins (in 1934) and Hayek (in 1935) retreated from Mises's "theoretical" argument to a mere denial of the practicability of socialism (which was itself said to have been answered by Lange in 1936).

The following discussion will offer a completely different picture of this piece of intellectual history. First I will describe the "formal similarity" arguments of Wieser and Barone, which, according to Lange and the standard view, proved (contra Mises) that rational central planning was "theoretically possible." However, these arguments will be found to be consistent with, and definitely not refutations of, Mises's argument. In addition to establishing that these two versions of the formal similarity argument have similar aims (to criticize the labor theory of value as a basis for central planning), some subtle differences between them will prove important for the elaboration later of the contrast between the Austrian and neoclassical paradigms.

I will then show that the "mathematical solution " of Taylor (1929) and Dickinson (1933), unlike the "formal similarity" arguments of Wieser and Barone, was an attempt to build a workable model of socialism on the foundation of the theory of the formal similarity of socialism to capitalism. One variation of this mathematical solution, the "equation-solving" argument, proposes to literally solve Walrasian general equilibrium equations (for example, through matrix inversion) as a method of central planning. When Hayek and Robbins responded to this equation-solving argument, besides reiterating Mises's argument they employed an additional "computation" argument that denied that any known mathematical procedure could feasibly solve the hundreds of thousands or millions of equations that would be required.[2]

Hayek doubted in 1935 that this literal equation-solving procedure could have really been what Taylor and Dickinson had in mind. He assumed instead that the mathematical argument meant to propose that the general equilibrium solution to the Walrasian equations is to be discovered by means of some kind of iterative procedure of searching for the solution by "trial and error." This variant of the mathematical solution has been developed in more sophisticated form in recent literature, but I will argue that whatever its theoretical value, it is inherently impracticable as a central planning procedure, for reasons cited by Hayek in the 1930s.

Two versions of the "formal similarity" argument

In classical economics it had been an established practice to postulate an ideal communist society as an abstract theoretical procedure, analogous to Crusoe economics, to aid in the explication of the labor theory of value. When value theory underwent a revolution after the 1870s, Friedrich von Wieser continued the classical practice by using the imaginary construction of an ideal communist world to explain

---

[2] See Robbins (1934a, p. 151) and Hayek ([1935] 1948f, p. 156).

the basic principles of the new marginalist value theory and to refute the labor value theory. One of the primary objectives of Wieser's 1889 book *Der natürliche Werth* (Natural value) was to show that "even in a community or state whose economic affairs were ordered on communistic principles, goods would not cease to have value" ([1899] 1956, p. 60). Wieser sought to demonstrate that "the elementary laws of valuation" are independent of the institutional framework of society and hence would have to be taken into account by the socialist community. Contrary to the views of many socialists of the time, even under communism "labour is valued according to its utility, value attaches to land and capital, and land rent, as well as interest on capital, is calculated among costs. If this were to be neglected, production would become chaos" (p. 66).

The imagined communist society plays the role in Wieser's analysis of an equilibrium state, and "natural value" is taken to be "value as it would exist in the communist state," or the equilibrium price (p. 60).

In his 1914 work, *Theorie der gesellschaftlichen Wirtschaft*, Wieser contrasts the "simple economy," which is the imaginary construction of "the economy of a single subject guided by a single mind" ([1914] 1927, p. 19), with the "social economy" in which "only a relatively small part of the [economic] process is carried forward under unified direction," but instead the "largest part by far is carried out independently by the private economies" (p. 149). Again, the simple economy with its single, conscious plan is used to demonstrate the logical skeleton of choice theory that Wieser treats as "an essential prerequisite" to the description of the "social economic process" of the real world. Wieser frequently criticizes classical economists for their occasional propensity to treat this simple economy as directly descriptive of the world rather than as merely a preliminary step in an abstract argument. "For the theory of the simple economy only explains the condition of the isolated and idealized individual economy that follows its laws of motion without restraint. But in the social economy these individual units meet from all directions. Indeed they clash with great force. We must, therefore, ascertain whether their conjunction does not alter their law of motion" (p. 151).

In the terminology of modern Austrian economics, one might say that Wieser's simple or natural economy abstracts from rivalry. Perfect consistency of plans is first assumed in order to show what basic elements of choice have to be taken into account even in a frictionless equilibrium world: "In its simplicity, purity, and originality it is so attractive, and at the same time so contradictory to all experience, that it is doubtful whether it can ever be more than a dream. So too we shall think of the communistic state as the perfect state. Every-thing will be ordered in the best possible way; . . . no error or any other kind of friction will ever occur" (p. 61).

Despite its unreality, Wieser uses this imaginary world as an ana-lytic tool for studying exchange value in the real world. Although exchange value is "disturbed by human imperfection, by error, fraud, force, chance" and so is not identical to "natural value," none-theless the latter "is not entirely foreign to that value which is re-cognized by the society of today" (pp. 61–2). Thus Wieser seeks to "investigate closely to what extent the phenomena of exchange value are of natural origin" and finds that such categories as rent and interest are "of natural origin" and not due merely to the distur-bances of a decentralized market order.

This demonstration of the universality of choice theory, abstracting from disturbances, is the "formal similarity" argument. All that follows from it is that under any economic system, decision making must take into account such categories as rent and interest because these reflect genuine scarcities.[3] It does not necessarily imply that private rentiers or bankers would have to collect these as incomes under socialism, nor does it say anything whatsoever about whether it will be possible to implement a socialist society. Wieser explicitly admits that "the ques-tion whether such a community can or ever will exist is one which does not in the least concern us" and that "natural value is a neutral phe-nomenon, the examination of which, whatever may come of it, can prove nothing for and nothing against socialism" (pp. 61, 63).

Reacting to the prevailing view among socialists of the time that the new marginalist/subjectivist economics was merely bourgeois apologia, Wieser stressed that "so little is natural value a weapon against socialism, that socialists could scarcely make use of a better witness in favour of it. Exchange value can have no severer criticism than that which exposes its divergences from the natural measure-ment, although, indeed, this forms no particular proof for the es-sence of socialism" (p. 63).[4]

---

[3] It may be recalled from the previous chapter that this is the same point that Mises made in his critique of labor hours as units of economic calculation when he argued that nature-given resources are genuinely scarce and that their producer evalua-tions cannot be directly calculated in units of labor time.

[4] Marx's condemnation of the anarchy of capitalist production, discussed in Chapter 2, bears a similarity to Wieser's point here. That capitalism is anarchically or sponta-neously organized rather than consciously organized implies that it is always in disequilibrium, or, in Wieser's language, necessarily departs from the "natural mea-surement," but the question remains as to whether conscious planning can better approximate equilibrium.

Although Wieser left open the possibility (and possible virtue) of achieving this communist equilibrium world, some of his remarks come very close to anticipating Mises's argument that the competitive order is the only practicable way to approximate to any degree the order that is perfectly achieved in this imaginary world:

The private economic system is the only historically tried form of a large society economic combination. The experience of thousands of years furnishes proof that, by this very system, a more successful social joint action is being secured, than by universal submission to one single command. The one will and command which, in war and for legal unity, is essential and indispensable as the connecting tie of the common forces, detracts in economic joint action from the efficacy of the agency. In the economy, though it have become social, work is always to be performed fractionally . . . *Part-performances of this sort will be executed far more effectively by thousands and millions of eyes, exerting as many wills:* they will be balanced, one against the other, far more accurately than if all these actions, like some complex mechanism, had to be guided and directed by some superior control. *A central prompter of this sort could never be informed of countless possibilities*, to be met with in every individual case, as regards the utmost utility to be derived from given circumstances or the best steps to be taken for further advancement and progress ([1914] 1927, pp. 396–7; emphasis added).

Enrico Barone's 1908 article, "Il ministro della produzione nello stato collettivista" [The ministry of production in the collectivist state] ([1908] 1935), was in the same vein as Wieser's formal similarity demonstration, being mainly directed at the labor theory of value and not at the possibility of realizing socialism. Like Wieser's article, it was intended to establish a revised formulation of the value problem that the central planning authorities would face, not a real mechanism by which this problem could be solved. The first part of Barone's article explains the formal logic of choice under the "individualist regime," after which a parallel formal case is made for the "collectivist regime." Like Wieser, Barone both makes it clear that he does "not write for or against Collectivism" (p. 245) and expresses serious doubts about the workability of a socialist system. His main aim is simply to eliminate certain "errors and contradictions" in the theoretical depiction of the collectivist regime.

Barone does consider it one of his main goals to differentiate his Walrasian/Paretian argument from that of Wieser's Austrian school. He proposes to prove "that to define the economic equilibrium – be it in a regime of free competition, in one of monopoly, or in the Collectivist State – there is no need to have recourse to the concepts of *utility*, of the *final degree of utility*, and the like," which he considers "metaphysical." Instead he employs the "old and simple ideas of demand, supply and cost of production . . . to construct into a system of equations the most important interrelations of economic quantities" (p. 246). He repeatedly denigrates the "vague" and "clumsy" arguments of his predecessors, who merely "perceived by intuition" the conclusions at which he has arrived by way of a "thorough demonstration . . . using mathematical analysis" (pp. 257–8). But despite his criticisms, he comes to substantially the same conclusions as his presumably less scientific Austrian precursors, asserting that "the system of the equations of the collectivist equilibrium is no other than that of the free competition" (p. 274). And like Wieser, Barone recognizes that one cannot conclude from this formal resemblance anything about the possible practicability of the collectivist program. Indeed Barone's own view that central planning cannot work in practice is even more emphatic than Wieser's. "It is obvious," Barone asserts, "how fantastic those doctrines are which imagine that production in the collectivist regime would be ordered in a manner substantially different from that of 'anarchist' production" (p. 289).

Barone believes that his approach to the "formal similarity" argument is more potent than the Austrian approach because it can concern itself only with the formal mathematical proof of the determinateness of equilibriums under the two social systems. He considers it an advantage of his argument that "all this theory of the economic equilibrium, in which we have compressed into a system of equations many varied circumstances, of which we take account at one moment—all this theory, we say, we have expounded without it being necessary to refer to any concept of utility" (p. 265).

In my view this exclusive concern with the rigorously mathematical aspects of value theory is a weakness rather than a strength of Barone's argument. His "precision" has been purchased at the expense of considerable explanatory power and relevance. The conclusiveness of his proof applies only to a formal equilibrium world—to an imaginary construct that is, as Wieser had put it, "so contradictory to all experience, that it is doubtful whether it can ever be more than a dream." Barone was far less clear about the divergence between his equilibrium world and the real world.[5]

[5] For example, whereas Wieser makes it clear that there could be no money in the simple economy ([1914] 1927, p. 49), Barone seems to believe that he can introduce money into his static world by simply adding an additional good with its corresponding equation (pp. 263–4). Barone neglects to explain how a world of complete plan coordination would find any point in the holding of cash balances.

Furthermore, by "compressing into equations" the complex of human interactions that underlie the phenomena of supply and demand, Barone has not merely made an economy of words; he has also diverted attention from some important issues. The economy is made to appear like a quantitative balance among things rather than a relationship among conscious, competing plans. Instead of causation in time, we seem to be talking about the timeless functional relationships among the variables of a system of simultaneous equations. Instead of inquiring into the causal processes by which real money prices are bid up or down, we find ourselves counting equations and unknowns in a mathematical problem in which "prices" are merely numerical solutions. The first forty pages of the article maintain that the necessary "data" concerning matters such as "the quantity of capital," "the relations in a given state of technique between the quantity produced and the factors of production," and "tastes" are available (p. 247). Only the last four pages discuss, in very vague terms, the question of how some of this data can come to be known. But Barone's conclusion that socialism is impracticable rests entirely upon this inadequately defended assertion that knowledge of these "givens" will be available to capitalist entrepreneurs but not to socialist managers.

If Barone were to resort to the device of the auctioneer, as did Walras, to explain how prices change and thus how knowledge is dispersed in his model, then his argument against socialism would be subject to the very reversal that Lange is thought to have accomplished against Mises. The Walrasian auctioneer can simply be replaced with a central planning board, and the socialists will have answered Barone's critique of socialism. Wieser's argument, on the other hand, which emphasizes the informational function of rivalry that is performed "by thousands and millions of eyes, exerting as many wills," is not so obviously susceptible to this Langean argument.

The mathematical solution and the computation argument

The contributions by Wieser and Barone, written before Mises's challenge, were considered abstract arguments that did not represent claims for the workability of central planning. The so-called mathematical solution, however, contends that the formal similarity demonstration can be fashioned into a practicable scheme of central planning and hence into an effective answer to Mises's challenge. Just as Walras and Pareto represented the interdependence of supplies and demands in the economy by means of the familiar simultaneous equations, so would the central planning board actually formulate and solve such equations as a method of central planning. This view holds that, as Hayek ([1935] 1948f, p. 152) phrased it, under the (question-begging) "assumption of a complete knowledge of all relevant data, the values and quantities of the different commodities to be produced might be determined by the application of the apparatus by which theoretical economics explains the formation of prices and the direction of production in a competitive system."

The standard view of the debate suggests that those early market socialists who discussed this mathematical solution were actually only restating the formal similarity argument and not proposing it as a serious method of planning.[6] The evidence shows, however, that at least some of the early market socialists were unquestionably advocating a central planning procedure, although some were not advocating the precise solving of equations, but rather the discovery of solutions to equations by some kind of trial and error procedure.

It is important to note that the mathematical solution in either variant may be seen as a plausible line of defense for the socialists to have tried to hold, although on close inspection it may prove unworkable. The reader may recall from the preceding chapters that the major economic reason for being of the central planning idea had been the subsuming of production under conscious, unified, nonrivalrous control. If a system of prices is to be reconciled with conscious planning, it would appear that the equilibrating process required to coordinate those who calculate with these prices would necessarily have to be carried out, as it were, on paper, or, as some contemporary theorists might say, in the computer. Plant managers would have to submit data to a central body that *precoordinates* their plans in advance of all economic activity. If this coordination is left to the a posteriori equilibrating process of rivalrous competition in markets instead of to the a priori process of formulating a conscious plan, an essential component of the original central planning program will have been abandoned.

One of the first English-language attempts to employ the mathematical solution as a central planning scheme (presumably as an answer to Mises) was Fred M. Taylor's December 1928 presidential address to the American Economic Association entitled "The Guidance of Production in a Socialist State" ([1929] 1964). Although it was published the next year in the *American Economic Review* it seems

---

[6] Hayek cites Taylor's article ([1929] 1964), as well as Tisch (1932), Dickinson (1933), and Roper (1931) as expositions of the mathematical solution.

to have been ignored at the time. But Taylor's brief statement was to set an important (and regrettable) precedent for most of the market socialist literature that followed in the thirties. Taylor divided the calculation problem into two parts and then paid almost exclusive attention to the first (in which he explicitly assumes the relevant knowledge to be available) at the expense of the second, in which he proposes little more than pure guesswork (trial and error) as a procedure for discovering such knowledge. Thus the precedent was established for the market socialists to minimize or ignore the dynamic aspects of the calculation argument and pay inordinate attention to the static aspects.

In the first part of Taylor's discussion, he poses the problem, How should socialist decision makers allocate resources? Under the assumption that they are able to make rational judgments of the "effective importance" (or the producer and consumer evaluations) of the resources in question. The effective importance of any factor is to be "derived from and determined by the importance of the innumerable commodities which emerge" from "the vast complex of productive processes in which it participates" and is to be "embodied . . . in arithmetic tables" that Taylor calls "factor-valuation tables" (p. 46). These tables are supposed to take the place of money prices under capitalism in supplying quantitative information concerning the relative "effective importances" of the various factors of production. For the first two-thirds of his paper, Taylor explicitly assumes "that the authorities of our socialist state will have proved able to ascertain with a sufficient degree of accuracy these effective importances or values of all the different kinds of primary factors" (p. 46), but the (dynamic) question of how to ascertain these values – that is, of how to fill in the factor-valuation tables with the right numbers – is taken up in fewer than five pages at the end of his paper.

It should be evident, in the light of the preceding chapter, that Taylor's first problem begs the question of the calculation difficulty that had been raised by Mises, whose argument was that money prices are the only workable indicators of the relative "effective importances" that Taylor assumes are already embodied in factor-valuation tables. It would surely not have surprised Mises that if one assumes that these tables contain the same knowledge that competitive bidding imparts to prices under capitalism, the calculation problem is easily solved. A similar assumption about knowledge permeates almost all of the market socialist literature, and those market socialists who venture beyond this question into the "dynamic" issues nonetheless devote the bulk of their analyses to these static problems. Despite the fame that Taylor has been accorded for his "trial and error" contribution to the dynamic issues, he considered the static part of his discussion to have been his "main task" (p. 50), and if the proportion of space allotted to an issue is any indication of the importance the writer attaches to it, then it seems that most market socialists agreed.[7]

Although Taylor's first problem may be considered merely an abstract "formal similarity" argument along the lines of Barone's, Taylor's second problem is undoubtedly intended to show the practicability of his scheme as an actual procedure for planning. It is difficult to see how otherwise to interpret Taylor's specific five-step procedure (p. 52) for discovering the correct values of his factor-valuation tables or his explicit remark (directed against those unnamed opponents who might "question the possibility of solving that problem at all under the conditions necessarily prevailing in a socialist state") that "in fact, the socialist authorities would find themselves quite equal to this task" (p. 51).

The brevity of Taylor's paper and the ambiguity of his remarks about "trial and error" make any clear-cut assessment of his proposal difficult. A more detailed and explicit proposal appeared in 1933 with H. D. Dickinson's "Price Formation in a Socialist Community." Unlike Taylor's contribution, Dickinson's immediately sparked a heated debate (in which Dobb and Lerner participated) and indeed can be considered the event that ignited the English-language calculation debate.

Although Dickinson said he was trying "to show that a rational pricing of instrumental goods is at least theoretically possible·in a socialistic economy" (1933, p. 238), there is no evidence that by "theoretical" he meant what Lange meant: an abstract description strictly confined to the assumptions of static equilibrium analysis. There is every indication that Dickinson was, on the contrary, talking about the real world and using the term *theoretical* in the broader sense in which it had been used by Mises. The static assumption is conspicuously absent from a preliminary section in which Dickinson

---

[7] Indeed the market socialist contributors were quite explicit about the fact that they viewed the formal, static, logical aspects of the issue as being of paramount importance. In his exchange with Lerner, Durbin concludes his discussion by saying, "Mr. Lerner and I are agreed upon the most important point of all – the applicability of the logic of the theory of value to the circumstances of the Planned Economy" (1937, p. 581). Lange (1937, p. 144) also expressed "perfect agreement" with Lerner that "the principle of equalizing marginal cost and the price of the product may be taken . . . as the most general rule ensuring the consistency of the decisions with the aims of the plan."

proposes to "first make clear the assumptions on which we shall base our argument" (p. 238). In fact, Dickinson makes his own distinction between theory and practice when he suggests that although socialism may be difficult in theory it will be much easier in practice:

Theoretically the task [of drawing up demand schedules for consumption and production goods] is a very difficult one, since the demand for one commodity is not a function of its price alone but of the prices of all other commodities. Practically, the task could be solved to an approximation sufficiently close for the guidance of the managers of industry, by taking groups of more closely related commodities (composite supply or joint demand) in isolation from other groups (p. 240).

Evidently Dickinson is not merely proposing a central planning scheme that is conceivable under unrealistic "theoretical" assumptions but one that he thinks will be workable in practice. The supreme economic council gathers statistics from which it constructs a Walrasian system of simultaneous equations, which it then solves. Dickinson makes it plain that he does not mean that these equations are to be "solved" metaphorically, the way consumers and entrepreneurs in a market "solve" them. He is not proposing a simulated market in production goods; he is really saying that the equations could be solved mathematically.

Once the system has got going it will probably be unnecessary to create . . . within the framework of the socialist community a sort of working model of capitalist production. It would be possible to deal with the problems mathematically, on the basis of the full statistical information that would be at the disposal of the [supreme economic council] (p. 242).

After describing "four kinds of functions" that the council would require to perform its computation, Dickinson concludes that "the whole thing could be resolved into a set of simultaneous equations, or, since only small deviations from an already established equilibrium need be considered, into a problem in calculus of variations" (p. 242). Other remarks in the article clearly imply that he believes his scheme will achieve equilibrium by solving these equations not simply under abstract theoretical assumptions but in actuality.

Dickinson relies heavily on the view that most if not all "ignorance of economic opportunities would be eliminated by the publicity of a planned economic system" (p. 245). He apparently believes that the problem of the dispersal of knowledge that Mises and Hayek described could be resolved simply by allowing for the "fullest publication of output, costs, sales, stocks, and other relevant statistical data," so that "all enterprises work as it were within glass walls" (p. 239). At this time Dickinson did not realize that the fullest publication of statistics cannot help if changes occur to render the data obsolete, but, contrary to Lange's view, he did not deliberately assume a static world. In fact he later (1939, p. 104) admitted that although he had believed in 1933 that this equation-solving solution represented a practicable procedure for planning, he had since abandoned this view because "the data themselves, which would have to be fed into the equation-machine, are continuously changing"–which was precisely the reason the Austrians rejected the mathematical solution.[8]

Hayek found this equation-solving interpretation of the mathematical solution so absurd that he doubted that it could have been what Taylor and Dickinson had in mind,[9] but he (and Robbins) nevertheless offered an additional argument against it. Their "computation argument" says that even if we presume that all of the relevant knowledge could somehow be gathered and continuously updated by the central planners, it would be practically impossible, given the computational methods available in 1935, for the hundreds of thousands or millions of simultaneous equations to be solved. The sheer complexity of the computation of such an enormous mathematical problem would bar the equation-solving solution from workability, even if all its other difficulties could be resolved.

In my next two chapters I will further substantiate my denial that there ever was a "retreat" from Mises to Hayek and Robbins, as the standard account contends. I will, however, suggest that Hayek and Robbins may have helped to cause the confusion that surrounds this issue when they hypothetically conceded a point that constitutes an essential pillar of their primary argument in order to advance a secondary *computation* argument against the equation-solving position. Only in this very restricted sense can they be said to have retreated. The arguments that they stressed however, were elabora-

---

[8] The Austrians were not the first to formulate this objection to the mathematical solution. As early as 1902, N. G. Pierson had offered a similar objection: "And as regards the fixing of prices, the socialistic State would soon find that no mathematical formula was of any avail, and that the only means by which it could hope to solve the problem were exact and repeated comparisons between present and future stocks and present and future demand; it would find that prices could not be fixed once and for all, but would have to be altered frequently. Not the theory of averages, but the value of things in exchange would, in most cases, have to serve as its guide in fixing prices; and why should it reject the services of that guide?" ([1902] 1912, p. 94).

[9] See Hayek [1935] 1948f, p. 157. Since the "computation" argument was directed at only this less plausible variant of the mathematical solution, the equation-solving argument, the computation argument clearly cannot have been the main point of Hayek's critique of central planning as the standard account of the debate suggests.

tions of the issue of the dispersal of knowledge that had been contained in the original Misesian challenge.

The fact that the response to Hayek and Robbins focused on this computation argument (which assumes the problem is merely one of solving fully formulated equations) rather than on the more fundamental calculation argument (which makes no such assumption) is probably due not so much to anything either economist wrote. Rather it is attributable to the fact that Hayek rather uncritically included in his *Collectivist Economic Planning: Critical Studies on the Possibilities of Socialism* (1935) his English translation of Barone's 1908 article. Barone *does* argue that planning on the basis of Walrasian equations is unworkable mainly because of "the difficulties – or more frankly, the impossibility – of solving such equations *a priori* . . . For the solution of the problem it is not enough that the Ministry of Production has arrived at tracing out for itself the system of equations of the equilibrium best adapted for obtaining the collective maximum in the well-known sense . . . It is necessary to solve the equations afterwards. And that is the problem" ([1908] 1935, pp. 286–7).

However, to at least Mises and Hayek, if not also Robbins, the problem was *formulating* the equations – not solving them. In a world of complexity and continuous change, the central planners would lack the knowledge of the coefficients that go into the equations. Unlike the "computation" argument, this more fundamental critique is applicable to both variants of the mathematical solution. Whether the solutions to general equilibrium equations are to be precisely computed or simply found by trial and error, a necessary prior step must be the formulation of the equations.

In Mises's own response to the equation-solving solution (1949, pp. 710–15), he emphasized that Walrasian equations can only describe the unrealizable state of equilibrium and cannot guide the decisions of real producers who are necessarily outside of this static world. Thus he argued that "for a utilization of the equations describing the state of equilibrium, a knowledge of the gradation of the values of consumers' goods in this state of equilibrium is required. This gradation is one of the elements of these equations assumed as known. Yet the director knows only his present valuations, not also his valuations under the hypothetical state of equilibrium" (p. 711). Mises treated the computation argument as merely a subsidiary point appended to his primary contention that the knowledge required to formulate the Walrasian equations is unavailable. The computation argument, which he refers to as an "algebraic" problem, is mentioned only once in his 1949 book, and in a manner that clearly signifies its secondary importance in his analysis: "There is . . . no need to stress the point that the fabulous number of equations which one would have to solve each day anew for a practical utilization of the method would make the whole idea absurd even if it were really a reasonable substitute for the market's economic calculation" (p. 715).

Although Robbins was not very clear on this issue, Chapter 6 will show that Hayek, like Mises, clearly treated the computation argument as subsidiary to the major point about the absence of the knowledge required to formulate the equations of general equilibrium. Unfortunately, Hayek muddied the waters when he said that he was relegating Barone's essay to the appendix of his 1935 collection of essays on economic planning "only because it is decidedly more technical than the rest of the book" (1935, p. 40) and not, presumably, because it represented what is in fact a substantially different point of view from the other contributions in the volume.[10] By not sharply differentiating the Austrian argument from Barone's, Hayek appears to have invited responses that, although they did not deal with the fundamental problem of formulating the equations, appeared to circumvent the lesser problem of solving them once they were formulated. Given both the secondary role that the computation argument played in Mises's and Hayek's critiques of socialism and the way the subsequent responses became preoccupied with this issue of solving equations, it is probably regrettable that the point was ever introduced.

"Trial and error" as a variant of the mathematical solution

Immediately after offering his computation argument against the equation-solving solution, Hayek goes on to say that it is "improbable that anyone who has realized the magnitude of the task involved has

[10] However, some of Barone's arguments against equation solving as a method of planning are very similar to the Austrian position and despite Barone's own quoted remarks to the contrary imply that the Walrasian equations are not merely insoluble but cannot be formulated at all. See, for example, his comments on the "economic variability of the technical coefficients" ([1908] 1935, pp. 287–8). Although Hayek later said that Barone "at least approached the problem" ([1935] 1948e, p. 140), Mises ([1922] 1936, p. 135) emphasized that Barone "did not penetrate to the core of the problem" as did Pierson ([1902] 1935).

seriously proposed a system of planning based on comprehensive systems of equations" ([1935] 1948f, p. 157). Rather they must have really believed that starting from a price system evolved from capitalism, only minor changes at the margin would be required to adjust prices to their equilibrium levels. Thus Dickinson (1933, p. 241) refers to "a process of successive approximation" and Taylor ([1929] 1964, p. 51) to a "method of trial and error . . . which consists of trying out a series of hypothetical solutions till one is found which proves a success."

Hayek interpreted Taylor's "trial and error" procedure as a nonrivalrous a priori process of first finding a full set of equilibrium prices that could then be used to implement the plan; hence to Hayek this amounts to only another species of the mathematical solution. Other interpretations of trial and error will be discussed in the next chapter, but here this rather literal interpretation will be examined, according to which the prices necessary to establish an economy-wide general equilibrium are supposed to actually be "found" by trial and error.[11]

Hayek's primary argument against the mathematical solution was not the computation argument but the more fundamental point that the relevant detailed knowledge of production processes cannot be considered "given" to the central planning board but rather resides and is continually regenerated in decentralized form throughout the economy. A plausible response to this argument might be that the plant managers in a decentralized production system could continually communicate with the planning board and somehow impart their knowledge of feasible factor combinations to the price-fixing planners. Tentative prices could be proposed by the board as a "trial," and plant managers could respond with tentative estimates of the quantities they would be able to produce at these prices, leading to "error" whenever supplies exceeded or fell short of demands. The board could then try another configuration of prices, and the cycle would be repeated until an equilibrium was "found."

This approach has been explored more deeply since the debate in a body of abstract theoretical central planning literature that has

[11] One immediate objection to this method is that, at least from the Austrian viewpoint, there is no way of knowing whether one has "found" an equilibrium, even if one supposes it could ever be attained. A subjectively defined equilibrium is not objectively verifiable. See Machlup (1958). For a systematic discussion of the limitations of equilibrium theory, see Kornai (1971, pp. 3–31).

been termed *planometrics*.[12] This approach includes a variety of sophisticated mathematical techniques (including linear and nonlinear programming, integer programming, much cybernetic decision analysis, and various computer-aided iterative approximation techniques) for finding an equilibrium set of prices, conceived as a substitute for a market's equilibrating process. In spite of very ambitious efforts of planometricians, even the most sophisticated models that have been developed so far have come nowhere near implementation. There has emerged a sharp dichotomy between central planning "theory," involving such planometric modeling, and central planning "practice," involving studies of the actual implementation of five-year, annual, and short-term plans.[13] As Martin Cave put it in his informative survey of the use of computers in Soviet planning: "Several writers have noted and regretted the gulf existing between two groups of investigators of economic mechanisms, the one group formulating abstract models of economic systems, the other studying existing systems" (1980, p. 26).

Although some Soviet models still propose to treat the planning process as a gigantic optimization problem to be solved by the central planning board, there is an increasing realization that such comprehensive modeling is, as Kornai once put it, "science fiction." Cave concludes that the "most fundamental" reason for the growing skepticism about planometric models as a substitute for markets is that "they do not, nor are they intended to, do justice to the complexities of a centrally-planned economy" (1980, p. 38).

Many enthusiasts of mathematical economics had confidently

---

[12] A voluminous literature in both the East and West has grown up on this subject. See Ames (1967), Arrow, Hurwicz and Uzawa (1958), Baumol (1958; 1972, pp. 70–190, 294–318, 515–35), Blaug (1968, pp. 410–12), Campbell (1961), Chenery and Kretschmer (1956), Dantzig (1963), Dantzig and Wolfe (1960; 1961), Dorfman (1953), Dorfman, Samuelson, and Solow (1958), Fadeeva (1959, pp. 99–102), Fedorenko (1974), Felker (1966), Fellner (1960), Gale (1960), Hahn and Negishi (1962), Hurwicz (1960; 1969; 1971; 1972), Kantorovich (1965), Köhler (1966, pp. 106–22), Koopmans (1951), Kornai (1974), Kornai and Liptak (1965), Lange (1970; 1971), Makower (1957), Malinvaud (1961; 1967), Marglin (1963), Marschak (1957), Montias (1967), Negishi (1962), Nemchinov (1964), Novozhilov (1969), Parker (1963), Rakovskii (1968), Scarf (1960), Sengupta (1972), Sherman (1969b, pp. 280–302), Sik (1976, p. 200), Swann (1975), Ward (1960; 1967a; 1971, p. 132), Weitzman (1970), Wilczynski (1970, pp. 24, 41), Zauberman (1976), and Zauberman, Bergstrom, Kronsjö, and Mishan (1967).

[13] See Grossman (1960a). Although the unrealism of much of planning "theory" is widely admitted, few realize that much of what constitutes the analysis of central planning "practice" is also far removed from the actual economic processes in socialist countries. Kornai (1959, pp. viii–ix) notes that most works on socialist practice, "instead of telling us how our economic mechanism really works, . . . merely describe how it would work if it worked as their authors would wish."

heralded the development of computers as the beginning of a new age for planning in which a comprehensive network of computers would replace the market as the equilibrating mechanism. Lange himself, in a retrospective on the calculation debate published in 1967, remarked that had computers been available in the 1930s he could have employed a much easier solution to Hayek's challenge than the "competitive solution" he offered then. By contrast with the exact procedures of computer-aided planometrics, Lange considers the market a crude and soon to be obsolete computing machine: "The market process with its cumbersome *tâtonnements* appears old-fashioned. Indeed, it may be considered as a computing device of the pre-electronic age" (1967, p. 158).

Yet after a few decades of planometric refinement, the idea of replacing markets with an all-encompassing, computerized central plan has been increasingly abandoned in the planning literature. Instead, planometrics is defended either as an intellectual pursuit interesting for its own sake or as a useful first stage (that of plan "formulation") to be combined with a later ("implementation") stage that relies on spontaneous market forces. Yet even those (for example, Hurwicz [1971, p. 81]) who offer the latter justification admit that the implementation stage consists primarily in adjusting the "plan" to market realities, rather than in shaping those realities to the elaborate planometric model. Belkin (1961, pp. 185–202) compares Soviet planning to an unguided missile that can only be pointed in the right direction but, once launched, is on its own.

The consensus in the planning literature seems to be that the computer plan should be, as Cave put it, "complementary to the extension of . . . independent accounting at the enterprise level" (1980, p. 5). Such independent profit and loss accounting, or *Khozraschet,* has been universal in the "central planning" systems of Eastern Europe since the failure of War Communism. The central "plan," as Roberts and Polanyi argue, seems to be more an *ex post* adaptation to the regulated market process of competition among plant managers for profit (among other goals) than it is an *ex ante* formulation and implementation of a true plan. Richard Judy (1967, p. 29) contends, as have many observers, that "so great is instability and so frequent the changes of the plan that by the end of the planned period, the plan is a document of only historical curiosity." Thus it can be argued that notwithstanding the remarkable advances in computer technology, the hopes of replacing the "cumbersome" market process with "exact" planometric procedures are no closer to realization today than they were in the 1930s.

The chief positive outcome of these modern explorations has been that they have established the extremely restrictive assumptions required to get a system to converge to a complete general equilibrium. Lange ([1936] 1964, pp. 70, 86) and Dickinson (1939, p. 103) presumed that even if one started with random prices the system would, after a few iterations, soon settle upon the "correct" prices. By contrast, even under very unrealistic simplifying assumptions, modern planometricians are much more hesitant to conclude that their models provide for convergence of prices toward equilibrium.

However, some practitioners of planometrics still claim that despite the failures so far, refinements of these procedures will one day make them workable as substitutes for a market.[14] Thus a few more comments about the inherent limitations of this approach are in order. An awareness of these limitations is implicit not only in Cave's recent assessment of planometrics but also in Hayek's 1935 response to Taylorian "trial and error."

As contrasted with its somewhat more sophisticated later developments in planometrics, the trial and error process that Taylor proposed in 1929 even more severely underestimated the extent and complexity of market change. Taylor (and, the next chapter will argue, Lange) seemed to think that upon the adoption of a central planning system, only small changes at the margin would be required to return the economy to and maintain it at the competitive equilibrium inherited from capitalism. Hence, it is suggested, no complete equation-solving procedure need ever be performed.

Hayek proposed two counterarguments. First, he doubted that the transition to socialism could be so moderate as to preserve the relevance of the price system that had been left by capitalism. To most adherents, then as now, market socialist or orthodox, socialism entails at the very least a massive redistribution of wealth that would inevitably have a drastic effect on prices ([1935] 1948f, p. 157).[15]

In addition, Hayek argued that the proposed method would be unworkable in a real world of continuous change. Each individual price change carries with it implications for innumerable other price

[14] See, for example, the comments by Wilczynski (1970, p. 24), who, while admitting that the "planometric centralist" model is "still beyond practical possibility," blames this on an "insufficiently developed network of computers" and a "shortage of trained personnel."

[15] Mises ([1920] 1935, pp. 109–10) had made the same point when he wrote that "the transition to socialism must, as a consequence of the levelling out of the differences in income and the resultant readjustments in consumption, and therefore production, change all economic data in such way that a connecting link with the final state of affairs in the previously existing competitive economy becomes impossible."

changes, all of which would have to be consciously adjusted by the central planners. "Almost every change of any single price would make changes of hundreds of other prices necessary, and most of these other changes would by no means be proportional but would be affected by the different degrees of elasticity of demand, by the possibilities of substitution and other changes in the method of production" ([1935] 1948f, p. 157). Given that detailed price fixing "would have to bring about as frequent and as varied price changes as those which occur in a capitalistic society every day and every hour," there is no likelihood of convergence toward a first equilibrium solution before new changes render this solution obsolete.

In his 1940 answer to Lange (to be examined in Chapter 6), Hayek wrote:

If in the real world we had to deal with approximately constant data, that is, if the problem were to find a price system which then could be left more or less unchanged for long periods, then the proposal under consideration would not be so entirely unreasonable. With given and constant data such a state of equilibrium could indeed be approached by the method of trial and error. But this is far from being the situation in the real world, where constant change is the rule ([1940] 1948a, p. 188).[16]

If the method is to actually "find" a configuration of prices that clears all markets, it would have to be modeled rather closely on the Walrasian auctioneer who calls out tentative prices and receives conditional answers from plant managers as to what they would supply and demand at these prices, until the equilibrium prices are discovered that will clear all markets. Then and only then can production on the basis of these equilibrium prices commence, and during the production period no changes of plan can be permitted. It was only under such stringent assumptions as these that Walras was able to prove that his model would achieve a complete general equilibrium.

Perhaps the most crucial difference between this imaginary auctioneer adjustment model and the real world has to do with the question of trading at "false prices." Contrary to the assumptions of the Walrasian approach, in actual market exchanges there is no way to prevent the data from changing before an equilibrium constellation

---

[16] In "The Use of Knowledge in Society" Hayek made this point even more emphatically when he indicated that "there are few points on which the assumptions made (usually only implicitly) by the 'planners' differ from those of their opponents as much as with regard to the significance and frequency of changes which will make substantial alterations of production plans necessary." Under conditions of minimal change the task of comprehensive planning "would be much less formidable" ([1945] 1948a, pp. 81–2).

of prices can be found. But this means that trading in the market will invariably take place at disequilibrium prices, and this is itself a disequilibrating force.

Ironically, many of the same theorists who explicitly recognize that the auctioneer model is unlike real market processes nonetheless endeavor to model central planning schemes after the Walrasian procedure. Indeed many advocates of planometrics insist that it is a strength of their approach that they can, by using an auctioneerlike approach, attain equilibrium more easily than real markets with their problems of "false trading." Thus Benjamin Ward, when he contrasts centralized and decentralized models of socialism, seems to consider it an advantage of centralized models that "no goods would be traded until the adjustment process, carried out by paper and pencil, or rather computer, had arrived at the optimal plan for quantities and prices" (1967b, pp. 32–3), whereas decentralized models have to contend with the "problem" of allowing irreversible exchanges to take place at disequilibrating prices.

But this is a peculiar way of looking at the issue of trading at false prices. Actually such trading, though perhaps a liability for formal general equilibrium analysis, is a definite advantage of real market processes over planometric models, and the fact that the latter have never proved practicable can largely be explained by the fact that they lack this "problem" of disequilibrium transactions. The chief strength of the real equilibrating process, as contrasted with the auctioneer models, is that it works tolerably well without eliminating exchanges at false prices and works in particular by taking advantage of the knowledge that is actively generated by the competitive process in disequilibrium.

If they are to avoid false prices, planometric price adjustment models must require that trading and production cease while supply and demand information throughout the structure of production is communicated to the ministry of production. The advantage of these schemes is supposed to be that the technological knowledge (the coefficients of production) need not be known by the central planners, this feature allegedly insulating them from Hayek's critique.[17]

---

[17] Chapter 6 will show that Hayek was more deeply dissatisfied with the assumption that such knowledge is objectively "given" to the central planning bureau than is generally supposed. Hayek was in fact denying that this knowledge is objectively given even to the decentralized decision makers. Rather, the relevant knowledge exists for the entrepreneur in an inarticulate form, as a "technique of thought" whose application fundamentally depends on one's being situated in a competitive market environment ([1935] 1948f, p. 155).

The difficulties that these schemes raise for any real-world implementation of central planning are often minimized. For example,
although Benjamin Ward makes some brief references to the mathematical "oversimplifications" of these schemes – for example, he
notes that they are static and usually linear (1967b, pp. 58–9) – he
underestimates some other potential difficulties. Ward claims that
the "communication between sectors and plan bureau . . . cannot be
a bottleneck to extension of the schemes" (p. 61). Such communication, he says, "involves at each round sets of numbers that should
not exceed n^2 for any one unit, where n is the number of sectors,
and is generally much less."[18] But if, as seems quite likely, "time
prevents completion of the iterations needed to generate an optimum," for the more sophisticated of these schemes "the process can
be stopped at an intermediate round and will produce a plan which
is consistent and an improvement over the starting feasible plan" (p.
61). With this comment Ward is abandoning the major raison d'être
of the auctioneer process. If producers are to hold up all economic
activity while the linear programming experts compute an equilibrium, only to achieve a "feasible" but nonoptimal configuration of
prices, why wait for such costly computation in the first place? The
non-*tâtonnement* processes of a decentralized market under an appropriate legal system can accomplish this imperfect result without the
intervention of planometricians.

But aside from the practical difficulties, one of the fundamental
problems with these models is that they, like the Walrasian approaches
from which they stem, trivialize the problem of market change in a
realistically complex economy.[19] Real-world production cannot afford
to await the incredibly complex discovery of the economy-wide implications of each step of production before embarking on it. It is easy
enough for theoretical planometrics to proceed as if all further
changes in the data can cease until the equilibrium is "found," but if
production were actually conducted in this manner it is doubtful that
even the first step of a single production project could ever commence.
Planometricians in a truly dynamic world would be perpetually chasing
after a continuously changing equilibrium solution.

[18] Although Ward speaks here of "sectors," for this to be a workable procedure n
  would have to be the number of separately priced items in the economy, a number
  that when squared and then multiplied by the number of necessary rounds could
  constitute a considerable bottleneck for even the most advanced communication
  system.
[19] A related and also fundamental problem with this approach is that it assumes that
  some of the "data" that are actually generated by competitive activity – i.e.,
  knowledge of "technology" – are at the outset available to socialist plant managers.

The limitations of static analysis

The "formal similarity argument," or the argument that the "formal analogy" between socialism and capitalism "makes the scientific technique of the theory of economic equilibrium which has been worked out for the latter also applicable to the former" was, in Lange's view, completely adequate to refute Mises's challenge ([1936] 1964, pp. 107–8). Lange and the other market socialists devoted the bulk of their analyses to demonstrating that the determination of an equilibrium configuration of prices is possible under socialism. Yet Mises seemed unconcerned with the static world of this formal argument[20] and explicitly acknowledged that under static assumptions there would be no calculation problem. A similar divergence over the significance of the static issues separates Barone's version of the formal similarity argument from Wieser's, and Dickinson's view of Walrasian equations from Hayek's view of them.

The gulf that separates these views on the significance of the "formal similarity" argument can be explained only by exploring the implicit differences between the Austrian and neoclassical paradigms. Since neoclassical theory is more familiar, this discussion will focus on certain features of the Austrian approach that differentiate it from the neoclassical approach.

Subjectivism

Mises and Hayek tended to take it for granted that ever since the completion of the marginalist revolution of the 1870s, all trained economists had been as subjectivistic as they themselves were. The primacy of "choice theory" in modern economics was understood to imply that economics is about ends and means strictly as they are

---

[20] It would be incorrect to infer that Mises found equilibrium theory unimportant. For Mises the static formulation establishes the logic of the equilibrium toward which market forces tend. If this equilibrium is inadequately described, systematic divergences between the real world and the theorists' equilibrium would persist. For example, if interest is not properly accounted for, as it had not been by the classical equilibrium theory, it will appear as an inexplicable regular income, which, despite competition for profit, never seems to get bid down to zero. If interest is understood as an explicable element of value theory involving the discounting of the future, then the systematic divergence of the equilibrium from reality disappears. Hence the internal details of the equilibrium state are important for Mises's or Wieser's rejection of the labor value theory or for any other approach that fails to properly account for all aspects of scarcity. Economic statics is necessary for the formulation of the value problem, which the calculation argument contends cannot be solved under central planning in a real – that is, nonstatic – world.

perceived by individual human minds and that the fundamental concepts of choice theory (such as cost) must therefore be understood in relation to the perceived alternatives to the particular choice being examined. Mises and Hayek seemed to think that with the general defeat of the classical value theory, the subjectivistic viewpoint had triumphed, and many contemporary neoclassical theorists would concur. But the modern Austrian school contends that a spurious objectivism has crept back into neoclassical economics and indeed that this counterrevolution had begun long before it became manifest in Lange's 1936 response to the calculation debate.

Although the concept of opportunity cost is considered a basic tenet of neoclassical economics, opportunity cost has come to mean objective opportunities displaced by a course of action, rather than the subjective alternatives perceived but forgone by the decision maker at the instant of his choice.[21] It is commonly presumed that money outlays correspond to the subjective value of all physically displaced alternatives, that these alternatives are equally known to all market participants, and that each decision maker has a predetermined indifference map that anticipates all conceivable options and mechanically yields the optimal among them whenever a choice must be made. Technological knowledge is distilled into objectively known production functions, equally "given" to all market participants and instantaneously revised with every technological advance.

This objectivization of choice can, of course, be thought of as purely an expository device and is so considered by many who employ it. But its serious limitations for the analysis of market processes are being increasingly recognized today, and it has undoubtedly led to many errors. The depiction of costs in terms of marginal and average cost curves for heuristic purposes has led many to presume that costs are objectively knowable, that from a systematic observation of economic phenomena the observer can somehow actually plot costs on graphs as a meteorologist plots cloud patterns. The essential insight of economic subjectivism — that costs are no more observable than the contents of the individual minds who incur them — has been forgotten by many economists who were trained in the neoclassical tradition.

Although the subjectivistic outlook is closely related to the calculation argument, the central problem that the calculation argument raises is not the subjectivistic insight that choice is always filtered

---

[21] See Thirlby (1973c) and Vaughn (1980a).

through individual minds.[22] The advocate of planning could readily concede that the central planning board's choice will also have to be filtered through the individual minds of the planners but could still contend that the central plan should concern itself as much as possible with production functions – that is, with the underlying objective possibilities of the transformation of resources into valuable commodities. As the example of Abba Lerner, a subjectivistic market socialist, should suggest, subjectivism per se, narrowly conceived as the approach that focuses on perceptions of reality by individual minds rather than directly on reality itself, does not constitute the primary issue of the calculation argument.

Rather, the key point of the calculation argument is that the required knowledge of objective production possibilities would be unavailable without the competitive market process. For central planning to be practicable, it is not enough that realized choices about production techniques be objectively measurable in some sense; unrealized alternatives that are forgone by such choices – that is, opportunity costs – must also be known. Implicit in the objective value theorists' outlook can usually be found the hidden assumption that technological and economic knowledge of the real production functions is "given." Thus it is not the subjectivity of value as such that undermines the hopes of central planning advocates; it is the fact that the requisite knowledge of the objective possibilities of production can only be generated by a rivalrous process that pits different plans against one another. Although it is true that this competitive market process cannot be understood without reference to the subjective perceptions of its contending participants, and thus that subjectivism is related to the calculation argument, the kernel of this

---

[22] James Buchanan, in his excellent study of subjectivism entitled *Cost and Choice*, contends that the Austrians in the debate overemphasized the "information problems" of central planning instead of the problem of subjective choice, which he considers "relatively . . . more significant." Thus, he argues, "Even if the socialist state should somehow discover an oracle that would allow all calculation to be made perfectly, even if all preference functions are revealed, and even if all production functions are known with certainty, efficiency in allocation will emerge only if . . . men can be motivated" or "trained" to "make choices that do not embody the opportunity costs that they, individually and personally, confront" (1969, pp. 96–7). Although I would agree that even if the problem of knowledge were overcome the problem of motivation would remain, it seems to me that it is the former that is the more fundamental. One could reverse Buchanan's argument and say that even if socialist managers could somehow, as he puts it, be "converted into economic eunuchs . . . to make decisions in accordance with cost criteria that are different from their own," the central difficulty of obtaining the relevant information would still remain. Even fully motivated planners would not know how to plan rationally.

argument is the issue of the generation and dispersal of knowledge about objective production possibilities.

Michael Polanyi's contributions to epistemology and the philosophy of science are extremely valuable in this context (1951; 1958). Polanyi points out that a great deal of the knowledge with which we live and work is inarticulate. We know how to do various things without knowing enough to objectively represent this knowledge in a formal, determinate system. Without denying that formalization represents an important step in the refinement of science, he stresses that any formal model necessarily stands on a foundation of inarticulate assumptions about what the model means and how it might be used. Polanyi distinguishes among three degrees of formalism— the "completely unformalized," the "completely formalized," and the "theoretically formalized." He places economics in the third category. The equations of formal economic theory, he says, "are valuable in exhibiting certain logical features of the problem to which they refer, but cannot be used for solving these problems." Among the basic reasons why economics is formalizable only "in theory," he cites the fact that most of the data on which the decision maker has to rely "can obviously not be given numerical values, or brought into mathematically specifiable relations to each other" (1951, p. 179).

Furthermore, Polanyi contends that much of our practical knowledge is embodied in skills that cannot be represented formally but can only be learned through apprenticeship, through practice in the proper context. For example, when one learns to ski or to play the piano one is not learning objective, articulated rules about when to lean uphill or how to apply the sustaining pedal. Rather one is cultivating unconscious habits through practice, by learning to use certain keys to adjust one's habits until the skill is mastered. Polanyi cites the example of the beginning cyclist who learns to keep his balance by turning in the direction toward which he starts to fall, thereby causing a centrifugal force that rights the bicycle, even though few cyclists are consciously aware of the principles underlying their skill. The key that the cyclist uses as he practices is his sense of balance that "tells" him which way he is tilting and thus which way to turn.

The practical use of cost accounting by an entrepreneur to guide production activity can be usefully viewed as the kind of skillful knowing that Polanyi describes. Only in the context of practicing within a competitive price system are "costs" meaningful keys that serve as "aids to the mind" in the entrepreneur's skilled direction of production toward more profitable undertakings. If costs were objective and universally known, choice could be reduced to obedience to specifiable, articulated rules, but since costs are subjective and strictly contextual, the skillful functioning of the entrepreneur cannot be replaced with objective criteria.

Aspects of choice

At the heart of this difference between neoclassical and Austrian views of cost is a fundamental difference in their respective theories of choice, a difference that has been sharply revealed only in relatively recent contributions of the Austrian school.

Both Austrian and neoclassical economics would agree with Lange's statement that "the economic problem is the problem of *choice* between alternatives" ([1936] 1964, p. 60) but there are subtle differences in what is meant by "choosing." This section will list three aspects of choice, only the first of which has been successfully incorporated in neoclassical analysis.

Maximization: The idea of maximizing choice is central to the question of rational economic calculation, for the purpose of accounting calculation is to aid the chooser in making the best possible, or optimal, choice – that is, to act economically. As Shackle (1972, p. 82) put it: "To be anti-economical is to be inconsistent, it is to engage in actions which are at odds with each other, it is to be less effective than one could be. The detail of a formal consistency . . . can be subtle and complex. It is this formal guidance that economics, in the sense of 'the pure logic of choice,' can give."

The pure logic of choice, that which underlies perfect competition, sees choice as the mechanical computation of the best among the known means for achieving a given end. But there is more to choice than this concept of pure optimization. Three major works in modern subjectivist economics – Mises's *Human Action* (1949), Shackle's *Epistemics and Economics* (1972), and Kirzner's *Competition and Entrepreneurship* (1973) – emphasize two other aspects of choice: futurity and alertness.

Futurity: "Action is always directed toward the future," Mises insisted, and the future is uncertain (1949, pp. 100). "Our knowledge," says Shackle, "is knowledge about the *present*, but choice is choice of what we hope for. We cannot *choose* the present: it is too late" (1972, p. 122).

The aim of all action, according to Mises, is "to render future conditions more satisfactory than they would be without the interference of action. The uneasiness that impels a man to act is caused by a dissatisfaction with expected future conditions as they would probably develop if nothing were done to alter them" (1949, p. 100). The actor forms alternative expectations of what the future will hold with respect to some end he values if he takes various imagined courses of action. From an inspection of these mental images of the future, the actor selects the course that he envisions will lead to the most desired future state of affairs. For example, the manager of a firm might imagine a causal stream of events likely to follow each of several possible decisions. He might, for instance, anticipate (1) greater demand and a depletion of his inventory, if he takes no action; (2) greater demand and a sufficient quantity of goods supplied, if he acts in an effort to expand output; or (3) unchanging demand and sufficient stocks, if he acts in an effort to raise his selling price to the right degree. Obviously, in any real-world case the number of such possible scenarios could be enormous. But actual decision makers must select a manageable sample of scenarios in order to compare *ex ante* the costs and advantages of each of the imagined causal streams—that is, in order to estimate through economic calculation the relative profitability of several possible choices. The degree of rationality of this calculation varies with (among other factors) the extent to which these expectational scenarios accurately conform to the evolving reality of history. More accurate expectational scenarios lead to a more rational allocation of resources through time.

Alertness: An optimization problem circumscribes the possible alternatives that are given to a decision maker but leaves unanswered the question of how these alternatives were noticed and not others. To the extent, then, that one works within a given ends/means framework, any other previously unnoticed alternatives are necessarily excluded.

Kirzner (1973, pp. 36–7) contrasts the Robbinsian optimizer with the alert actor. The pure theory of choice distills from the idea of a decision all such "impurities" as the imperfect knowledge of the relevant resources, techniques, and constraints. "Where a clearly identifiable framework of ends and means is held relevant by a decision-maker before his decision, we may explain his decision quite satisfactorily as yielded mechanically by calculation with the ends–means data." But there is nothing in this pure logic of choice that can tell us "how . . . one pattern of relevant ends—means comes to be replaced by another." Acting man must be not only an optimizer but also an alert noticer—or one might say creator—of optimizable alternatives.

The concept of the entrepreneur embodies these latter two aspects of choice that are missing from the pure logic of choice. The Austrian view of choice includes and emphasizes this entrepreneurial role. Actors formulate plans for future choices on the basis of their expectations of future circumstances.

The fact that both of these latter aspects of choice, so often neglected by economists, have been emphasized by the Austrians underscores the open-endedness and creativity of the Austrian view of choice. Economists have tended to overemphasize the aspect of choice that involves maximizing from given alternatives, as if every actor had at hand a complete list of options from which he or she merely has to select the optimal one. Shackle has perhaps been the most eloquent critic of this narrow notion of action.

In general, in life at large, in history, business, politics, diplomacy and public affairs, where can any list be found, of detailed answers giving all relevant particulars? There is no source of such a list, except what the expectation-former can conceive in his own mind. The list, if we allow ourselves to call it such, is the work of his own thought, unbounded in its scope except by what experience or formal instruction or logic tell him is outside the principles of Nature or the Scheme of Things. Since there is nothing in principle to limit the length of future time whose situations or events may seem relevant, the diversity of the sequels he is free to conceive of seems on this ground to be beyond all reckoning . . . The expectation-former is provided with no given and ready-made list of relevant sequels to any one of the rival courses open to him. Such sequels are for him to conceive, to invent. He has no grounds for supposing that the process of conceiving ever-different sequels will be brought to an end by their exhaustion. May not the process of inventive thought be inexhaustible? Expectation is not a passive, finished and settled state of thought but an activity of mind which can at no time say that it has completed the imaginative exploitation of its data; for these data are mere fragmentary suggestions in a paradoxically fertile void (1972, p. 366).

Neoclassical equilibrium models, of which the perfect competition model is one variety, are attempts to include all alternatives in a given framework—that is, they presuppose a world of Robbinsian optimizers who have preset adjustment ready to meet any change that is anticipated under a given framework. There are no fundamental surprises, no genuinely new ideas, no alertness to unimagined alternatives – in short, no genuine changes. The only adjustments are adjustments in price or quantity within the limits established by the original decision matrix. Constraints may change, and so may the optimal choice, but the framework of alternatives itself is rigid. Given the available options, the model specifies which options are chosen under which circumstances. But the question of which options are to be considered in the first place is never raised.

The neoclassical world of general equilibrium is populated with automatons who are programmed by the standard of profit maximization to respond to price changes in such a way as to make $MC = MR$, or, in the case of perfect competition, $MC = P$. In Chapter 5 I argue that Lange's world is populated by similar automatons who are instructed to produce at the quantity where $MC = P$. Potential opportunities for profit have all been mapped out clearly ahead of time, and the Robbinsian optimizers merely produce the quantity at which marginal costs equal price. Profit isn't found – it's maximized. The element of entrepreneurship is absent not only from the end state of equilibrium itself – as it must be – but also from the proposed process of adjustment toward that equilibrium.

But the market society envisioned by the Austrians is populated with human actors. They, first of all, do not merely respond. Their alternatives have not all been given them from day one. The products themselves, and not just their prices and quantities, are subject to change. Future demand must continuously be estimated ahead of time. The entrepreneur does not simply react to exogenous demand changes; he anticipates changes by taking action himself. He does not adjust only to actual surpluses and shortages; he adjusts to anticipated surpluses and shortages on the basis of his comprehension of other actors' plans.

The pure logic of choice makes sense only in an imaginary world from which genuine change has been abstracted, a world of "equilibrium." If the means/ends framework employed by decision makers covers all contingencies, if no true surprises confront anyone, then "choice" may be modeled in terms of the mechanistic constrained-optimization problems familiar from intermediate microeconomics texts or planometric exercises. But if, as the Austrians maintain, the real world never reaches equilibrium, the explanatory power of the "pure" aspects of choice theory is necessarily diminished, and that of the disequilibrium aspects of choice – futurity and alertness – is correspondingly enhanced.[23]

Equilibrium and equilibration

A great deal of the confusion that prevented the opponents in the debate from understanding one another can be traced to their different ways of looking at equilibrium. In the more neoclassical contributions such as Barone's ([1908] 1935) and Lange's ([1936] 1964), equilibrium is presented as an objectively observable, quantitative matching of current "supplies" to current "demands" and seems to be thought of as the usual condition of an economy, from which it is only occasionally and temporarily disturbed. The paradigm case seems to be the kind of pure-exchange Marshallian fish market from which time and its associated complications have been abstracted. Prices are simply adjusted until supply equals demand and that is the end of it. The only idea of any sort of "equilibration" process is the instantaneous adjustment of a price until the market is cleared.

By contrast, the Austrian view of equilibration or coordination is concerned with "approaching" an equilibrium in the sense of developing production plans that prove, over the course of time, to be compatible. Its paradigm case of an equilibrium would be time-consuming production activities that prove, upon completion, to have been consistent with one another, as if all market participants had correctly anticipated the independent projects of their fellows. As Hayek put it in his essay "Economics and Knowledge,"

---

[23] Most contemporary advocates of planning have not yet realized the significance, for the Austrian critique of planning, of the distinctively Austrian view of choice as involving alertness and futurity. A notable exception is the book by Estrin and Holmes (1983, pp. 38–9) on French economic planning. The authors recognize that "writers in the Austrian tradition have always been dissatisfied with static equilibria and the treatment of uncertainty as a special case of certainty through the use of certainty equivalents. They focus on the consistent uncertainty and disappointment of agents who are driven to make entrepreneurial profits by out-guessing each other in the market place." Unfortunately, the only response these writers make to this distinctively Austrian critique of planning is the comment that because of "economies of scale in the gathering and processing of information," we need indicative planning by the state "to make useful suggestions in an informationally imperfect world." Making "useful suggestions" is a far cry from the traditional ambitions of national economic planning, but it is also not clear why, if such informational economies of scale really exist, large corporations fail to take advantage of them and profit by supplying the needed information. In any case, as Vera Lutz (1969) has shown, the usefulness of the suggestions made by the French planning bureau has been highly questionable.

It appears that the concept of equilibrium merely means that the foresight of the different members of the society is in a special sense correct. It must be correct in the sense that every person's plan is based on the expectation of just those actions of other people which those other people intend to perform and that all these plans are based on the expectation of the same set of external facts, so that under certain conditions nobody will have any reason to change his plans ([1937] 1948b, p. 42).

Thus to the Austrians equilibrium should not be confused with the mere matching of quantities currently supplied with those demanded. The Marshallian market-clearing price can often be reached, whereas the price needed for general equilibrium, Mises argued, "will never be attained" (1949, pp. 244–5), since its attainment would imply the miraculous coincidence of the perfect compatibility of plans that Hayek was talking about. For the Austrians, that world where no opportunities for profit lurk around an uncertain corner, where there is a perfect coordination of plans, and where all expectations prove correct, will never arrive.

Most modern general equilibrium theorists such as Debreu (1959) recognize this disparity between the world they occupy and the one they formalize. Certainly any theory must abstract from aspects of reality that are irrelevant in order to examine in isolation those aspects under investigation. The real world is a bewildering network of simultaneous causal strands running through historical phenomena. No theory could ever get off the ground unless one selected particular causal sequences to analyze, *ceteris paribus*. "Other things being equal" is a meaningful and indispensable theoretical step in all of those sciences, including economics, whose purpose is to comprehend a single causal sequence within a multicausal complex.

In any science one can imagine "what would happen if," even when one cannot conduct empirical tests. In economics we can hypothesize specific economic circumstances in order to decide the implications of those circumstances, *ceteris paribus*. By examining individual strands of causal forces mentally, we can learn what makes an economy tick. For example, by imagining a world in which the future is certain, we can better elucidate those aspects of the real world that differ from that imagined world, and we will thereby have isolated the specific aspects of our world that are implied by the existence of an uncertain future.

Mises was to set forth this method briefly in *Human Action:*

The specific method of economics is the method of imaginary constructions ... An imaginary construction is a conceptual image of a sequence of events logically evolved from the elements of action employed in its formation ... The main formula for designing of imaginary constructions is to abstract from the operation of some conditions present in actual action. Then we are in a position to grasp the hypothetical consequences of the absence of these conditions and to conceive the effects of their existence (1949, pp. 236–7).

In this method it is no criticism to say that the imaginary construction is unrealistic; the construction is usually intended to be unrealistic, since it is by its usefulness as a contrast to reality that it renders services to the economic theorist. The state of economic equilibrium is a very commonly used imaginary construction, and, like most, it is not realistic. What we imagine happens in this unreal world does not directly tell us anything about what would happen in the real world.

With the use of these mental tools the economist investigates the different functional aspects of action. Mises writes in *Human Action* that the central concept of his theory, the entrepreneur, "means acting man in regard to the changes occurring in the data of the market" (p. 254). There is an entrepreneurial aspect to all real-world action, but the economist, in order to isolate the specific real-world resultants of this aspect of all action, postulates a world in which just this element of action is missing (Mises calls this world the "evenly rotating economy"). This unreal construct is contrasted with the real world, where, we know, entrepreneurship is present, and in this manner the entrepreneurship function is elucidated. In the evenly rotating economy there is no change in the data; there is no uncertainty; prices are all at the level where supply equals demand; plans are perfectly consistent.

As Robbins (1934b, p. 466) once remarked parenthetically in describing the limited role and purpose of the theory of equilibrium, "No assumption is made that this condition is necessarily achieved in any existing economic system or that the tendencies operative would necessarily achieve it if undisturbed. The sole purpose of the inquiry is to illuminate, by contrast, certain problems of movement." To the extent that the evenly rotating economy is different from the economy in the real world (where changes do occur; where all prices are not clearing prices; where expectations are frequently mistaken), there is scope for entrepreneurial action, and, if it is successful, for entrepreneurial profit. In the real world there is always scope for entrepreneurial action – that is, in the real world we are never in equilibrium.

Equilibrating forces, all driven by entrepreneurial action, never actually work to their completion before changes in the data (some of which these forces themselves have caused) disrupt the situation.

Economic theory conceives of the operation of these equilibrating forces by formulating mental constructs. In the real world, Shackle reminds us, "The parameters of any model are inevitably permeated by noneconomic influences of commanding importance, from politics, diplomacy and power-hunger in general; from demagogic rivalry; from the intense pursuit of technological improvement. Ceteris paribus is a mere pedagogic device or means to insight, and cannot be turned into practical experimental insulation" (1972, p. 75).

Equilibrium, to the Austrian economist, is an intermediate tool of thought used in extracting from our understanding of human action certain of its functional aspects (such as time preference, resource ownership, and entrepreneurship) and in analyzing the way in which these aspects of action are reflected in a market order in corresponding categories of returns (such as interest, rent, and profit). This whole analytic process of category formation and functional delimitation is the essence of the Austrian theoretical method. To the Austrian economist the "theory" is not confined to the analytics of an equilibrium model, although theory may employ such a model; rather "theory" is the collection of concepts that are both abstractions from and descriptions of the real world.

The virtue of the market economy as opposed to a centrally planned economy, according to Mises's calculation argument, is that it has an equilibrating process that is driven by the struggle among entrepreneurs for profit. The virtue is not claimed to be that a market economy can achieve a competitive equilibrium that is Pareto-optimal whereas a planned economy cannot. Although the market socialists believed that they had answered Mises by offering a socialist *equilibrium* to supplant the "competitive" equilibrium of capitalism, what was required was to show a socialist process of *coordination* to supplant the competitive economy's entrepreneurial equilibration process.

Institutions and institutionalism

The market socialists took it for granted that knowledge of "production functions" (the specific knowledge necessary for economic production) is equally available to producers regardless of the institutional setting in which they find themselves. The Austrian school, on the other hand, is noted for its attention to the role that institutions play in the economy. However, when Lange called Mises an "institutionalist," lumping him in this regard with Marx and the historical school, Lange was criticizing rather than praising. Mises, according to Lange, thought that "the economic principles of choice between different alternatives are applicable only to a special institutional set-up, i.e., to a society which recognizes private owner-ship of the means of production." This, Lange argues, represents a "spectacular contradiction" of both Mises's own avowal of "the uni-versal validity of economic theory" and also of the arguments of the entire "Austrian school, which did so much to emphasize the universal validity of the fundamental principles of economic the-ory" ([1936] 1964, p. 62).

But to read Mises's calculation argument as a denial of "the univer-sal validity of the fundamental principles of economic theory" is to completely reverse his point.[24] Mises, on the contrary, was contending that the principles of choice theory – the abstract logic concerning the application of means to achieve ends – must find application in any mode of production if that production is to be rational and to attain a sophisticated technological level. This, however, is only to restate the problem of economic calculation. The question remains whether a society in which the socialist institution of common ownership of the means of production is established has the capacity to solve this prob-lem. Postulating an equilibrium formulation along the lines of Bar-one's, in which the problem is assumed away, does little to aid the search for a solution in a real, disequilibrium world.

If, as Lange seems to imply, anyone who holds that institutions (such as private capital markets) matter is an institutionalist, then Mises (along with the entire Austrian, Marxian, historicist and, no doubt, other schools) is an institutionalist. The Austrian school is not only noted for its explication of the universality of certain basic propositions of choice theory; it has also made seminal contributions to our understanding of the evolution, nature, and importance of social institutions. Menger's idea of "organic" institutions and his specific analysis of the origin of money; Hayek's work on the signifi-

[24] Hayek ([1940] 1948a, pp. 182–3) was astonished at this reversal of Mises's argu-ment, which has become a commonplace in the standard account of the debate, despite Hayek's criticism of it. It was Mises, Hayek wrote, who had "pointed out that if the socialist community wanted to act rationally its calculation would have to be guided by the same formal laws which applied to a capitalist society. It seems necessary especially to underline the fact that this was a point made by the critics of the socialist plans, since Professor Lange and particularly his editor (Lippincott, [1938] 1964, p. 7) now seem inclined to suggest that the demonstration that the formal principles of economic theory apply to a socialist economy provides an answer to these critics. The fact is that it has never been denied by anybody, except socialists, that these formal principles *ought* to apply to a socialist society, and the question raised by Mises and others was not whether they ought to apply but whether they could in practice be applied in the absence of a market."

cance of legal institutions as a framework for a market order; and Mises's analysis of the informational role of the institution of profit/loss accounting procedures – these are but a few instances of this Austrian "institutionalism." In fact all three of these institutions – money, law, and economic calculation through accounting methods – are depicted by the Austrians as mutually reinforcing one another and thereby contributing to the "equilibration" or coordination of the economic choices involved. The Austrian notion of equilibration, unlike the idea of equilibrium, presupposes a particular kind of institutional environment.

Austrians, however, differ from other "institutionalists" precisely in that they try to explain the emergence and survival of any social institution by reference to the purposes of the individuals whose interactions sustain it. Institutions are seen as "guide posts" that help individuals to orient themselves with others – that is, institutions are regarded as indispensable components of a coordination process. To the Austrian economists, as contrasted with "institutionalists" in the usual sense of the word, identifying specific historical institutions is not the end of an analysis but only the beginning. These institutions are themselves explicable in terms of the interacting purposes of those individuals who use them. Thus Austrian choice theory is seen as a tool for the study of social institutions.

By contrast, the neoclassical choice theory that Lange employs completely ignores institutions. In a static equilibrium world, such guide posts for coordination are redundant, since the coordination problem is assumed to have been solved. Little wonder, then, that Lange sees no calculation problem for socialism, since in his model all of the significant institutional differences between capitalism and socialism have been abstracted away. As Dobb pointed out,

Naturally, if matters are formulated in a sufficiently formal way, the 'similarities' between one economic system and another will be paramount and the contrasting 'differences' will disappear. It is the fashion in economic theory today for propositions to be cast in such a formal mould, and so devoid of realistic content, that essential differences . . . disappear . . . The distinctive qualities of the laws of a socialist economy and of a capitalist economy . . . are not, of course, given in the rules of algebra, but in assumptions depending on differences existing in the real world (1935a, pp. 144–5).[25]

[25] Similarly, Dobb had remarked in 1933, in responding to Dickinson, that to apply "the postulates of a static equilibrium" to a changing world is a "barren feat of abstraction." Economics, he argued, should be seen as more than "a formal technique . . . , a system of functional equations, a branch of applied mathematics, postulating a formal relationship between certain quantities" (1963, p. 589).

The static answer to Mises reconsidered

Mises's basic error, according to Lange, was "a confusion concerning the nature of prices" ([1936] 1964, p. 59). Referring to one of the most subjectivistic price theorists in economics, Philip H. Wicksteed ([1910] 1933, p. 28), Lange distinguishes between a narrow and a broad meaning of "price." According to Lange, Mises asserted that money prices "in the ordinary sense, i.e., the exchange ratio of two commodities on a market" are necessary. Lange contends that only prices in the broader sense of "terms on which alternatives are offered" (that is, abstract accounting prices, or the prices arrived at by using Taylor's factor-valuation tables) are "indispensable to solving the problem of allocation of resources" ([1936] 1964, pp. 59–60). Lange then proceeds to point out how "prices" in this wider sense would be available to socialist producers and could supplant the function of money prices under capitalism.

The economic problem is a problem of *choice* between alternatives. To solve the problem three data are needed: (1) a preference scale which guides the acts of choice; (2) knowledge of the "terms on which alternatives are offered"; and (3) knowledge of the amount of resources available. Those three data being given, the problem of choice is soluble ([1936] 1964, p. 60).

Aside from the semantic redundancy of speaking of "data" being "given," note the more important analytic redundancy of posing "the economic problem" as a maximization exercise in which the knowledge that Mises had argued could not be generated and dispersed is simply assumed to be available. "It is obvious," Lange asserts, "that a socialist economy may regard the data under 1 and 3 as given, at least in as great a degree as they are given in a capitalist economy."[26] As for the data described in item 2, Lange alleges that

a careful study of price theory and of the theory of production convinces us that, the data under 1 and under 3 being given, the "terms on which alternatives are offered" are determined ultimately by the technical possibilities of transformation of one commodity into another, i.e., by the production functions. The administrators of a socialist economy will have exactly the same knowledge, or lack of knowledge, of the production functions as the capitalist entrepreneurs have (pp. 60–1).

---

[26] Since Lange concedes the need for a genuine market for consumer goods, the data described in item 1 would be as available under his scheme as it is under capitalism, but the data described in item 3 is far more problematic than he suggests. Determining what is and what is not a "resource" itself depends on having an adequate procedure of value imputation.

But this last assertion is precisely what Mises and Hayek repeatedly denied. To the neoclassical participants in the debate, the relevant knowledge is assumed to be given to market participants, and the main analytic conclusion is that under certain static assumptions the capitalist equilibrium is determinate. It is a small step from this analysis to the adoption of similar assumptions and the arrival at similar conclusions for socialism.

However, as my last chapter showed, Mises's calculation argument was not about the determinateness of equilibrium "under socialism;"[27] it was about real social institutions and their causal interconnectedness under disequilibrium conditions. Mises was not confusing money prices with abstract accounting prices in terms of a *numeraire;* he was expressly contending that only money prices can serve as "aids to the mind" or disperse knowledge in such a way as to enable the extension of technology to proceed to its modern level of complexity, a level far beyond that possible for a single mind. Abstract accounting prices can of course be imagined to be at general equilibrium levels, but only by assuming a perfect compatibility of all plans—that is, by assuming away the problem of knowledge dispersal. Since Mises maintained that it was by their active bidding against one another that entrepreneurs push money prices in equilibrating directions, this coordinating process would have to be replaced by something if the means of production are commonly owned. To simply assume from the outset that all of the relevant knowledge is somehow "given" to the central planners is to profoundly miss the point.

A possible reason why Lange misunderstood Mises's challenge that rational calculation is "theoretically impossible" under socialism is that *theoretical,* to Lange, may have suggested the pure, institutionless logic of choice of neoclassical theory. Certainly if Mises had denied the universality of choice theory, his argument would already have been refuted, in essence, by the arguments of Wieser and Barone.[28] Mises's remarks about the static world, added in 1936 to the English

---

[27] Indeed, what it means for a static world to be "under socialism" or "under capitalism" is not at all clear. In a world where production plans are perfectly coordinated, it would seem that neither a central planning bureau nor a private property legal framework has any function. It is very difficult to imagine what laws, contracts, prices, or money would be like in a world where all plans are perfectly compatible. Any meaningful contrast between economic systems will have to take place outside the confines of equilibrium theory.

[28] The static argument was not conceded by all participants in the debate, however. Dobb, in his response to Dickinson, denied "that the categories of economic theory are equally valid in a socialist as in an individualist order" (1933, p. 589), although he later seemed to withdraw this denial (1955).

translation of his 1922 book, leave no doubt that his "theoretical" case against socialism involves the question of the practicability of central planning in the real, continually changing world:

It is clear that under stationary conditions the problem of economic calculation does not really arise. When we think of the stationary society, we think of an economy in which all the factors of production are already used in such a way as, under the given conditions, to provide the maximum of the things which are demanded by consumers. That is to say, under stationary conditions there no longer exists a problem for economic calculation to solve ... To use a popular but not altogether satisfactory terminology we can say that the problem of economic calculation is of economic dynamics: it is no problem of economic statics ([1922] 1936, p. 139).

CHAPTER 5

The market socialists' "competitive" response: rivalry ignored

As the standard account of the calculation debate describes their arguments, Hayek and Robbins retreated in the face of the early market socialist responses to Mises by conceding that a rational central planning system is conceivable but contending that it is impracticable because of the complexity of the equations it would have to solve. The famous "competitive" solution of Oskar Lange and others is generally described as an effective demonstration of a workable system of planning under which such equations need not be solved by a central planning bureau, thus answering Hayek and Robbins.

The next two chapters will present an alternative version of this stage of the debate, according to which it will be argued first (in this chapter) that the market socialists posed and attempted to solve a substantially different problem from the one posed by Mises, and then (in the next chapter) that the contributions of Hayek and Robbins constitute effective rejoinders to the type of solution the market socialists offered. It should be noted that in these chapters many contributions by Mises, Hayek, and Robbins that preceded Lange's 1936 essay ("On the Economic Theory of Socialism," [1936]), and that the latter is thought to have answered, are not described until after the Lange solution. The reason for this departure from strict chronology is that the competitive solution is being interpreted here as an answer to the static "computation" argument described in the preceding chapter rather than as an answer to the main arguments of the Austrians, which will be discussed later. In other words, Mises's, Hayek's, and Robbins's discussions will all be treated as (in some cases anticipatory) answers to the competitive solution.[1]

The market socialists, I suggest, never grasped the essence of the

---

[1] For Hayek and Robbins to have effectively anticipated the Lange solution did not require any feats of intellectual prophecy. In the German-language debate in the 1930s, somewhat vague proposals for introducing pseudocompetition into central planning had already been made, and by 1934 and 1935, when Hayek and Robbins joined the English-language debate, such ideas were, so to speak, "in the air."

Misesian challenge. They proposed a competitive solution that, on the strength of its own ambiguity, appears to successfully steer a path between a centralized, nonrivalrous planning that would be subject to the Austrian critique of statics and a decentralized market that would circumvent this critique only to abandon all vestiges of genuine planning.

I will describe this competitive solution primarily by reference to Lange's classic exposition but will also refer to related arguments of Durbin, Dickinson, and Lerner. The purposes of this description will be to illuminate the general structure of the market socialist argument, to suggest its possible relevance to the computation argument, and to point out that as an answer to the calculation argument it is ambiguous and question-begging. This task is somewhat complicated by the fact that in my view the contributions of these four market socialists contain fundamental contradictions, not only among one another but also within each of their expositions. The interpretation presented here will represent only the most plausible resolutions of such contradictions that I have been able to achieve, but articulating the specific distinctive features of these proposals is not the central concern of this examination. These proposals are more important, from the point of view of this study, for what they all assume without argument and for the substantive issues that they all manage to avoid.

Lange's extension of the "formal similarity" argument

We saw in the previous chapter that the Wieser and Barone versions of the "formal similarity" argument contended that the same principles of choice should govern socialist decision making as govern this process under capitalism. It was taken for granted that what distinguishes socialism from capitalism is not the choice problem that each faces in the abstract but rather the practical method by which each proposes to solve this problem: for socialism by deliberate planning, for capitalism by a competitive market. In other words, it was held that the same equilibrium theory would pertain to socialism as to capitalism but that their respective equilibrating processes – conscious planning or spontaneous competition – would differ.

By contrast, we saw that Taylor's 1929 planning model, described in "The Guidance of Production in a Socialist State," was advanced as a practical solution on the grounds that its equilibrating process, characterized as "trial and error," is analogous to that of capitalism. Socialism and capitalism apparently not only face a similar problem in the abstract; they can also employ similar practical solutions. Because of the brevity of Taylor's discussion it was difficult to determine precisely how closely analogous this trial and error process was supposed to be to competition under private ownership, and we will see in the following section that a similar ambiguity plagues Lange's more lengthy treatment. Hayek was to interpret these two versions of trial and error differently, calling the earlier one a mathematical solution and the later a competitive solution, although Lange believed himself to be simply elaborating on Taylor's innovation.

Of more direct interest here is the specific form of the Lange-Taylor argument. As was mentioned in the last chapter, the argument proceeds by breaking the calculation problem into two separate parts. In the static part it is assumed that all of the specific decentralized knowledge of production processes, tastes, and the availability of resources, as well as all equilibrium prices, are "given" to plant managers. It is then meticulously demonstrated that under these knowledge assumptions there is no difficulty in performing economic calculation. Part two, the presumably dynamic part, then relaxes only one of these knowledge assumptions – the correct prices are no longer assumed given – and the trial and error process is advanced as a procedure by which these prices are "found."

But the Lange-Taylor procedure of breaking the calculation problem into these two issues amounts to a significant reformulation of the problem that they were trying to solve. In effect, the market socialists never properly formulated the original calculation problem and for this reason never answered it either. By relaxing only the one datum, prices, and retaining the assumption that all of the other data were available, this approach reduces the problem of knowledge dispersal to one of computing the equilibrium prices for a set of fully specified Walrasian equations. In other words, Lange and Taylor offered answers to the computation argument rather than the calculation argument. Although their demonstration may be considered relevant to Barone's neoclassical critique of socialism, in which the difficulty of solving such equations constituted the central problem, it necessarily fails to provide an answer to Mises and Hayek, for whom this computation argument was merely a secondary point.

Lange, in his 1936 article, "On the Economic Theory of Socialism," begins his "formal analogy" between capitalism and socialism by recounting what he calls the "textbook exposition of the elements of the theory of economic equilibrium," which shows how a determinate equilibrium is computed in a perfect competition world ([1936]

1964, p. 72). He cites three conditions for reaching this optimal state: "(A) all individuals participating in the economic system must attain their maximum position on the basis of equilibrium prices; and (B) the equilibrium prices are determined by the condition that the demand for each commodity is equal to its supply. We may call the first the subjective, and the latter the objective condition." The third condition "expresses the social organization of the economic system," which in this case states that "(C) the incomes of the consumers are equal to their receipts from selling the services of the productive resources they own, plus entrepreneurs' profits (which are zero in equilibrium)" (pp. 65–6).

In standard neoclassical fashion, Lange shows how in perfect competition the subjective condition of equilibrium A is achieved when consumers maximize their utility and producers maximize their profit. The former case leads consumers to equate the ratios of their marginal utilities to prices for all commodities, whereas the latter leads producers to equate the ratios of the marginal productivities to the prices of each factor and to produce at the scale of output where marginal cost equals the price of the product. Total industry output is based on free entry and exit, which "makes the total output of an industry such that the price of the product is equal to the average cost of production" (pp. 66–8). This gives us the total output and demand for the commodities and factors on the market as a determinate solution.[2]

Lange then shows how condition C tells us that "incomes of consumers are determined by prices of the services of ultimate productive resources and by profits so that, finally, prices alone remain as the variables determining demand and supply of commodities" (p. 69). Using the objective condition B, which says that demand equals supply, we can determine the set of prices that equilibrates the market. "As Walras has brilliantly shown," Lange concludes, "this is done by a series of successive trials (*tâtonnements*)" (p. 70). For Lange, "the *theoretical* solution of the problem of equilibrium on a competitive market" consists of a proof of the determinateness of equilibrium "under capitalism," but the actual solution to the problem, he argues, is achieved by Walrasian *tâtonnements* – that is, by a kind of trial and error where, "if . . . the quantities demanded and the quantities supplied diverge, the competition of the buyers and sellers

---

[2] I should note in passing that Lange jumps casually from a tautological condition of incomes (C) to a *causal* determination of incomes. The difference between a mathematical determination, as in $y = f(x)$, and causal determination – x causes y – is often obscured in the market socialist discussions.

will alter the prices . . . And so the process goes on until the objective equilibrium condition is satisfied and equilibrium finally reached" (p. 71).[3]

Having shown how an equilibrium "for capitalism" is both determinate "theoretically" and, at least to Lange's satisfaction, actually attained in practice, Lange proceeds to show how in a socialist community the equilibrium can also be determinate "theoretically" and how a similar process of trial and error can find this equilibrium.

The subjective equilibrium condition is met, Lange asserts, by permitting consumers to maximize their utility in the market for consumer goods, as with capitalism, and by having producers, no longer guided by the standard of profit maximization, obey two rules imposed upon them by the central planning board.[4] Rule 1 must supplant the perfect competition model's characteristic that profit maximization leads producers to equalize their marginal products for each factor, so here the central planning board instructs the producers to choose the combination of factors that minimizes the average cost of production. Rule 2, Lange says, must replace the perfect competition model's characteristic that the optimal scale of output is brought about by means of profit maximization such that marginal cost equals the price of the product. Thus rule 2, addressed to the managers of plants, instructs them to produce at that level where marginal cost equals price (pp. 75–6).

Total industry production is then set "by addressing the second rule also to the managers of a whole industry . . . as a principle to guide them in deciding whether an industry ought to be expanded . . . or contracted." This "performs the function which under free competition is carried out by the free entry of firms into an industry or their exodus from it" (pp. 76–7).

These rules are then to be interpreted by the decision makers on the basis of the prices given to them for their relevant costs of production and output prices. In this model, the prices of consumer goods and wages are determined by a market, whereas the factor prices are fixed by the central planning board. The decision makers are to be instructed to use these prices in their accounting, thus

---

[3] More will be said later about Lange's implicit assumptions here both that an equilibrium can be "reached" and that it could be recognized as such if it were ever attained.

[4] Both the extent to which Lange's rules represent a fundamental retreat from the traditional concept of planning, as well as the argument that the rules would be unenforceable, will be addressed in the next chapter. This section is strictly concerned with the role of the rules in Lange's extension of the formal similarity argument.

establishing the "parametric" function of prices – that is, the prices are "parameters determining the behavior of the individuals," and to the extent that these prices represent true relative scarcities they will guide choices toward the optimal allocative-productive arrangement (p. 70).

Lange finishes the analogy by arguing that the objective equilibrium condition – supply equals demand – is met by "trial and error" price corrections by the central planning board when surpluses or shortages appear.[5] Here the planning board supplants the market for capital goods in the function of clearing markets. Thus the socialist community has formally the same determinate equilibrium as the perfectly competitive model and discovers this equilibrium by the same Walrasian trial and error process.

In perfect competition, Lange argued, the conditions of equilibrium are met through consumers' utility maximization, producers' profit maximization, and free entry and exit, giving the equilibrium set of prices when, by Walrasian trial and error, supply equals demand. In socialism, Lange asserted, the same conditions can be met by consumers' utility maximization and by imposing the two rules for producers (minimize average cost, and produce at the level where $MC = P$) and by instructing plant managers to use the planning board's prices in their accounting. The equilibrium set of prices is achieved when, by Taylorian trial and error, supply equals demand.

It cannot be denied that as an answer to the computation argument, Lange's demonstration is an impressive accomplishment, and indeed it would seem that neoclassical economists who doubt the workability of socialism face a difficult task in responding to this demonstration. If the equilibrating process of real-world capitalism is explained by recourse to a Walrasian auctioneer, it is not clear why a planning bureau could not similarly function as a coordinating agent. If there is a satisfactory refutation of Lange, it must be one that is as critical of this "auctioneer" equilibrating mechanism as it is of the central planning board, and for essentially the same reason. Neither auctioneer nor planning board could have the requisite knowledge.

Throughout his demonstration, Lange retains the assumption that

[5] Although all of the market socialists casually employ the terminology of "supply and demand," none of them explicitly offers any explanation of the basis upon which individuals who own no title to the means of production are supposed to express "demand" for factors. To simply assert that socialist managers should act so as to equate supplies and demands is to gloss over the underlying legal framework within which supply and demand have meaning.

alternative production techniques and data on the availability of resources, as well as on the set of tradable commodities, are known by either capitalist entrepreneurs or socialist plant managers. The only ignorance built into this neoclassical formulation of the problem is a temporary ignorance of the "correct" prices, which, it is argued, may be obviated by a process of trial and error. For any conceivable configuration of relative prices it is assumed that each plant manager can simply read from known cost curves the optimal quantities he has to produce in order to equate his marginal costs to the selling price of his product.

It is only by assuming objectively known costs that the function that profit maximization fulfills under capitalism can plausibly be replaced with a pair of rules issued by the central planning board to plant managers. If costs are unknown to the planning board, it would be impossible for it to tell whether or not plant managers are obeying the rules.

Thus the problem of knowledge dispersal that Lange proposes to solve by trial and error is a much narrower problem than that which Mises raised. By assuming that all of the information required for general equilibrium except the correct prices is given, Lange and his school trivialize the complex process by which the dispersion and acquisition of knowledge takes place. Each producer is assumed to already have at his disposal a complete set of technologically feasible production methods into which he need only plug the planning board's computed prices in order to decide the best combinations of resources.

In the Austrian view, by contrast, producers discover feasible and more efficient methods of production only by trying different ones and by either failing or succeeding, success being revealed only in profit and loss figures. The advantages of the non-*tâtonnement* equilibrating process is that it depends on the competition of separate private owners who disagree about which techniques are better. This competition permits different entrepreneurs to try their hands at proving their views on the market by making a profit. Those with more accurate expectations and more efficient technological methods struggle rivalrously against those with less. Market competition is thus what Hayek calls a "discovery procedure" in which the extensive knowledge that neoclassical economists graphically depict in production possibility surfaces is not in fact inherently in the mind of the plant manager any more than it could be at the disposal of the central planning board. Without an ongoing competitive discovery process, the manager too would be ignorant about what methods are more efficient.

Hayek's discussion of the difficulties of centralizing the dispersed knowledge of an economy has frequently been interpreted as meaning only that the producers' choices of optimal production techniques must be decentralized but that the adjustment of prices could still be performed by a central planning board equipped with a sufficiently powerful computer. This dichotomy between the discovery of correct prices and the discovery of efficient production techniques is an artificial theoretical procedure that begs the essential questions of the calculation debate. In the real world's market process, the trial-and-error testing of techniques and of prices are inextricably bound together. Actual producers simultaneously bid prices up and down as part of their experiments with production techniques, and without this competitive process they would not know what techniques are better. But, it might be argued, if one does not assume that the entrepreneur has this knowledge under capitalism, then how does a capitalist price system offer him the knowledge he requires to make rational decisions? The point is that apart from what he has learned from the competitive process, the entrepreneur has very little technological knowledge. He gradually learns that which is relevant to a limited range of relative prices by experimenting and revising his plans in accordance with profit and loss information. It is only through a process of interacting with the price system that an entrepreneur gains a technological knowledge of prices, a knowledge that pertains to the limited range of relative prices he has experienced. This learning process is missed by a mode of analysis that assumes that enough knowledge is available initially to yield a determinate solution of simultaneous equations.

Thus Lange and his school offer a discovery process for only a small segment of the knowledge that the Austrians hold is dispersed throughout the price system – that is, knowledge needed to set the correct prices themselves. The next section will further examine Lange's conflicting remarks about this notion of trial and error, but my aim in this section has been to show the important role that the trial and error process plays in Lange's overall argument. For him, socialism does not simply face the same equilibrium logic of choice as capitalism; socialism is to employ a procedure for equilibration similar to that ostensibly employed under capitalism, a Walrasian *tâtonnement* process. Thus the formal analogy of socialism to capitalism that led Wieser and Barone to doubt that socialism was practical is extended by Lange to a practical analogy used to show that socialism is as practicable as capitalism.

The crucial ambiguity of "trial and error"

Any assessment of the significance of Lange's version of the formal similarity argument depends on how this trial and error process is interpreted with respect to the issue of rivalry.[6] But on this crucial issue Lange and the other market socialists are surprisingly ambiguous. Although some passages lend themselves to the interpretation that Hayek called the mathematical solution, the general thrust of other arguments seems more consistent with what Hayek called the "competitive solution." Underlying this ambiguity is failure (due to an overly narrow formulation of the knowledge dispersal problem) to recognize the disequilibrium aspects of choice. By considering only the optimization aspect of choice, Lange failed to recognize that his own scheme, like capitalism, would inevitably always be in disequilibrium and consequently that production plans would be in a continuous state of rivalry among one another. But this unrecognized necessity of rivalry undermines the "competitive" solution with respect to both its practicability and its presumed status as a species of central planning.

Lange variously refers to this process as "the same process of trial and error by which prices on a competitive market are determined" ([1936] 1964, p. 87) and as "a method of trial and error similar to that in a competitive market" (p. 86). If trial and error is exactly the same process as competition among private owners, then it does not constitute a socialist model at all, and if it is different but similar then it would seem incumbent upon Lange to specify the differences. If, as his argument entails, his model of socialism is to be rendered plausible on the basis of its similarity to capitalism, we will have to know which aspects of capitalism are to be retained. Only if these retained aspects are sufficient to generate a coordinating process in the face of continuous, unexpected change can the model be accepted as an answer to the Mises-Hayek challenge.

---

[6] Both E. F. M. Durbin ([1936] 1968, p. 151; 1937, pp. 580–1) and Dickinson (1939, p. 213) argued for "financial independence" and profit/loss accounting on the part of plant managers under socialism without recognizing that this contradicts the principle of common ownership of the means of production. Dobb had good reason for remarking that in debating with the "elusive" Lerner he was "embarrassed by a sense of battling with an invisible opponent" (1935a, p. 144). Such comments as the following by Lerner hardly help to dispel the confusion: "And by a price system I do mean a price system. Not a mere *a posteriori* juggling with figures by auditors, but prices which will have to be taken into consideration by managers of factories in organizing production" (1935, p. 152). "The competitive price system has to be *adapted* to a socialist society. If it is applied *in toto* we have not a socialist but a competitive society" (1934b, p. 55).

As Hayek points out, in order for central planning to work, the knowledge that is dispersed in a decentralized system would have to be "concentrated in the heads of one or at best a very few people who actually formulate the equations to be worked out" ([1935] 1948, p. 155). Both Hayek and Robbins ridicule the notion of centralizing all the knowledge of technological processes in the ministry of production. The main purpose of Lange's essay was to deny that such centralized knowledge would be required for a socialist system. However, it should be noted that Lange was not able to entirely free himself from the assumption of most socialists of his time that the central planning board would have vast reserves of knowledge at its disposal. Although Lange clearly intended to develop a scheme that would be immune from Hayek's charge ([1935] 1948f, p. 155) that the central planning board would have to maintain "complete lists of the different quantities of all commodities which would be bought at any possible combination of prices of the different commodities which might be available," nonetheless much of Lange's discussion appears to assume that such knowledge is available to the planning board.

For example, when arguing that his scheme would be free of business cycles, Lange contends that whereas a business failure under capitalism may lead to a chain reaction of failures, socialism can localize mistakes. In making a correction for one mistake, "*All* the alternatives gained and sacrificed can be taken into account," and the "secondary effect of a cumulative shrinkage of demand and of unemployment of factors of production" can be avoided ([1936] 1964, p. 106). Underlying this suggestion must be the assumption that the central planning board will somehow possess such intricate knowledge of the structure of production that it can weigh *all* (the emphasis was Lange's) the complex alternative sequences of events implicit in each mistake. Yet if the planning board is presumed to have such knowledge, why should it allow discretion on the part of mistake-prone plant managers in the first place? Surely the reason that Lange's model permits such discretion and individual mistakes – that is, the impossibility of centralized knowledge – also argues for the inability of the planning board to foresee the complex, rippling implications of such mistakes throughout the structure of production.

Dickinson (1933) had based his whole adjustment process on this assumption of the availability of complete knowledge, contending that since production would no longer be private and secret but would take place behind what he called the "glass walls" of socialism,

it would be easy, through empirical estimation of supply and demand curves, to find the equilibrium configuration of prices. Although Lange did not adopt this position, he was apparently not
entirely disabused of the assumption that the relevant knowledge is
somehow available to the planning board. Lange and Dickinson both
refer to the deliberate construction and use of demand and supply
schedules derived from statistics by the planning board as if such
devices were practical tools of discerning stable empirical conditions
rather than mere heuristic tools of analysis. Although Lange (pp.
89–90) does not believe that "a knowledge of the demand and
supply schedules derived from statistics" is necessary, as Dickinson
(1933) believed, he contends that such knowledge would be available
and "may be of great service."

Indeed Lange eventually arrives at the confident conclusion that
"the Central Planning Board has a much wider knowledge of what is
going on in the whole economic system than any private entrepreneur can ever have and, consequently, may be able to reach the right
equilibrium prices by a *much shorter* series of successive trials than a
competitive market actually does" (p. 89).

But this comparison between the central planning board and the
competitive market is improperly formulated in two respects. First,
Lange's comparison should not be between the knowledge possessed
by the planning board and that of a single private entrepreneur. No
one ever suggested that a single participant in the market knows
how to set equilibrium prices in an entire economic system. The
relevant comparison would have to be between the knowledge consciously possessed by the planning board and that which is unconsciously reflected in a competitive price system. The calculation
argument contends that a competitive price system utilizes the dispersed particular knowledge of all of its numerous participants. The
issue depends on whether the planning board could ever consciously
master all of the knowledge that is contained in a competitive price
system but that is not mastered by any individual entrepreneur.

Second, Lange is comparing the speed with which the two systems
are supposed to be able to "reach the right equilibrium prices,"
whereas under realistic assumptions of continuous change, neither
can ever reach equilibrium. Lange's failure to realize that any real
economy would invariably find itself in disequilibrium at all times
leads him to disregard the crucial disequilibrium aspects of choice
(futurity and alertness) and thus to trivialize the equilibration process. In place of profit-seeking entrepreneurs unconsciously bidding
prices toward an equilibrium that none of them knows how to find,

we have rule-following plant managers consciously equating marginal costs to the equilibrium selling prices that are deliberately "found" and given to them by the central planning board.

Compared to his predecessors, however, Lange does seem sensitive to Hayek's charge that the crucial knowledge about the technological transformation of some commodities into others cannot realistically be assumed to be available to the central planning office. Lange concedes that the full centralization of all such knowledge as would be required for the equation-solving model of central planning may be, if not inconceivable, at least impracticable. Lange's trial and error solution appears to be offered primarily as an effort to develop a theory of partially decentralized planning according to which prices of capital goods are set by the board but factor combinations on the basis of these prices are chosen by decentralized plant managers, using their special technological knowledge.[7]

Lange rests his whole justification for the workability of this trial and error method on its similarity to the spontaneous price adjustment that regularly occurs under capitalism. He responds to the computation argument that the planning board would be unable to solve millions of equations by denying that the board would have to perform this task at all. "Exactly the same kind and number of 'equations,' no less and no more, have to be 'solved' in a socialist as in a capitalist economy, and exactly the same persons, the consumers and managers of production plants have to 'solve' them" (pp. 88–9).

Apparently Lange wants to rely on a spontaneous, decentralized solution to the Walrasian equations rather than a deliberate mathematical solution. Market-clearing prices will be found by observing the fluctuations of supply and demand. However, to preserve at least some vestige of "planning," Lange proposes that, as in the neoclassical model of perfect competition, all market participants are to be pure price takers, while all price adjustment is to be carried out by the planning board instead of the auctioneer.

As Lange explicitly points out, "This method of trial and error is based on the *parametric function of prices*" (p. 86) according to which

[7] Lerner (1935, p. 153) appears to take a similar view when, in arguing against Dobb's apparent assumption of a supertechnician who can subsume all production under a single plan, he argues that "it is possible to enlist each producer's separate knowledge of the ratio between marginal productivities of factors in his own workshop, and to integrate this knowledge in the service of society by the use of the price mechanism. If every producer so regulates his production as to make the marginal productivities of factors proportional to their prices on a market, and if the prices are moved so as to equate the producer's demands to the supply, the problem can be solved without waiting for the supertechnician."

all decision makers are assumed to be pure price takers. "All accounting has to be done *as if* prices were independent of the decision taken. For purposes of accounting, prices must be treated as constant, as they are treated by entrepreneurs on a competitive market" (p. 81).

But this is precisely what real entrepreneurs do not do. As Kirzner has shown, the reason that the perfect competition model fails is because within it there is no procedure by which prices can ever change. The "entrepreneur," in this view, does not treat prices as parameters out of his control but, on the contrary, represents the very causal force that moves prices in coordinating directions. In other words, Lange claims that his trial and error process will work on the grounds that it at least resembles, if not duplicates, the equilibrating process of capitalism. This he represents as a Walrasian auctioneer trying prices until a configuration is found that equilibrates all markets. From the point of view of the Austrian economists, this very similarity of Lange's model to Walras's establishes its unworkability.

Lange seems to admit that the real capitalist world bears little resemblance to the perfect competition equilibrium model: "The capitalist system is far removed from the model of a competitive economy as elaborated by economic theory" (p. 107). But he rejects this equilibrium as descriptive of reality only to supplant it with other equilibrium constructs, those of Robinson and Chamberlin, which employ a notion of choice that is equally restricted.[8] Thus his argument against capitalism is that it attains the wrong equilibrium, but he nevertheless is assuming that an equilibrium can be attained.

He deems it a virtue of his model that unlike under capitalism, where monopolists frequently can have an effect on prices to their own advantage, plant managers under his scheme will have to act as pure price takers. But this supposed virtue would be seen from the Austrian perspective as a serious defect. Precisely because all initiative for price changes must come from the planning board, the equilibration process of Lange's model would be at best extremely cumbersome. In contrast to a market, where a multitude of entrepreneurs, situated in the interstices of the capital structure, can continuously bid prices up and down on the basis of their specialized

---

[8] Other participants in the debate, such as Lerner (1934a) also seemed to view the fact that the real world differs from perfect competition as a defect of capitalism that socialism can at least potentially correct, rather than a defect of the model. For the argument that monopolistic and imperfect competition theories preserve the static limitations of perfect competition theories and add some additional limitations of their own, see Kirzner (1973, pp. 112–19).

knowledge and expectations, the prices in Lange's model can be changed only when the planning board notices observable shortages or surpluses of stocks.

Let the Central Planning Board start with a given set of prices chosen *at random*. All decisions of the managers of production and of the productive resources in public ownership and also all decisions of individuals as consumers and as suppliers of labor are made on the basis of these prices. As a result of these decisions the quantity demanded and supplied of each commodity is determined. If the quantity demanded of a commodity is not equal to the quantity supplied, the price of that commodity has to be changed (p. 86).

This process of trial and error, we are told, is repeated until "equilibrium prices are finally determined" (p. 86).

What remains unclear in this discussion is just what is supposed to be happening while the planning board is conducting its trials and somehow identifying its errors. Depending on the answer to this question, two fundamentally different kinds of trial and error models can be reconciled with Lange's presentation. If, as in the Walrasian auctioneer model, no activity begins until the full implications of tentative demands and supplies are worked out, then we would have a nonrivalrous "planometric" model that would involve the misleading "static" assumptions that were examined in the preceding chapter. If, on the other hand, production activity proceeds during a rivalrous trial and error process, then we would have trading at false prices, which would, as it does under capitalism, prevent the system from ever attaining general equilibrium.

The failure of the capitalist system to ever reach equilibrium is not fatal for its trial and error process of equilibration, since decision makers can orient themselves to one another by using the decentralized guide of money profits or losses, but the corresponding failure of Lange's socialist system would seem to be more serious. Having rejected profits as a signal, the market socialists have not shown how they could differentiate a successful from an erroneous "trial" in their trial and error process once a system-wide equilibrium is acknowledged to be unattainable.

Lange's trial and error procedure of reaching equilibrium may be plausible for a virtually static world in which economic changes are assumed to be occasional disturbances to an equilibrium that normally exists. Where only "small variations at the margin" are necessary to maintain this equilibrium (p. 88), these adjustments could be made by the planning board and the economy could quickly be returned to equilibrium.[9]

In Lange's presentation the process of finding equilibrium prices appears to be a simple matter of observing the inventories of finished goods. "The right prices are simply found out by watching the quantities demanded and the quantities supplied and by raising the price of a commodity or service whenever there is an excess of demand over supply and lowering it whenever the reverse is the case, until, by trial and error, the price is found at which demand and supply are in balance" (p. 89).

Thus Lange seems to believe that all that is needed to adjust prices is the observation of certain objective and verifiable facts concerning the levels of stocks, apparently a task that either plant managers or bureaucrats in the planning board could undertake and that higher authorities could continually monitor. He believes that it will be a relatively easy matter to "find" an economy-wide general equilibrium by having the planning board adjust prices on the basis of observed supplies and demands. Yet this proposition is nowhere defended explicitly, and Lange seems to think it follows from the fact that a "similar" process of trial and error takes place in existing capitalist markets.

Now in a static model such as a pure Marshallian fish market, one may imagine the equilibration process to be this simple a matter of equating current supply and demand. In such a world, by construction, only the present matters, because the fish will soon spoil. As with the Walrasian auctioneer, the market-clearing price can be found by calling out either prices or quantities until no excess supplies or demands are being expressed.

Such highly simplified market models may be useful heuristically precisely because of their simplicity, but their equilibration process cannot be considered representative of those of real-world markets, for at least two reasons. First, the ends/means framework within which decisions are made, involving the complete definition of all products (and product quality) and the full specification of administrative units assigned to produce them, is assumed given. Choice is viewed as purely routine optimization within this given framework, thus excluding any possible alertness to innovations in product definition or institutional organization.

---

[9] Dickinson (1939, p. 103) also seems to believe that an economic system can be expected to actually "converge to a definite end position," after which "small adjustments will be sufficient to keep the system in equilibrium."

Second, in the real world, where production takes place through time, supplies and demands are not simply observed as objective data such as inventory stocks; they have to be anticipated. The evaluation of means of production must be made on the basis of expectations of future conditions. It will not suffice for a producer who is now launching a ten-year project – say, building a factory – to be told to observe whether the stock of similar factories that are unsold is rising or falling. If he waits until excess supplies and demands are manifest in actual stocks before acting on them he will be forever too late.

Thus the essential weakness of Lange's approach is the very weakness that was found in the arguments of the earlier market socialists: The analytic framework for studying "choice" is too narrow for the problem at hand. The Lange scheme could work only in a world populated by pure mechanistic optimizers, selecting the best among known alternatives, but could not work to the degree that choice is a matter of entrepreneurial alertness to new opportunities or a matter of making judgments about possible future opportunities.

Variations on the Lange theme

This chapter has concentrated on Oskar Lange's presentation because of its prominence in the standard account of the debate as the definitive answer to Mises and Hayek. Relatively little has been said about the other market socialists whose arguments appeared at about the same time and in most respects duplicate points made by Lange. The main criticisms that I have made of Lange's formulation of the problem and of his trial and error solution also apply to the contributions that will be discussed in this section. But rather than reiterate these points it might be more fruitful to examine these variants of Lange's response to Mises in order to see if we can find in their underlying notions of choice those specific elements of alertness or futurity whose absence constituted the most serious defect of Lange's scheme. We will look, in the contributions of Durbin, Lerner, and Dickinson, for any clues that they could be found innocent of the charges the Austrians leveled against Lange. We might, indeed have hopes for finding such clues, since there were definite "Austrian" influences on all of these writers. E. F. M. Durbin (1934), for example, made an important contribution to the exposition of the Austrian theory of the trade cycle, and many elements of this theory, such as that concerning the time structure of production, can be found in the books by Lerner (1944) and Dickinson (1939) as well. But in terms of the specific meaning that I attach to "Austrian" as opposed to neoclassical economics in this study, I conclude that despite these influences the essential perspective of the Austrian school was absent from the contributions of these writers to the calculation debate.[10]

Durbin

The contribution of E. F. M. Durbin ([1936] 1968) may appear superior to Lange's in certain respects; Durbin differentiates among the three branches of marginalist economics, acknowledges the unworkability of socialist schemes constructed on the basis of the Walrasian, general equilibrium analytic framework, and proposes one or both of the other approaches as alternatives. In light of the central part that the distinctiveness of the Austrian branch of marginalism plays in this study, Durbin's approach may seem more congenial than the standard procedure of viewing the three marginalist schools as identical. However, we will see that on the crucial question of the assumption made about knowledge, Durbin too fails to discern those distinctive features of the Austrian approach that I have stressed.

Durbin answered Hayek's and Robbins's computation argument by contending that it constitutes an argument only against the Walrasian-Paretian analytic apparatus. However, he believed that either a "solution by way of marginal products" along the lines of the theories of Cannan, Pigou, and Böhm-Bawerk, or a solution constructed in terms of Marshallian supply and demand curves would be immune from Hayek's and Robbins's charge ([1936] 1968, p. 141). As Durbin pointed out, "the whole point" of his 1936 article was "to try to suggest a more *practicable* method of calculus than Dr. Dickinson's simultaneous equations" (1937, p. 578).[11]

Like Lange, Durbin proposed two "rules" to guide plant managers under socialism to get them to take the kind of actions that would

---

[10] For an in-depth discussion of the intellectual context of the early English democratic socialists (Durbin, Lerner, and Dickinson) see Elizabeth Durbin (1984). As she stresses, these writers were, at the time of the debate, groping for solutions to the serious depression that was plaguing the world's economy. Although there are few hints in their contributions to the debate, they were all soon to opt for Keynesian macroeconomic policy as their primary tool for economic planning.

[11] Evidently, contrary to Lange's view of Dickinson's 1933 essay, Durbin saw this essay as an attempt at a practical solution upon which Durbin was trying to improve, and not as merely an abstract "formal similarity" argument.

result in an approximation of competitive equilibrium.[12] Yet the chief component parts of these rules – average or marginal costs – are themselves resultants under capitalism of a process of active competition for profit among private owners. To simply assume that knowledge of these costs would be equally available to the passive recipients of the central planner's rules is to continue to beg the important question. Thus Durbin's proposal assumes explicitly that "the ability to discover marginal products is not dependent upon the existence of any particular set of social institutions" (p. 143) and implicitly that the demand curves are known (pp. 145–50). Like Taylor and Dickinson, Durbin has glossed over the essential question concerning how the knowledge of marginal costs can be acquired. Once this knowledge has been assumed it is not clear why the Austrian or Marshallian method is any more (or less) capable of revealing the implications of this knowledge in an equilibrium set of prices than the Walrasian method of solving equations would be. Under perfect-knowledge assumptions, little but style of exposition differentiates the three marginalist schools.

Durbin's refusal to extend his analysis beyond this assumption of objectively known costs is quite deliberate. He considers such questions (for example, the question of how decision makers could in practice discover such bits of knowledge under socialist institutions) to be beyond the realm of economic theory. Durbin explicitly admits, "It may be very difficult to calculate marginal products. But the technical difficulties are the same for capitalist and planned economies alike. All difficulties that are not accountancy difficulties are not susceptible to theoretical dogmatism" (p. 143).[13] Thus all questions concerning how knowledge is to be dispersed without the competition of private owners are deemed "practical questions" upon which the theorist cannot pronounce judgment. "In the realm of economic theory, then, the marginal productivity solution seems adequate. As long as the socialised factories calculate marginal products, and mobile resources continuously move to the highest margins, the problem of calculus will be solved" (p. 143).

[12] Durbin's rules are not quite the same as Lange's: They are "(a) that [plant managers] shall calculate the marginal productivity to them of all mobile resources; (b) that mobile resources shall everywhere be moved to the positions of highest calculated product" (pp. 142–3). He then modified these marginal cost instructions with average cost criteria, for which Lerner severely criticized him.

[13] This, as well as Chapter 1 of Lerner's *Economics of Control* (1944), suggests that any point of view that rejects the mixed economy in favor of laissez faire capitalism or complete central planning must ipso facto be "dogmatic." This idea is often itself asserted without supportive argument – that is, dogmatically.

This procedure of refusing to discuss practical issues, such as the specific institutions by which central planning is supposed to operate, the nature of property rights under socialism, or the dispersal of knowledge in the absence of competition, reflects a consistent pattern in all the market socialist arguments. Indeed this relegation of all discussion to the abstract formulation of the optimum at which planning should aim, at the expense of any consideration of the mechanism by which this aim might be realized, only became intensified in the subsequent development of market socialism. What began as the question of the workability of socialist institutions ended as the refinement of the welfare economic guidelines toward which socialists should strive, regardless of any "mere" practical question of how this might be brought about.

Dickinson

The systematic book by H. D. Dickinson (1939) might be thought a likely candidate for an exposition of market socialism that extends the argument beyond the pure static logic of choice into the sphere of dynamic issues. Beyond the sheer size and comprehensiveness of the volume, which suggests that more topics may be covered than in the briefer discussions of Lange and Durbin, there is the hopeful sign of some specific grappling with subjects such as risk and entrepreneurship. Furthermore, recalling from the previous chapter that Dickinson, on the basis of dynamic considerations, abandoned his earlier belief in an equation-solving solution to the calculation problem, we have some reason to expect him to take up such matters in this book.

However it appears that Dickinson's retreat was not as complete as it might have seemed and that even this modified presentation retains a basically static perspective. His discussions of risk and entrepreneurship will serve to illustrate that although he tries to cope with these essentially dynamic issues, he leaves off his discussion at just the point where they begin to become interesting.

On the issue of risk, the Austrians have often cited Frank Knight's classic book *Risk, Uncertainty and Profit* ([1921] 1971) in support of their distinction between risk and uncertainty. Many neoclassical economists would doubt the value of this distinction, but interestingly enough Dickinson begins his discussion by citing Knight (in a footnote) and pointing out that some risks are "uninsurable" and so "constitute true economic uncertainty." Once this is admitted, Mises and Hayek would contend, it follows that socialist institutions would be unable to cope adequately with such true uncertainty.

But Dickinson (1939, pp. 93–8) goes on to argue that planning can eliminate some of these uninsurable risks outright and can cover the rest by adding a special "uncertainty-surcharge" to the usual elements of cost such as wages, rent, and interest. The uncertainty that he believes planning can completely eliminate includes all of those risks that are "due to the simultaneous action of a number of entrepreneurs ignorant of each other's decisions" (p. 93). Still referring to the "glass walls" of socialism, Dickinson seems to believe that tracing out and reconciling the detailed implications of producers' plans in advance of their execution is not only a practicable goal but one of the chief virtues of the planned economy. "The object of genuine economic planning . . . is to substitute a conscious and direct relation of production to human needs for a relation arrived at by an indirect mechanism through the unconscious pushes and pulls of innumerable private interests in the market." Dickinson offers no argument to support his contention that this uncertainty that is due to the simultaneous construction of rivalrous plans can be eliminated under socialism (p. 10). Surely the fact that each decision maker is ignorant of the detailed plans of his rivals is not, as Dickinson implies, essentially a result of industrial secrets kept behind the "opaque walls" of capitalism.[14] Each producer could inundate his rivals with information about his plans without significantly reducing their ignorance about the concrete implications of his plans for the feasibility of theirs. It is only when they actually clash in competition and the economically stronger rivals succeed in winning profits that anybody learns about these concrete implications. To assume they could be learned without the aid of this rivalrous pursuit of profit by the relative degrees of the various "pushes and pulls of innumerable private interests in the market" is again to beg the question.

But, Dickinson concedes, there are some uninsurable risks that are "inherent in all production in anticipation of demand," both because there may be changes in "the method of production" and because there may be "new needs or changes in the relative order of urgency of old needs" that require adjustment. In these cases, he says, uninsurable risks would be accounted for by attaching a surcharge to the price of the commodity whose production involves uncertainty. "The calculation of a surcharge for uncertainty is," Dickinson says, "a more difficult task than the determination of a rate of interest" (p.

---

[14] See Dickinson (p. 9). Of course individuals or corporations may and do keep secrets under capitalism, and in particular instances this may be considered an antisocial act. But to prohibit such secrecy would not only fail to solve the calculation problem; it would also intrude unnecessarily on the privacy of innocent persons.

97). But since "in the individualist community it is largely a matter of guesswork," he contends that uncertainty should present no special problem for socialist costing that is not already a problem for capitalism. He concludes his treatment of uncertainty by speculating that the socialist community "might in time evolve a statistical treatment of uncertainty based on the frequency distribution of sales and of price changes" (pp. 97–8).

But as Knight's distinction between insurable and uninsurable risk was intended to show, it is in the very nature of uninsurable risk that its cost cannot be reduced to a specific value based on a frequency distribution. It is hardly a satisfactory answer to problems of true certainty to end up assigning just such a value to uninsurable risk.

However, the clue to the limitation of Dickinson's treatment of uncertainty lies in his remark that coping with uncertainty, even under capitalism, is merely a matter of "guesswork," under which category he includes "unconscious judgment, based on old-standing habit and a mass of assimilated experience" (p. 97). Such "judgment" represents what Michael Polanyi called "inarticulate knowledge," and its skillful exercise depends on the context within which the decision maker acts. This context includes the "assimilated experience" of relative prices and their implications for profitable production methods. Thus, to the Austrian economists, this is precisely the kind of choice that stimulates the competitive discovery process and that socialist institutions would be hard pressed to replicate, whereas to Dickinson this kind of choice is dismissed as arbitrary guesswork.

Section 3 of Chapter 9 in Dickinson's book, entitled "The Entrepreneur in a Planned Socialist Economy," is the only part of the book that deals with the important question of the locus of ownership and responsibility in the market socialist society. Here the reader might expect to be offered an explicit reconciliation, on the basis of the delegation of responsibility for decision making, of the apparently contradictory goals of centralized conscious direction of production and decentralized choice according to the guidance of prices. Unfortunately Dickinson again cuts off his discussion at precisely the point in his argument when it comes closest to the crucial question.

He begins the section by admitting that he has borrowed substantially from elements of capitalism, including the use of (but not the exclusive reliance upon) profit and loss accounting, in terms of money prices, by decentralized and financially independent enterprises. This, he points out, "raises the problem of the powers and remuneration of the individuals who are to manage" these enterprises (p. 213).[15] His answer to this pertinent question is that if the economic system is to "realize its economic advantages to the full, a very large degree of independence must be given to the managers" and that they "must be free to experiment with new products, with alternative methods of production, and with the substitution of one kind of material, machine, or labour for another" (pp. 213–14). Further, Dickinson admits that "independence involves responsibility," and thus that the "manager's personal remuneration must in some way reflect his success or failure as a manager." Without this correspondence between the manager's payment and his firm's prospects, Dickinson points out, the manager would either be "tempted to embark on all sorts of risky experiments on the bare chance that one of them will turn out successful," or else "the attempt to check irresponsibility will tie up the managers of socialist enterprises with so much red-tape and bureaucratic regulation that they will lose all initiative and independence" (p. 214).

One could not find a more forthright argument in defense of private ownership in the writings of Mises or Hayek. If managers must be free to exercise initiative, bearing the burdens and reaping the benefits of their own risk judgments, then what is left of the professed goal of planning, which was to create "a deliberate, conscious control of economic life" (p. 16)? It seems that Dickinson has deflected this argument by conceding the need for the very feature of capitalism he had set out to prove unnecessary: independent, private decision making.

The only difference between Dickinson's scheme and capitalism seems to be that in the former the manager's "bonus" should not, in general, be equal to profit, since "the emergence of profit is not necessarily a sign of efficiency, but may denote a failure to expand output" (p. 219). This implies that the planning board that examines the individual profit and loss accounts must be in a position to distinguish genuine profit from monopoly gain in the standard sense. However, this evades the question under consideration, since the calculation argument contends that the planning board would lack the knowledge that decentralized initiative generates and that this

[15] It is significant that Dickinson equates the "entrepreneur" with the "manager" throughout his discussion. In fact he attributes to Mises the view that modern capitalism is still typified by small firms in which the functions of manager, owner, and entrepreneur are combined in a single individual. However, this is a serious misreading of Mises. For Mises, entrepreneurship is embodied in all action to varying degrees, including action that takes place within a large modern corporation. See also Kirzner (1979, pp. 91–106).

knowledge is revealed only in profit and loss accounts. There is no superior store of knowledge against which profit figures can be compared, so that the manager's remuneration can be correspondingly altered.

Similarly, Dickinson's suggestions that the planning board offer "an incentive to experiment" (p. 219) in order to preserve decentralized initiative presupposes that the bureau knows what kinds of experiments it ought to encourage with incentives. The idea of specified incentives as a deliberate planning device is contradictory to the idea of experimentation as a genuinely decentralized discovery procedure. If the central planning board does not have the knowledge necessary to differentiate bold initiative from reckless gambling, it could not allocate incentives among managers to encourage the one and discourage the other.

As with his discussion of risk, Dickinson's treatment of the entrepreneur slips into the assumption of complete knowledge just at the point in the argument when he takes up the question of uncertainty.

Lerner

Abba Lerner's contribution to the debate did not take the form of direct responses to the Mises-Hayek challenge. Rather, it consisted of articles published in the 1930s in which Lerner commented on the responses made by Dickinson, Durbin, Dobb, and Lange and of further comments that he made in his systematic book on welfare economics, *The Economics of Control,* published in 1944. His arguments are no less confined to static issues, or, as he puts it, to "pure economic theory," than the other market socialist formulations, although he was perhaps more careful and systematic. His dissatisfaction with Dickinson's article (1933) was only that the argument was "not sufficiently refined," and he cited minor errors and weaknesses that, he said, "do not seriously detract from the merit of Mr. Dickinson's work" (1934b, p. 52). Against Durbin's and Lange's two rules for approximating the conditions of a perfect competition equilibrium, Lerner insisted that the planning board go "direct to the more fundamental principle of marginal opportunity cost" that is supposed to be the virtue of the competitive equilibrium (1937, p. 253). In fact, not only was Lerner as guilty of making the assumption of complete knowledge as those market socialists he debated, but he can be seen as the most explicit advocate of retaining this assumption.

For example, Lerner concluded his critique of Durbin with the simple statement that "price must be made equal to marginal cost.

This is the contribution that pure economic theory has to make to the building up of a socialist economy" (1937, p. 270). In that essay Lerner's main difficulty with Durbin was that Durbin had ventured beyond this "pure" question into the entirely different matter of motivation, that is, the problem of getting producers to comply with the planner's rule(s). Durbin (1937, p. 579) had argued, in support of his "average cost" rule, that it would be more likely to be complied with than the theoretically more desirable "marginal cost rules" advanced by Lange and Lerner. Lerner's cryptic rejoinder to Durbin in 1938 compared him with "the schoolboy in the examination room who wrote 'I do not know the social effects of the French Revolution, but the following were the Kings of England'" (1938, p. 75). In other words, by dealing with what he called "the practical problem," Durbin was answering the wrong question. But surely if it was Mises's challenge that the market socialists were trying to answer, then it was Lerner who was answering the wrong question.

In the same vein Lerner criticized Lange for trying too hard to replicate the mechanism of competition, when the proper question was rather to articulate the welfare conditions defining the ideal, regardless of the method by which this ideal is to be realized.

Methodologically my objection is that Dr. Lange takes the state of competitive equilibrium as his *end* while in reality it is only a *means* to the end. He fails to go *behind* perfect competitive equilibrium and to aim at what is really wanted. Even though it be true that if the state of classical static perfectly competitive equilibrium were reached and maintained in its entirety the social optimum which is the *real* end would thereby be attained, it does not follow that it is by aiming at this equilibrium that one can approach most nearly the social optimum that is desired (1936, p. 74).

For various rather convincing reasons, Lerner doubts that aiming at the "perfectly competitive equilibrium" will result in actually approaching the "social optimum that is desired." Thus whereas Lange had sought to duplicate the perfect competition equilibrium, Lerner instead emphasized going directly to the principle of marginal opportunity cost. "If we so order the economic activity of the society that no commodity is produced unless its importance is greater than that of the alternative that is sacrificed, we shall have completely achieved the ideal that the economic calculus of a socialist state sets before itself" (1937, p. 253). Even though Lerner entitled the essay in which this sentence appeared "Statics and Dynamics in Socialist Economics," Lerner's solution is just as "static" (in the sense used in this study) as Durbin's, Lange's, and Dickinson's had been. That sentence clearly states the basic economic allocative problem in static terms. We should indeed produce the commodities that we find most important. But production, like all action, takes time, and changes occur as time passes. The product that is considered more important today may no longer be by the time it is produced. The $MC = P$ rule will optimize allocation within a given framework of means and ends as long as future costs are expected to be the same as current costs. This is a world of static expectations, which are reasonable in a static world. In a world of continuous change, however, an entrepreneur must try to anticipate demand, to form expectations, and to act on them. He should view his costs on the basis of the specific alternatives that appear available to him at the time of his choice. Both his estimate of revenue and his estimate of costs depend on his expectations at the time of decision.

Lerner had tried to simplify Lange's rules to the one "marginal cost principle," but the "rule" for achieving rational economic calculation, if there is such a thing, would have to read something like this: Set expected marginal costs for some period equal to expected price. But of course, such a rule could never be put into practice. What bureaucratic inspector can observe a decision maker and verify whether he is, in good faith, acting optimally *according to his own expectations?*

Ironically, Lerner himself had raised the issue of expectations against Hayek in a different context when Lerner remarked that the cost of capital goods "depends not on the present price" of the products for the production of which the capital goods are employed "but on the *expected future price*" (1937, p. 269). This is indeed true and significant, but it raises all of the thorny questions about futurity that Lerner's own marginal cost rule evades. These questions are again dismissed as outside the province of economic theory. "The question is then the sociological one, whether the Socialist Trust is able to estimate this future value more accurately or less accurately then the competitive owner of the hired instrument, and here we leave pure economic theory" (p. 269).

Lerner briefly takes up the issue of expectations again in his book, where he distinguishes the "productive speculator," whose function is beneficial and is to be preserved in the controlled economy, from the aggressive or monopolistic speculator (1944, pp. 69–70). The difference is entirely a matter of the motives for which the speculative activity is undertaken, and Lerner offers no guidance as to how the officials in control would be able to ascertain such motives. But a more important problem with Lerner's exposition is the fact that in his entire discussion of speculation he does not address the problems arising from the fact that people will be taking risks with other people's money. Without private ownership, what will prevent the speculator from undertaking either too timid or too adventurous projects? Since speculative activity by its very nature involves the unknown future, the planning bureau cannot be presumed to know whether its subordinates are being too careful or not careful enough with society's resources. All of the advantages to be gained from speculation – even from incorrect speculation – that Lerner describes in Chapter 8 of his book depend on private ownership of the resources that are being risked. Yet Lerner has nothing to say about the legal property rights institutions underlying his model.

It is common in market socialist literature to segregate the strictly short-run "$MC = P$" rule, in which capital is assumed to be constant, from the long-run optimal investment theory, in which additions to or deletions from capital are considered. Thus expectational complications are relegated to the latter (and even there are treated only in aggregate) and are conveniently avoided in the analysis of marginal cost pricing. This method, however, depends on drawing a sharp distinction between a producer's day-to-day market activities and industry investment activities.

But for Mises (1949, p. 296), "What happens in the short run is precisely the first stages of the chain of successive transformations which tend to bring about the long run effects." The decision maker surveys a different time horizon for different actions, but he ignores futurity at his peril. Abram Bergson noted the essential ambiguity of marginal cost pricing in this regard: "In practice what we have to reckon with is not a unique marginal cost for a given level of output, but a complex of marginal costs, each of which is pertinent to a particular period of time. As a longer period of time is considered, more of the 'fixed factors' become variable" (1948, p. 427).

Surely a rule that includes such an ephemeral, subjective phenomenon as marginal cost as its major element is unenforceable, and not merely because there may be a lack of the desired motivation on the part of the rule followers. The relevant expectations of future costs are both necessary for rational choices and necessarily must also be in the minds of the individual users of resources, rather than centralized in a central planning board.

In all of these models, rules in the socialist economy are supposed to supplant the role of profit maximizing in the market economy. But this is the replacement of a dynamic and active force by a static commandment to passively obey certain price signals. In a market firm, expected demand guides producers to bid for factors – that is, the producers' collective actions bring about the coordinative prices of factors. In the socialist scheme, the plant manager must take as given the prices of all factors as well as the price of the product, and is told to produce at least cost under these static assumptions.

Since rule-following behavior cannot legitimately be inferred from the existence of a published rule, the analyst must apply choice theory to explain the self-motivated actions that people are likely to take when confronted with the rules under consideration. As soon as a rule is proposed as a substitute for directly self-motivated action, such issues as how to distinguish compliance from disobedience, how to provide sanctions for disobedience and rewards for compliance, and the extent to which the desired actions can be articulated in explicit rules must be examined.

The fundamental difference between the self-directed action of profit seeking and the other-directed action of rule obedience is completely overlooked in the market socialists' discussion. Nothing is said of the allocation of responsibility that would have to supplant the legal institutions of private ownership. No justification is made for the implicit claim that this ruled behavior will conform to the intentions of the rule makers.

The reason such issues were avoided has to be traced to the fact that they were deemed to be outside the legitimate province of economic theory. The job of the economist was only to state the principle that, if followed, would produce the optimal result, and it was a matter for political, sociological, and psychological debate to resolve how to properly motivate people to obey the principle.

Of the market socialists, Lerner was the most explicit and consistent advocate of this view, but they all insisted that the economist's attention be confined to the problem of formulating a precise principle by which socialist planners ought to guide production. The "practical" problem of how the plant managers can be gotten to act in accordance with this principle was consciously excluded from discussion as but a matter of "incentives," which reduces to sociological and psychological issues beyond the expertise of the economist. All the economist can do is insist that plant managers be instructed to follow the dictates of welfare economics.

But there are two entirely different kinds of "incentives," corresponding to different kinds of obstacles that might prevent a plant manager from obeying such a rule. He may simply lack the motivation, but he may also lack the knowledge necessary to carry out the directive. The first obstacle has been widely discussed in central planning literature, but very little has been said about the second.

Consciously devised "incentives" to get plant managers to do explicit, known, perfectly describable tasks are not the same as the profit "incentives" that spontaneously inform market participants of which tasks ought to be tried.

The market socialists offered a response to the wrong argument. Lange's response is incisive for those neoclassical economists who are content to represent the coordinating function of the capitalist price system solely by reference to the Walrasian auctioneer and who see the auctioneer as merely removing the agents' ignorance about prices, in a system from which all other ignorance is assumed away. Replace the auctioneer with a central planning board, and the problem is solved. But this response does not at all answer the Misesian challenge. The calculation problem, as we have seen, is not merely the static computational difficulty of solving Walrasian equations to obtain the equilibrium values of the prices; it involves the deeper problem of the rivalrous dissemination of knowledge, including, but not limited to, the knowledge of prices. Even where the market socialists expressly tried to get beyond statics in some of their discussions of trial and error, risk, and entrepreneurship, they ultimately failed to equip the agents of their models with the nonstatic aspects of choice – alertness and futurity – that agents in a truly dynamic world require. Indeed they by and large agreed that we should not let such practical questions, which they took to lie outside the proper realm of economics, intrude on the analytical elegance of their static proofs.

CHAPTER 6

The Austrian rejoinder:
learning from rivalry

The purpose of this chapter will be to show that the contributions by
Mises, Robbins, and Hayek to the calculation debate constitute a
single coherent argument that underwent important refinement and
clarification as it was redirected at the competitive solution but was
not fundamentally changed during the course of the debate. Robbins and Hayek did not say the same thing that Mises had said, but
what changes there were are misrepresented in the standard account
when they are called a "retreat." It makes more sense to say that
Robbins, and especially Hayek, expanded on the Misesian argument.
The first section of the chapter examines the main statements that
Robbins and Hayek made concerning the nature of the calculation
problem and its relationship to the empirical evidence of planning in
the Soviet Union. The second section discusses their early reactions
to the embryonic suggestions for a "competitive solution" to the
calculation problem. Hayek's later, more complete critique of the
competitive solution as it had been articulated by Lange and Dickinson is described in the next section, as well as some of his important
essays on knowledge and competition that significantly clarify his
meaning. I conclude by describing Mises's own reaction to the competitive solution, both before and after Lange's and Dickinson's explicit formulations of it appeared.

Robbins and Hayek: retreat or restatement?

Robbins's alleged retreat

At the beginning of his discussion of the calculation argument (section 7 of Chapter 7 of *The Great Depression*, 1934a, pp. 148–56),
Robbins indicated in a footnote that in his own opinion he was
primarily restating Mises's arguments ([1922] 1936) – with which he
was intimately familiar – and certainly made no concession that he

was "retreating" in any way (1934a, p. 148).[1] The following examination of Robbins's arguments will find them to closely parallel, not retreat from, those that Mises had employed fourteen years earlier. They differed mainly in the fact that Mises's major opponents in the debate, whose arguments Robbins wished to meet, had retreated in the interim, moving from a largely implicit Marxian central planning theory to two new market socialist positions, the "mathematical" and "competitive" solutions.[2]

Robbins begins his section entitled "The Central Difficulty of a Planned Society" by asking "On what basis is planning to take place?" and "Whose preferences are to govern the organization of production?" His answer – and most socialist economists had already conceded the point by this time – was that for a "democratic community," the "preferences of consumers" must guide social production. The only "mechanism . . . available for ascertaining the complex and changing tastes of the millions of different individuals constituting the community" is a market for consumer goods (1934a, pp. 148–50). At the outset Robbins considers not Marxian socialism but a market socialism in which there is common ownership of the means of production, with centralized direction aimed at supplying a genuinely competitive market for consumer goods. Consumers can be "given sums of money" and be "left free to bid for the various commodities available," and the planning board, guided by these market-revealed preferences, "would seek so to distribute its productive resources that the demand for all commodities was satisfied to the same level of urgency" (p. 150).

However, although imaginable, such a procedure may be entirely unworkable. Robbins points out that "it is one thing to sketch the requirement of the plan" but "it is another thing to conceive of its execution." Although no doubt some market socialists took this as a retreat from Mises's position, Robbins is in fact simply restating Mises's argument that although the planning authority may perhaps

---

[1] Robbins had translated the parts of Mises's 1922 book that pertain to the central calculation argument (i.e., essentially the 1920 essay discussed in Chapter 3, only slightly revised) and had supplied a draft of this to his friend J. Kahane, who then completed the translation, cited in this work as Mises ([1922] 1936]). The history of the translation is recounted in an unpublished interview conducted by Richard M. Ebeling for the *Austrian Economics Newsletter*.

[2] Strictly speaking, one should refer to the socialist movement as a whole as having retreated from Marxism to the new market socialist positions. As Elizabeth Durbin has pointed out to me, the English market socialists were never Marxists, and to the best of my knowledge Lange, although sympathetic to much of Marxism, never endorsed the Marxian theory of planning.

be able to discover consumer evaluations by permitting a free market to operate in that sector, "this is not enough" (p. 150). Mises had argued that even if we assume that consumer evaluations are decided upon, either by authoritarian dictate or through the operation of the consumer market, "once this decision has been taken, the real task of rational economic direction only commences, i.e. economically, to place the means at the service of the end" ([1920] 1935, p. 103). In other words, the planning board must also estimate the *producer* evaluations or "the relative efficiencies of the factors of production in producing all the possible alternatives" (Robbins, 1934a, pp. 150–1). Both Mises and Robbins argue that for rational producer evaluations to be possible there must be a capital market, a competitive market in factors of production among private owners. Yet this would be incompatible with the notion of centrally planned production.

At this point in his argument, Robbins pauses to dismiss the mathematical solution, which, although it may offer a solution "on paper," offers in practice "no hope . . . of discovering the relative sacrifices of alternative kinds of investment" (p. 151). Next Robbins explains how the calculation problem is solved in a decentralized manner under capitalism, or "under competitive conditions"–that is, "by comparison of costs and prices." Each individual capitalist compares his "expectations of price" with his "expectations of cost" in order to decide "in what line to extend his enterprise" (pp. 151–2). The money prices he uses in such decentralized calculations embody more information than is consciously possessed by anyone and thus enable him to engage in far more complex production plans than could be designed under a centrally planned system. These prices contain such information because of the rivalrous pressures generated by the competing bids for resources by entrepreneurs. Robbins argues that "the prices of the various factors of production, which are the resultant of the competitive bidding of the different *entrepreneurs*, tend to reflect the value of their contribution to the production of different products . . . Computations of costs and prices under competitive conditions are, as it were, a short cut to the solution of the millions of equations" (p. 152). Thus Robbins contends that the accounting practice of estimating profits and losses serves as a guide to decentralized decision makers, directing them to "better" avenues of investment.

By "better," Robbins of course meant "better" from an economic as opposed to a "technical" (or technologically feasible) point of view. In the absence of a price system, the planning board "could no doubt erect an apparatus which, from the technical point of view, would be very imposing," but it could not ascertain "at what sacrifice of other goods its products would be secured, at what economic, as distinct from technical, efficiency, it functioned." In other words, the economic costs of its projects could not be known. Like Mises, Robbins attached great significance to this distinction "between the technical and the economic" and asserted that the conflation of these concepts "lies at the root of nearly all the major confusions of contemporary economic discussion" (p. 155).

Robbins does not elaborate on this distinction here but refers the reader to discussions in the second chapter of his famous *Essay on the Nature and Significance of Economic Science* ([1932] 1935), as well as in a note on "production" that he had contributed to the *Encyclopedia of the Social Sciences* (1934b). In the latter he explains that "if there is only one end – then the problem of activity is entirely technical. Or if there are many wants but the means for satisfying them are completely specialized, again the problems of satisfying them are technical problems. But as soon as the means are capable of various uses, then a problem which is not technical – an economic problem – arises" (1934b, p. 465).[3]

Hence it is not enough to establish the technological feasibility of a production plan; it is also necessary to determine its economic cost – that is, the value of the opportunities forgone by this plan. The complexity of deliberately tracing out such cost implications of each plan necessitates that this be done unconsciously by relying on the information supplied by a price system.

This comprises Robbins's restatement of the Misesian critique of centralized planning. There are no grounds for characterizing this as a retreat from Mises's argument. Indeed, although in his later years Robbins was to distance himself from the Austrian school in many respects, ultimately renouncing most of the 1934 book in which his contributions to the debate appeared, he never substantially altered his Austrian perspective on the calculation problem. In his autobiography, which hints strongly at the importance of the

---

[3] Compare with Mises (1949, pp. 206–7): "The mere information conveyed by technology would suffice for the performance of calculation only if all means of production – both material and human – could be perfectly substituted for one another according to definite ratios, or if they were all absolutely specific." I understand that this distinction is due to Hans Mayer. The criticisms of this distinction by Kirzner (1967, pp. 127–37) and Rivett (1955, pp. 217–19) are aimed largely at demonstrating that there are no purely technological choices in the real world and that this distinction cannot be used to separate economic science from other disciplines. This, however, does not deny the analytic value of the distinction.

Misesian calculation argument in the development of his general point of view in economics, he writes:

[Mises's] main contentions that without a price system of some sort, a complex collectivist society is without the necessary guidance and that, within the general framework of such a society, attempts to institute price systems which have meaning and incentive in a dynamic context are liable to conflict with the main intention of collectivism – these still seem to me to be true and to be borne out by the whole history of totalitarian societies since they were propounded (1971, p. 107; see also 1976, pp. 135–50).

Hayek's "retreat" and the question of the Soviet economy

Hayek begins the first of his two 1935 essays on the calculation debate, "The Nature and History of the Problem" ([1935] 1948e, pp. 119–47), with a clarification of the difference between the economic and the technological problems of choice that Mises and Robbins had stressed. "The common character" of the latter is "the singleness of their purpose in every case, the absolutely determined nature of the ends to which the available means are to be devoted" (p. 121). By contrast, "The economic problem arises . . . as soon as different purposes compete for the available resources." The "criterion" of the presence of an economic as opposed to a technological problem is that for the former, "costs" in the sense of "the advantages to be derived from the use of given resources in other directions" have to be "taken into account" (p. 123).

After a digression on what he calls a "Decay of Economic Insight" in the historical school and in Marxism that he believes has diverted attention from economic issues, Hayek proceeds to outline the nature of the calculation problem. Like Mises and Robbins, he places primary emphasis on the distinction between the ends and the means of the socialist program and stresses that however the ultimate ends of the socialist society (in terms of a scale of consumer evaluations) are decided upon, the crucial problem is whether planning can constitute a workable means for the achievement of those ends.

Thus Hayek sums up the calculation problem:

[The] fact that one central authority has to solve the economic problem of distributing a limited amount of resources between a practically infinite number of competing purposes . . . constitutes the problem of socialism as a method. The fundamental question is whether it is possible under the complex conditions of a large modern society for such a central authority to carry out the implications of any such scale of values . . . with a degree of success equaling or approaching the results of competitive capitalism (pp. 130–1).

Having stated the basic problem in general terms, Hayek then describes various "types of socialism" to which this problem applies. Here he points out that the "most widely advocated" variety of socialism at this time had already conceded the need for a market in consumer goods and labor but retained the requirement of collective ownership of and control over the means of production. However, Hayek notes that "recently . . . there has arisen . . . a tendency among socialist thinkers to reintroduce a certain degree of competition into their schemes," even in the sphere of factors of production. He resolves to take these up later, noting that a certain "minimum assumption consistent with the idea of collective ownership" must be retained if the competitive socialism is to be regarded as a species of planning rather than a full concession to Mises's critique. The minimum assumption, he asserts, is that the question of who is to exercise command over a given quantity of resources for the community or of what amount of resources is to be entrusted to "entrepreneurs" will have to be decided by one central authority (pp. 133–34).

If even this "smallest degree of central control" consistent with the community's "command over the income derived from the material means of production" were relinquished, then "planning . . . ceases to be a problem. It becomes unthinkable." Instead we would have the "separate problem of state intervention in a capitalist society." Concerning this policy, Hayek only remarks, citing Mises's 1929 book on interventionism, that "it can be easily shown, not that such a thing is impossible, but that any isolated measure of this sort will cause reactions which will defeat its own end" since "well accepted analysis" has shown that authoritative fixing of minimum or maximum prices leads to surpluses or shortages, and since interventionism cannot in any case sensibly be considered a variety of central planning, such "partial planning" is "excluded from our considerations" (p. 134).

Hayek then warns against interpreting his dismissal of interventionism as a defense of "complete laissez-faire in the old sense" or of "the historically given legal institutions." He differentiates between interventionism and those changes that seek to find "the most appropriate permanent framework which will secure the smoothest and most efficient working of competition," noting that the latter issue has been "sadly neglected by economists" (pp. 134–5). The "essential distinction" he describes in this context represents what he later was to refer to as the difference between *nomos* and *thesis* approaches to law (see especially his 1973 and 1976 books). *Nomos* describes "a permanent legal framework so devised as to provide all the necessary incentives to private initiative to bring about the adaptations required by any change"; *thesis* involves "a system where such adaptations are brought about by central direction" (p. 135).

Thus Hayek contrasts two kinds of "rules" that may guide production decisions (which have been confused with one another in Lange's competitive solution): there may be *thesis* "rules" in the form of specific commands transmitted down a decision-making hierarchy in which genuine initiative must reside at the top, or there may be a general framework of *nomos* "rules" as constraints within which decentralized initiative can operate smoothly.

As Hayek's later elaborations of this distinction emphasize, rules in the sense of *nomos* law are not and cannot be employed to serve specific purposes, since they provide only an ordering framework for a multiplicity of conflicting purposes, the resultant of which is in principle unpredictable in advance. The virtue of such abstract rules is their flexibility in coping – or rather in permitting those who operate under them to cope – with unforeseen changes. By contrast, rules of an organization, or *thesis* law, must consist of specific commands chosen to advance known purposes and thus can only permit a limited degree of discretion on the part of those who are supposed to obey them.

The market socialists' marginal cost rules can be reexamined in the light of this distinction. They seem to be defended as components of a central planning system – that is, as *thesis* rules of organization, in accordance with conscious, centralized decision making. Yet they also are intended as functional replacements for the unconscious operation of private owners competing for profit under a *nomos* legal system of rules concerning property titles. The only way in which this substitution of *thesis* for *nomos* rules can be considered plausible is if the choices being examined can be reduced to purely routine optimization under a completely specified ends/means framework, in which case genuine initiative on the part of the rule followers is unnecessary.

The remainder of this first essay by Hayek is concerned with the historical development of the calculation argument culminating in Mises's "complete and systematic exposition" in 1922. Nowhere in Hayek's essay can there be found any indication that he is retreating from this Misesian formulation, which he says "represents the starting-point from which all the discussions of the economic problems of socialism, whether constructive or critical, which aspire to be taken seriously must necessarily proceed" (p. 143).

Such effusive praise is hardly indicative of a retreat, but two of

Hayek's remarks, one of which was later quoted by Lange ([1936] 1964, pp. 62–3) as evidence of a retreat, require explanation. Hayek said, "It must be admitted that [Taylor and Dickinson's model of socialism] is not an impossibility in the sense that it is logically contradictory" ([1935] 1948f, pp. 152–3) and explicitly chided Mises for having "occasionally used the somewhat loose statement that socialism was 'impossible' while what he meant was that socialism made rational calculation impossible." Hayek then concedes, "Of course any proposed course of action . . . is possible in the strict sense of the word, i.e., it may be tried" (pp. 145–6).

These statements have been interpreted as indicating a substantive retreat from Mises's more extreme position and as a concession that socialism is possible in theory but not in practice. It is assumed that Hayek was covering up his retreat by suggesting that Mises had only been careless with words, rather than wrong, in asserting that socialism was "impossible."

Two different (and incompatible) versions of this story of Hayek's alleged retreat from Mises can be found in the literature, reflecting two meanings of the word *impossible*. One version (for example, Köhler 1966, p. 69 and Seligman 1971, pp. 107–8) says that Mises denied the "logical credentials" of socialism (to use Schumpeter's phrase), after which Hayek and Robbins, convinced by Barone's "formal similarity" argument, retreated to a "practicability" position. More will be said shortly about this "theoretical" controversy, but since, as we have already seen, Mises never took the position that this version attributes to him, Hayek and Robbins could hardly have "retreated" from it.

The other version of this retreat story, more often hinted at than clearly articulated, suggests that Mises denied the practicability of socialism whereas Hayek and Robbins, convinced by Soviet experience, admitted in principle the practicability of socialism but simply contended that it would result in waste and other problems (see, for example, Misra 1972, p. 188, and Tangri 1967, pp. vii–viii). To answer this charge will require an examination of the meaning of "socialism" and the extent to which Soviet experience constitutes a genuine instance of a socialist economy.

Let us assume for a moment that Mises was not careless with words but really meant that socialism is impossible. Even in this case, there would be no substantive difference between his and Hayek's positions. Mises (and most socialists of the time) often included in the notion of "socialism" the goal of improving or at least retaining the technological productivity of capitalism, whereas Hayek meant by "socialism" only the method of planning, regardless of its consequences.[4] Hence, although Mises said that "socialism" is impossible and Hayek said that "rational calculation under socialism" is impossible, both were making the same point: that attempts to replace market institutions with the central direction of production would lead to a significant drop in standards of living, and that if the use of prices in economic decision making both internally and internationally were permanently and completely abandoned, nothing short of complete economic collapse and reversion to the conditions of a primitive peasant economy would eventually result. In this sense an economy that is both genuinely centrally planned and technologically advanced is, according to Mises, Hayek, and Robbins, truly impossible.

One can nevertheless agree with Hayek that Mises's choice of words was in some respects most unfortunate. Many assumed that he was doubting the possibility of something that has, since 1920, been etched in history, and some critics consequently dismissed his argument without giving it the serious examination it deserved. It is incorrect but understandable to interpret Mises's "impossible" (unmöglich) as a prediction that any attempt to realize "central planning" is bound to immediately usher in complete economic ruin. Comparative economics texts frequently cite Soviet experience as a refutation of Mises's view that rational economic calculation under socialism is impossible. Surely, it is argued, if this theory predicts complete economic collapse, then it does not stand up to historical evidence.

At the time when Mises's statement was first published, this extreme interpretation of his views may have actually lent support to his position, since the failure of the Lenin regime (1919–22) was as complete a collapse as any in economic history, and it seemed to be further corroborated by the explicit reversion to market institutions in the period of the New Economic Policy. However, the at least ostensible return to central planning in Russia in the early 1930s with the introduction of Stalinist-style five-year plans, seemed to weigh against this extreme interpretation. Although modern economic historians acknowledge that the Soviet economy has produced waste on a far greater scale than was generally thought fifty years ago, it cannot, however inefficient, be said to have produced the utter "destruction and annihilation" that the Soviet economy suffered in the early 1920s.[5] It seems likely that the limited success and

---

[4] I owe this observation to David Ramsey Steele (see Steele 1978).
[5] These were the words Mises ([1920] 1935, p. 125) used to describe the ongoing performance of the Soviet economy under Lenin.

gradual development of the Soviet economy has suggested to many observers of the theoretical debate that central planning is, if not efficient, at least possible, and that Mises's position must therefore have been too extreme.

But neither Mises nor Hayek ever asserted that all *attempts* to institute a system of "planning" would necessarily produce total economic collapse. Both argued only that such attempts would decrease the standard of living of the people below that which they could achieve by relying on competitive forces, whereas advocates of planning had made confident claims for its greater productivity over the wastefulness of anarchic production. Attempts to realize the socialist program, Mises wrote, would result in a society in which "the provision of goods of a lower order [consumer goods] for human beings . . . is diminished" ([1920] 1935, p. 130); in Hayek's view, such attempts would result in a "decline in general wealth" (Hayek [1935] 1948e, p. 146). Both Hayek and Mises explicitly stated that an advocate of socialism who is willing to acknowledge the fact that socialism will reduce the general level of wealth is immune from their critique.[6]

It is one thing to argue that the *persistent* pursuit of a particular goal will inevitably lead to disaster and quite another to contend that actual advocates of this goal will be persistent enough, in the face of mounting difficulties, to bring about such a disaster. To say that genuine central planning (the complete substitution of deliberate control for market institutions as the ordering mechanism of the economy) is "impossible" is not to say that attempts in practice, such as in the Soviet Union, to establish something called "central planning" will necessarily lead to immediate economic catastrophe. It depends on the extent to which such economies consistently adhere to central planning by abolishing all remnants of the price system. Indeed the very difficulties of a consistent pursuit of central planning make it improbable that any regime would persist very long in this direction; it is more likely that such a regime would instead radically modify its "central planning" to make it more compatible with a price system.

[6] Mises had admitted that "whoever is prepared himself to enter upon socialism on ethical grounds" despite its diminished productivity "or whoever is guided by ascetic ideals in his desire for socialism, will not allow himself to be influenced in his endeavors by what we have said" ([1920] 1935, p. 130). And Hayek agreed that if those who advocate socialism are willing to suffer such a reduction of wealth in order to achieve other goals and "if this attitude is based on a clear realization of what this choice implies," then "there is no more to be said about it" ([1935] 1948e, p. 146).

In his second calculation debate essay, "The Present State of the Debate" ([1935] 1948f, pp. 148–80), Hayek further clarifies the relevance of the Russian experiment to the calculation argument. He remarks that although "the actual existence in Russia of a system which professes to be planned has led many of those who know nothing of its development to suppose that the main problems are solved," in fact this experience "provides abundant confirmation" of the calculation argument (p. 148).

Hayek refers to the study by Boris Brutzkus ([1922] 1935), that explains the unmitigated failure of the "War Communism" period as a necessary consequence of the deliberate attempt on the part of the Bolsheviks to abolish the market and the price system.[7] Early Soviet history bears out Mises's contention that such market institutions as money, prices, capital accounting, and profits are indispensable for advanced technological production, for, as Brutzkus shows, the conscious attempt to eradicate these institutions produced "catastrophe" (pp. 101–9).[8]

It is well known that the New Economic Policy that followed War Communism involved a "restoration of the market" (Brutzkus, pp. 109–22), but it is usually argued that with the inauguration of the Stalinist-style five-year plans the centralized planning of the early years was reintroduced. This second attempt at "central planning" did not result in catastrophe and despite its problems has been used by many students of the Soviet economy as "proof" that Mises was mistaken.

But, as Brutzkus had pointed out, the "fundamental difference between this second [Stalinist] scheme and the first [Leninist] lay in the fact that [the second] was planned on the lines of a money economy and not those of natural socialism" (p. 97). In other words, although the Stalinist economy "professes to be planned," to use Hayek's phrase, it in fact relies on the outcome of the clash among rivalrous, decentralized decision makers–that is, it is anarchically rather than consciously organized.

---

[7] As Brutzkus ([1922] 1935, p. 102) pointed out, the label of "War Communism" and its description as a series of temporary emergency measures were only applied later. At the time, the methods of this period were advanced as deliberate policies for hastening the arrival of communism. Polanyi (1951), Roberts (1971), and Steele (1978) have now demonstrated this beyond any reasonable doubt.

[8] Brutzkus summarizes the results of Lenin's policies: "In 1920 production is said to have fallen to 13 percent of that of the pre-war period. The cause of this decline was not only the war, but also, to a large extent, the utterly defective distribution of the means of production under the system of natural [i.e. Marxian] socialism . . . It almost never happened that production goods allotted to an undertaking by various Governing Boards were matched in quantity or quality" ([1922] 1935, pp. 106–7).

The point is not only that the Soviet model has performed badly but also that the extent to which the Soviet economy has managed to muddle through corresponds to the degree to which its planning agencies have relinquished effective control over economic decisions to the plant managers. In a very important sense the Soviet economy is not really a centrally planned economy at all.[9] As Eugene Zaleski concluded in his monumental study of the Soviet economy, "The centralization of power does not imply an equal concentration of decision-making authority, and the formal appropriation of all power does not carry with it the ability to exercise that power." As his research shows, "The existence of . . . a central national plan, coherent and perfect, to be subdivided and implemented at all levels, is only a *myth*. What actually exists, as in any centrally administered economy, is an endless number of plans, constantly evolving, that are coordinated *ex post* after they have been put into operation" (1980, pp. 484–5). In short, what exists is not planning but economic rivalry.

Of course the fact that the Soviet economy has not been an example of true central planning does not imply that it is identical to a free-market economy. Although the government has withdrawn from the early attempts to completely eradicate market institutions, it has not withdrawn from attempts to direct production from the center. Thus, paradoxically, both the limited success of the Soviet economy since the New Economic Policy and that economy's failures are consistent with, and can helpfully be explained by, the calculation argument. The ultimate reliance on money prices for economic calculation illustrates Mises's argument that this element is indispensable, just as the numerous obstacles in the USSR to fluid changes of prices and to decentralized control over resources (especially the absence of an open stock market and financial market) prevents the system from working as well as a system that more closely resembled the free market would.

Hayek tries to clarify the relationship between the theoretical argument concerning planning and the assessment of practical experiments with planning, by noting that "it was not the possibility of planning as such which has been questioned . . . but the possibility of successful planning, of achieving the ends for which planning was undertaken" (1948f, p. 149). The criteria for judging success or failure are not as simple as sheer survival versus utter breakdown.

[9] This claim was first made by Michael Polanyi during the Stalinist years and has since been supported by the research of Nutter (1983), Roberts (1971), Besancon (1978; 1980), and Zaleski (1971; 1980).

"There is no reason to expect that production would stop, or that the authorities would find difficulty in using all the available resources somehow, or even that output would be permanently lower than it had been before planning started" (p. 150).

Rather, in such a restricted price system we would find output to be lower than it would have been if the price system had been allowed to operate freely. Some lines of production would be over-developed at the expense of others, "at a cost which was not justified by the importance of their increased output." Thus technological excellence may be in evidence for certain specific products, but economic efficiency on the whole will be greatly diminished.

By the "only two legitimate tests of success" that Hayek considers appropriate to use in judging the Soviet system – the ability to produce consumer goods and the degree of "rationality . . . of the decisions of the central authority" – he concludes that the system has failed (pp. 150–1). Judging the experience both before and after the Soviet retreat to the use of money and prices, Hayek concludes that

the anticipations based on general reasoning have been thoroughly confirmed. The breakdown of "war communism" occurred for exactly the same reasons, the impossibility of rational calculation in a moneyless economy, which Professors Mises and Brutzkus had foreseen. The development since, with its repeated reversals of policy, has only shown that the rulers of Russia had to learn by experience all the obstacles which a systematic analysis of the problem had revealed (p. 151).

Today there is a growing consensus that the contemporary Soviet economy serves the consumer very poorly (e.g., see Goldman 1983), but this criticism is often accompanied by a concession that the Stalinist model is suitable for rapid development and fails today only because it lacks the flexibility to foster continued growth in a technologically advanced economy. We should recall, however, that a generation ago economists were apologizing for the low standard of living of the Soviet population by contending that the economy was building up productive capacity for the future. Now that the future has arrived and the standard of living remains embarrassingly low, we are told that the great gains of the Stalinist model were in the past. It seems that the only accomplishments that this model can boast about are statistics on certain investment goods such as steel production, which were achieved at the long-run expense, rather than for the promised long-run benefit, of the Soviet citizen.

Thus one would be hard pressed to try to draw a distinction between the viewpoints of Hayek and Mises on the basis of their reactions to the empirical evidence. Both theorists argued that wherever and to the extent that central direction of economic life is tried it will lead to results that are contrary to the intentions of its own advocates: It will cause a substantial reduction of the general wealth of society, and, if this attempt is uncompromisingly pursued, will result in serious economic collapse.

Robbins's and Hayek's early critique of the competitive solution

Robbins (in 1934) and Hayek (in 1935) did not only restate the Misesian challenge to central planning and explain its relevance to Soviet experience. They also offered elaborations of the argument against the newer proposals for a "competitive" scheme of planning such as was to be articulated at length by Lange (in 1936). Robbins, after having argued that the complex determination of the economic costs of a production plan exceeds the capacity of the human mind and thus requires the aid of separate profit/loss calculations, explicitly considers the competitive solution – the possibility that a planning authority might also rely on such decentralized "computations of costs and prices." This too must be rejected, says Robbins, because

the possibility of computations relative to profitability of this sort involves the existence, not merely of a market for final products but also of markets for all the multitudinous elements entering into costs: raw materials, machines, semi-manufactures, different kinds of land, labour, expert guidance and, last but not least, free capital – with the *entrepreneurs* constituting the sellers and buyers, each acting according to his anticipation of the prices in the various markets in which they operate (1934a, pp. 152–3).

That is, for Robbins as for Mises, rational calculation of the relative profitability of various productive alternatives presupposes markets for intermediate goods, and such markets presuppose rivalrous bidding among private owners of resources whose bidding intensities reflect the value of alternative uses. "But," Robbins comments, "by definition, the central planning authority has abolished all that"; therefore "it does not seem to be in a position to keep accurate accounts" (p. 153).

It is not enough for socialist managers to "*play* at competition," to "bid against each other for factors of production, sell their products competitively, in short behave *as if* they were competitive capitalists." Robbins points out that "the propounders of such schemes conceive of the problem in altogether too static and *simpliste* a manner. They conceive of competitive prices as springing from the demands of

clearly demarcated administrative units whose continuity can be postulated without destroying the hypothesis that competitive prices are
realised" (pp. 153–4).

In other words, the "fictitious markets" solution necessarily depends on a given framework of ends and means within which each
manager merely optimizes. It retains a static conception of choice
that, as was argued in Chapter 4, excludes the disequilibrium aspects
of alertness and futurity relevant to a world of continuous change.[10]
Only by abstracting from genuinely unexpected change are the market socialists able to plausibly replace capitalist entrepreneurs with
socialist managers who routinely obey marginalist rules passed down
to them.

Contrary to this static view, Robbins points out that in the real
world tastes, technology, the availability of resources, and supplies of
labor and capital are "in process of continual alteration." As a result
of this, "The entrepreneur must be at liberty to withdraw his capital
altogether from one line of production, sell his plant and his stocks
and go into other lines. He must be at liberty to break up the administrative unit." Such freedom to dispose of property "is necessary if
the market is to be the register of the varying pulls of all the changes
in the data," and yet it is clearly incompatible with "ownership and
control at the center" (p. 154).

If economic choice is reduced to pure optimization, then the difference between a private owner's and a civil servant's choice disappears. All is merely routine behavior, and the best alternative need
only be read off the appropriate cost curves. It would seem in this
case to be of little consequence whether the producer is motivated to
select the optimal factor combination by private profit or by public
conscience.

But if we acknowledge that in the real world choice always involves
uncertainty and requires the specification of ends/means frameworks, this difference between the private owner and the socialist
plant manager correspondingly grows in significance. The "best"
factor combination for any particular constellation of prices is no
longer a given datum but has to be treated as an educated guess in
which someone has to invest some degree of confidence and some

---

[10] It is interesting to note that by this interpretation of Robbins he himself is offering
a critique of what Kirzner calls the narrow "Robbinsian" notion of choice. Although
Robbins's more general statement of "the economic problem" in his *Nature and
Significance* may lend itself to Kirzner's interpretation, many of Robbins's specific
uses of choice theory place him closer to the Austrian than the neoclassical view of
choice.

amount of risk capital. Rival producers under capitalism may contend with one another about what factor combination is more likely
to promise success. Where capital ownership is dispersed, the accrual
of money profits acts as a signal to guide production toward "better"
factor combinations. Where capital ownership is common, all decision makers are part of a joint project and thus cannot contend with
one another in this manner. In such a case there can be no struggle
among decision makers in their willingness to risk "their" capital in
various uncertain avenues, but rather "society's" capital has to be
consciously allocated in the "better" ways. Lacking profit and loss
signals, these "better" ways would simply be unknown.

Although Robbins also employed the "computation" argument
against the mathematical solution – an argument that the competitive
solution can be said to have answered – his comments about artificial
competition are more potent and were left unanswered by the market socialists. The profit and loss system, driven by the rivalrous
bidding of entrepreneurs, continually generates the knowledge without which a dynamic system could not be coordinated. This very
knowledge that Robbins contends is a resultant of competition is, in
the market socialist schemes, simply assumed to be "given" to plant
managers. Thus the market socialists failed to recognize the essential
problem of knowledge dispersal to which Robbins, following Mises,
had drawn attention.

This contrast between the Austrian view of a process of knowledge
dispersal and the neoclassical market socialist assumption of "given"
data was clarified further not only in Hayek's three contributions to the
debate but also in much of his subsequent work. Unlike Robbins,
Hayek had clearly used the computation argument as only a subsidiary
argument against the mathematical solution. His major argument was
a fundamental critique of the idea that the knowledge necessary for
economic production can be formulated into Paretian equations. This
more fundamental issue is as relevant to the competitive solution as it is
to the mathematical solution at which it was mainly directed.

Although we have seen that the later market socialists conceded
the need for at least some decentralization in their competitive solution, Hayek's specific grounds for asserting the impossibility of centralizing the knowledge necessary for production is pertinent to
their solution. Responding to Hayek's argument that the relevant
data cannot be considered objectively "given" to the central planners, they had proposed a solution that assumes such data to be
objectively given to the decentralized plant managers instead. But
Hayek's critique of the assumption of "givens" goes deeper than the

market socialists realized, although his most persuasive presentations of this viewpoint were only to emerge in a series of subsequent essays on knowledge and competition (to be discussed in the next section). As a result of their misreading of Hayek's critique of "givens," the market socialists never properly formulated the Misesian problem of knowledge dispersal that their competitive solution was invented to resolve.

When Hayek considers the mathematical solution, he notes that many of these mathematical schemes are defended only as a kind of "rear-guard action where all that is attempted is to prove that 'in principle' a solution is conceivable," with "little or no claim" being advanced that it would be "practicable" (1948f, p. 149). Hayek thus adopted the same position as Mises had, but his statements were taken by Lange ([1936] 1964, pp. 62–3) and the standard view as evidence of a retreat from Mises's position.

We have already seen that this standard interpretation represents a serious misreading of Mises, but Lange also misinterprets Hayek's position. Lange describes Hayek's (and Robbins's) position as the view that "theoretically prices in the generalized sense of 'terms on which alternatives are offered' are admitted to be given . . . without an actual market" and the problem is reduced to providing "a method of allocating resources by trial and error" ([1936] 1964, p. 64). Lange then shows the parallels, in both the formal conditions for a determinate equilibrium and in the trial and error procedures for "finding" equilibrium, between the neoclassical perfect competition model and his market socialist scheme and concludes on this basis that the Hayek-Robbins thesis is refuted. Thus Lange read the Hayek-Robbins "theoretical" concession as more than an admission that one can imagine a static world; he read it as an acceptance of the neoclassical formulation of the problem. However, that was not Hayek's meaning. In the very section in which he admits that the mathematical solution is conceivable, he offers an argument against this neoclassical formulation of the problem.

Hayek first points out that an immense amount of knowledge of specific resources, production techniques, and other factors would somehow have to be made available to the planning bureau for it to successfully plan. He then proceeds to what he calls "another problem of even greater importance," the question of whether the necessary knowledge can be considered "given" even to decentralized decision makers. "The usual theoretical abstractions used in the explanation of equilibrium in a competitive system include the assumption that a certain range of technical knowledge is 'given' " (1948f, p. 154).

The idea that this knowledge could be "concentrated in the heads" of the few people who devise a central plan "is an absurd idea even in so far as that knowledge is concerned which can properly be said to 'exist' at any moment of time" (p. 155). Such general scientific knowledge, for example, which is contained in libraries or taught in the academic community, would, in a truly centralized scheme of planning, have to be concentrated in the offices of the planning board. Although this may prove an insurmountable problem in itself, it does not seem inconceivable that, perhaps with a sophisticated communications network, such existing knowledge could be put at the disposal of the planners.

"But," Hayek continues, "much of the knowledge that is actually utilized is by no means 'in existence' in this ready-made form." Rather, "Most of it consists in a technique of thought which enables the individual engineer to find new solutions rapidly as soon as he is confronted with new constellations of circumstances" (p. 155). In such cases it is virtually impossible that those who possess such knowledge would be able to communicate it to the central planning board.

Although directed at the mathematical solution, this argument against the assumption of given data is equally potent against Lange's competitive solution and was so employed by Hayek. In 1935, Hayek, like Robbins the year before, specifically considered proposed solutions to the calculation problem that revert to a "reintroduction of competition." At this time some explicit formulations of such competitive schemes had appeared in German, whereas in English, "thought on these lines" was "still in an embryonic stage." But Hayek's comments were not directed only at the German variants of the competitive solution. Hayek also had in mind those embryonic English proposals that had already been circulating in London among "some of the younger economists" and to which he had been exposed "in conversations and discussion" (pp. 160–1).

Hayek summarized these schemes as follows:

The common fundamental idea is that there should be markets and competition between independent entrepreneurs or managers of individual firms and that in consequence there should be money prices, as in the present society, for all goods, intermediate or finished, but that these entrepreneurs should not be owners of the means of production used by them but salaried officials of the state, acting under state instructions and producing, not for profit, but so as to be able to sell at prices which will just cover costs (p. 161).

Hayek's first reaction to these proposals is to doubt that they can be legitimately considered species of planning at all. In terms of his distinction between *nomos* and *thesis* approaches to rules, the competitive solution appears to fit into the category of *nomos* and "not to involve much more planning than the construction of a rational legal framework for capitalism . . . within which concrete action would be left to individual initiative" (p. 161). If this is a fair assessment of the competitive solution, then it would not constitute an answer but rather a complete concession to the Misesian challenge. But in Hayek's more detailed look at two possible variants of the competitive solution, he finds their problems to be "not so very different" from those of the more traditional central planning models (p. 172).

The two models of what he calls "pseudocompetition" that Hayek examined in 1935 were similar to, but not quite the same as, Lange's 1936 model. In the first, which Hayek calls the "World of Competing Monopolies," he considers the possibility of going "halfway" and permitting "competition between industries only" (p. 162) and not within any industry. This model is based on a scheme for "competing trusts" that had appeared in the German literature (see Hoff [1949, pp. 153–65]). In this model, individual plants within each industry are to be guided not by profit and loss but by rules that instruct them to produce at that quantity where their marginal costs of production equal their selling price.

In the second model, profit and loss are viewed as the guiding criteria, and competition is extended to the intraindustry as well as interindustry level. In this proposal, the planning agency is viewed as a kind of superbank to which privately earned profits from each plant are passed and from which funds for capital investment flow. Public ownership of capital goods is still to be retained, but the conduct of individual plants is to be guided largely by profit and loss considerations.[11]

The market socialist proposals examined in the preceding chapter do not fit neatly into either of these classifications but seem rather to borrow features from each. Marginal cost rules like those depicted in Hayek's first scheme are retained, but not the sharp distinction between industry and plant competition, whereas the superbank notion finds some support, especially in scattered remarks of Lerner and Dickinson. Nonetheless, some of Hayek's responses to these two versions of the competitive solution are applicable to the English variations that appeared subsequently.

Hayek's primary objection to the first of these schemes is that its

---

[11] This model bears more similarity to contemporary market socialist schemes than it does to the market socialist theory of the 1930s.

marginal cost "rule" is impracticable, an objection that applies with full force to the rules of Lange and the English market socialists. Hayek argues that marginal cost rules cannot in principle replace profits, which "under dynamic conditions . . . serve a necessary function, and . . . are . . . the main equilibrating force which brings about the adaptation to any change" (p. 170). Hayek asks, "Does the instruction that [managers] should aim at prices which will just cover their (marginal) cost really provide a clear criterion of action?" Those who propose such marginal cost rules, he says, "attribute to the notion of costs in general a much greater precision and definiteness than can be attached to any cost phenomenon in real life" (p. 167).

This assumption of objectively given costs, as has been argued in Chapter 4, seems to result from an exclusive concentration on the static world of equilibrium. "But as soon as we leave the realm . . . of a stationary state . . . the question of what exactly are the costs of production of a given product is a question of extreme difficulty which cannot be answered definitely on the basis of any processes which take place inside the individual firm or industry" (p. 168). Hayek goes on to argue that costs depend on expectations of future conditions and on the plans of competitors for alternative uses of the factors in question. In other words, it is only the context of a rivalrous struggle among different owners to employ factors in a variety of ways that gives any concrete meaning to "costs." In short, "The competitive or necessary cost cannot be known unless there is competition," and that must mean competition not only among but also within industries (p. 170).

A basic problem, then, with marginal cost rules is that they depend on costs being objectively known, whereas when property is privately held, costs are estimates that are "verified" only by the earning of profits. Thus there is a fundamental difference between, on the one hand, the tendency for producers, impelled by competitive profit seeking, to equate price to marginal cost and on the other the explicit instruction to directly attain this marginal "cost equals price" result.

It might be thought that Hayek's second scheme, in which more competition is permitted and in which profits are employed as a guide for decision making, represents a total capitulation to capitalism. But even those who would be "prepared to go the whole hog and to restore competition completely" would not necessarily be conceding the need for private ownership of capital. They are interested in restoring competition only "so far as in their view this is compatible with the state retaining the ownership of all the material means of production" (p. 161). This, Hayek says, "evades most of the objections to central planning as such" but raises "extremely interesting" problems of its own concerning "the rationale of private property in its most general and fundamental aspect" (p. 162).

Thus the question is no longer whether a nonrivalrous conscious plan can supplant the coordinating function of rivalrous competition among private owners but the related question of whether rivalrous competition can perform its function when the competitors are not private owners. The basic issue in dispute no longer directly concerns whether knowledge can be centralized but concerns "whether decisions and responsibility can be successfully left to competing individuals who are not owners or are not otherwise directly interested in the means of production under their charge" (p. 162).

Specific directives from a central planning office are no longer to be the regulators of production decisions; instead, investment capital is to be issued by the central planning board to subordinate plant managers who are to use their specialized knowledge to transform these general resources into concrete production projects. Ultimate responsibility over the use of existing capital goods and the flow of new investment is supposed to rest with a central body, but control over the details of production is to be delegated to plant managers.

Clearly, wherever responsibility for decisions is delegated to managers in the lower levels of the hierarchy of an organization, there must be some procedure for monitoring their performance. If plant managers were given free rein, there would be no validity to the claim that ownership of the means of production is common, but if their every move were determined by central decree we would be back to a noncompetitive, centralized model. If the competitive solution is to be judged according to its own advocates' aims, it will have to lie somewhere between these extremes. Plant managers must be given authority to decide the details of production, but ultimate responsibility for the performance of managers must be retained by the central office.

For this to work there must be some way for the planning board to determine who can be entrusted with society's resources. Hayek suggests that the board cannot simply lend funds to the highest bidder, since "it would lend to persons who have no property of their own," and thus the board would have to "bear all the risk" (p. 172). But if the risk bearing is centralized, he asserts, then so must be the function of forming the expectations on the basis of which risks are to be borne (pp. 173–4) – and hence we are back at the problem of the centralization of knowledge.

Hayek, in 1935, focused primarily on the question of who is to decide how to allocate investment resources in the absence of private ownership, and on what basis. Perhaps his argument might have been more powerful had he tried to explain in more detail how such decisions are made under private ownership, rather than denying that they could be made under competitive schemes of socialism. But considering the fact that Hayek was writing before the English market socialist models were described in print, it is striking how few of the questions he raised were ever answered. When Hayek returned to the debate in 1940, so little attention had been paid to what he had said in 1935 about these issues of risk and expectations in the absence of private ownership that he felt compelled to quote his earlier remarks, including his conclusion:

> To assume that it is possible to create conditions of full competition without making those who are responsible for the decisions pay for their mistakes seems to be pure illusion. It will at best be a system of quasi-competition where the person really responsible will not be the entrepreneur but the official who approves his decisions and where in consequence all the difficulties will arise in connection with freedom of initiative and the assessment of responsibility which are usually associated with bureaucracy. ([1935] 1948f, p. 176, and [1940] 1948a, p. 203).

Hayek's later rejoinders to the market socialists

The standard account of the debate rarely even mentions the fact that Hayek rejoined the debate in 1940, after Lange's response had been published. This section will describe the essay in which Hayek answered Lange and Dickinson, as well as the series of essays on knowledge and competition in which Hayek substantially clarified his position.

Hayek begins his rejoinder to Lange and Dickinson, "The Competitive 'Solution'" ([1940] 1948a, pp. 181–208), by assessing the development of the calculation debate up to this time. The first two stages of the debate, representing the Marxian and mathematical models of planning, he says, "may now be regarded as closed" (p. 181). The controversy has now shifted to a third stage, the proposal "to solve the problems of determining values by the reintroduction of competition" that he had tentatively examined five years earlier, before any "systematic exposition of the theoretical bases of competitive socialism" had been available (p. 184). But, he says, the solutions proposed by Lange in 1936 and by Dickinson in 1939 finally offer

such a systematic exposition, which can now be critically examined
on its merits. Hayek summarizes the two positions as follows:

They both rely to some extent on the competitive mechanism for the determination of relative prices. But they both refuse to let prices be determined
directly in the market and propose instead a system of price-fixing by a
central authority, where the state of the market of a particular commodity,
i.e., the relation of demand to supply, merely serves as an indication to the
authority whether the prescribed prices ought to be raised or lowered (p.
185).

Hayek proposes to consider three issues concerning this centrally
directed competitive price system: (1) "how far this kind of socialist
system still conforms to the hopes that were placed on the substitution
of a planned socialist system for the chaos of competition" (p. 186); (2)
"how far the proposed method of central price-fixing, while leaving it
to individual firms and consumers to adjust demand and supply to
given prices, is likely to solve the problem which admittedly cannot be
solved by mathematical calculation" (pp. 186–7); and (3) "how far" the
specific proposals are "applicable" to a real economy (p. 186).

Hayek's answer to the first question is brief and definite. Clearly
the original aim of replacing the anarchy of capitalism with a consciously planned social order has, at this third stage of the debate,
been abandoned. The reintroduction of competition, which to
Hayek implies a rivalrous struggle among conflicting plans, constitutes a very significant concession, as indeed many socialist critics of
these competitive schemes have pointed out. Most of Hayek's essay is
devoted to the latter two questions, which in effect ask whether the
Lange-Dickinson solution can work, even on its own terms, in whatever realm it may be found applicable, and whether that realm is
coincident with or even close to the real world.

Hayek's second point concerns the question of whether it is possible to use a centrally directed trial and error procedure as an equilibrating process for discovering the prices that will solve the equations which cannot be solved by direct mathematical methods. Hayek
says that he cannot understand how trial and error could begin to
address the problem at hand. "This seems to be much the same
thing as if it were suggested that a system of equations, which was
too complex to be solved by calculation within reasonable time and
whose values were constantly changing, could be effectively tackled
by arbitrarily inserting tentative values and then trying about until
the proper solution was found" (p. 187). Surely, Hayek reasons, if
the equations were too complex and the changes in the data too

frequent for a mathematical solution to be practicable, these same considerations apply to the likelihood of guessing the correct solutions.[12]

Hayek points out that Lange and Dickinson are quite unclear and inconsistent in their explanations of how this price fixing by the planning board is supposed to proceed (as I also argued in the last chapter). For example, are price changes to be made "at the end of the accounting period," as Lange said, or "constantly" – as he also said ([1936] 1964, pp. 82, 86)? That is, what is the period for which prices are to be treated by market participants as parameters? The inconsistency of Lange and Dickinson on such central questions, Hayek suggests, "makes one almost doubt whether they have made a real effort to visualize their system at work" (p. 191).

With respect to the third of Hayek's questions, involving how far the proposed model is applicable to the real world, the Lange-Dickinson model does not fare much better. Both authors "overlook a very important field to which their method appears to be simply inapplicable" – that is, those cases in which we are concerned with "commodities which cannot be standardized." In those industries whose products are "produced on individual orders, perhaps after invitation for tenders," for example, "identical products are rarely produced twice in short intervals" (pp. 188–9).

In such cases the market socialists' instruction to the planning board to fix prices so as to equalize supply and demand has no meaning. If prices for unique products are to be centrally fixed, the authorities would have to examine the entire production process to ensure that all the costs borne were necessary. They would need to inspect the plans of all potential suppliers and purchasers, none of whom have objective, realized accounting records that are directly relevant to the price in question.

If a society's matrix of products and production techniques were fully standardized, Hayek admits, one can conceive that prices could

---

[12] Some might argue here (contrary to the conclusion of Chapter 5) that Hayek is showing that Lange's answer was ineffective not only against the calculation argument but also against the computation argument. However, Hayek's objection holds only if one rejects (as I believe Hayek did, at least implicitly) the Walrasian explanation of how capitalism works. For any neoclassical theorist who takes his Walrasian auctioneer seriously, Lange's formal analogy argument shows quite plausibly that his central planning board can do as well at finding a general equilibrium configuration of prices as the auctioneer could. Thus no doubt Lange would have responded to Hayek that if the planning board could not find the right prices, then neither could capitalists. Within what I have called the "neoclassical" perspective, this response would be unanswerable.

be decreed from above. But, it has been argued, such cases involve a narrow optimizing notion of choice in which the framework of ends and means is given in advance. In this realm, choice is a mechanical-solution to a constrained optimization problem for the exercise of which the central planning board may be as well equipped as an entrepreneur/capitalist could be. But, Hayek contends, such problems constitute only a fraction of the choices that would have to be made by a planning board.[13] In all decisions concerning nonstandardized products, the planning board would have to make entrepreneurial judgments itself (thereby returning to the problems of centralized knowledge for which the competitive solution was proposed) or else simply offer official sanction for private entrepreneurs to make the judgments, in which case "the process of price-fixing would become either exceedingly cumbersome and the cause of infinite delay or a pure formality" (p. 189).

Underlying both of these issues – the limitation of trial and error for finding prices even for standardized products and its complete inapplicability for nonstandardized commodities – is what Hayek calls "the modern preoccupation with stationary equilibrium" (p. 191). Unfortunately, Hayek devotes very little effort here to a direct critique of this preoccupation with "statics" and instead tries to analyze the practicability of the Lange-Dickinson model in the dynamic context.[14] In other words, he does not elaborate why he has posed "the problem" as necessarily one of disequilibrium but simply examines the model in terms of the problem as he understands it. He asserts, for example, that "the practical problem is not whether a particular method would eventually lead to a hypothetical equilibrium, but which method will secure the more rapid and complete adjustment to the daily changing conditions in different places and different industries" (p. 188).

Given that this is the problem to be solved, the Lange-Dickinson model is then shown to be inadequate. But, as we have seen, this

[13] Hayek points out that "much machinery, most buildings and ships, and many parts of other products are hardly ever produced for a market, but only on special contract" ([1940] 1948a, p. 189). Today probably an even greater proportion of economic production is nonstandardized than was the case forty years ago. Even more fundamentally, the question of which standards ought to become dominant is itself decided through a rivalrous process during which a multiplicity of "standards" compete for the privilege of becoming widely adopted. Without this process, imposed standards that did not have to win acceptance in a prior competitive struggle would tend to be inferior to those that competition would discover.

[14] He does, however, refer in footnote to his paper "Economics and Knowledge" ([1937] 1948b) in which he had discussed the nonstatic nature of "the economic problem."

does not appear to be the problem that Lange and Dickinson were trying to solve. It would seem, then, that a more fundamental approach on Hayek's part, a clearer articulation of the problem and how it is solved under capitalism, rather than a detailed discussion of how poorly the proposed socialist solution would work, would have been more effective.

Nevertheless, although Hayek does not specifically refer to the methodological differences between the Austrian (disequilibrium) and neoclassical (equilibrium) approaches as such, most of the essential elements of an Austrian methodological critique of Lange and Dickinson are presented in various parts of his essay. In the process of examining various aspects of the competitive solution, he repeatedly raises issues that are far more general than the question of the workability of these particular schemes.

For example, while discussing the specific procedures by which the central planning board would change prices, Hayek points out that in any practical implementation of the program the board would not only be slower in responding to changes, as has been mentioned, but its recommendations would also be less refined. Implicit in Hayek's comments here is the Austrians' methodological distrust of aggregates. Given the practical limits of information gathering, the board would have to aggregate the huge mass of particular data into broader, more manageable categories, so that there would be "less differentiation between prices of commodities according to differences of quality and the circumstances of time and place" (p. 192). Therefore those details that are based on "special circumstances of time, place and quality" would "find no expression" in the price-fixing process. "This means . . . that the managers of production will have no inducement, and even no real possibility, to make use of special opportunities, special bargains, and all the little advantages offered by their special local conditions, since all these things could not enter into their calculations" (p. 193).

Another example of a fundamental methodological issue that Hayek raises almost incidentally in the course of his argument is his remark that the Lange-Dickinson argument seems to proceed "as if the cost curves were objectively given facts." By contrast, from the radically subjectivistic perspective of the Austrian school, costs are not objectively given but subjectively estimated and continually being discovered. "What is forgotten is that the method which under given conditions is the cheapest is a thing which has to be discovered, and to be discovered anew, sometimes almost from day to day, by the entrepreneur" (p. 196).

Thus the basic problem with marginal cost pricing rules is not merely a matter of the "loyalty or capacity" of the managers, whom both Mises and Hayek explicitly assumed to be capable and motivated. The basic problem is whether the manager will have at his disposal the requisite knowledge when he does not face competitive rivals who are trying to outbid him for resources. He may sincerely want to produce at minimum cost but he may simply not know what the minimum cost is if he is not involved in a rivalrous, competitive discovery process. "The force which in a competitive society brings about the reduction of price to the lowest cost at which the quantity salable at that cost can be produced is the opportunity for anybody who knows a cheaper method to come in at his own risk and to attract customers by underbidding the other producers" (p. 196).

To assume that the knowledge of the relative costs of alternative projects is available is, as Hayek says, to miss the whole point. Hayek admits that in some sense, all the knowledge that is dispersed throughout the economy, "taken together" is equally "given" to the participants in a socialist or capitalist society. But the question is, How can this dispersed knowledge be "effectively used by the planning authority" in the absence of a competitive process? "It is the main merit of real competition that through it use is made of knowledge divided between many persons which, if it were to be used in a centrally directed economy, would all have to enter the single plan" (p. 202).

Hayek elaborated further on this critique of the assumption of "given" knowledge in some of his other essays. In his 1937 *Economica* paper, "Economics and Knowledge," for example, he refers to an equivocal use of the term *datum* in much economic theorizing, according to which those data that "are supposed to be objective facts and the same for all people" are confused with "those facts and only those facts, which are present in the mind of the acting person" ([1937] 1948b, pp. 38–9). This confusion comes from the unanswered question of whom the facts are supposed to be given to – whether to "the observing economist" or to "the persons whose actions he wants to explain" (p. 39). This same confusion between objective and subjective knowledge appears to underlie the market socialists' solutions.

In Hayek's best-known paper on knowledge, the 1945 *American Economic Review* article "The Use of Knowledge in Society," he clarified the distinction between his concept of "the economic problem" and that of the market socialists. The latter pose the problem in these terms: "*If* we possess all the relevant information, *if* we can start out from a given system of preferences, and *if* we command complete knowledge of available means, the problem which remains is purely one of logic" ([1945] 1948g, p. 77). In other words, in this formulation "the answer . . . is implicit in our assumptions." This formal exercise establishes the equilibrium conditions for economic optimality and as such comprises "an important step toward the solution of the economic problem of society." "The conditions which the solution of this optimum problem must satisfy . . . are that the marginal rates of substitution between any two commodities or factors must be the same in all their different uses" (p. 77).

This optimality problem, to which we have seen that Lerner explicitly and the other market socialists implicitly reduced the Misesian challange, "is emphatically not the economic problem which society faces," according to Hayek, because "the 'data' from which the economic calculus starts are never for the whole society 'given' to a single mind which would work out the implications and can never be so given" (p. 77).

The crucial distinction that Hayek introduces in this regard is between "scientific knowledge" and "unorganized knowledge," or "the knowledge of the particular circumstances of time and place." The latter, he insists, cannot be available except to the "man on the spot" (pp. 80–3). It is only by employing such particular knowledge in conjunction with the "telecommunications" system of prices (p. 87) that rational economic decisions can be made, and only a price system that is driven by the forces of competition can facilitate this dispersal of knowledge.

Hayek's views on the function of competition in this process of knowledge dispersal and his critique of perfect competition models were further developed the following year in "The Meaning of Competition." There he concludes with the succinct statement that "competition is essentially a process of the formation of opinion: by spreading information, it creates that unity and coherence of the economic system which we presuppose when we think of it as one market" (1948d, p. 106).

One more contribution by Hayek that crystalizes his approach to these issues has to be mentioned: his "Competition as a Discovery Procedure." There, more clearly than ever before, he describes rivalrous competition as "a procedure for the discovery of such facts as, without resort to it, would not be known to anyone, or at least would not be utilised" (1978a, p. 179).

In all of these essays, Hayek was elaborating an approach to economics that seeks to replace the neoclassical welfare criteria of

Pareto-optimality or efficiency with the criterion of plan coordination. Had this distinction been articulated at the time of the calculation debate, much of the debate's confusion might have been avoided. Hayek explains that one cannot in principle judge the efficiency of the competitive process, because "if we do not know the facts we hope to discover by means of competition, we can never ascertain how effective it has been in discovering those facts that might be discovered" (1978a, p. 180).[15]

Mises's own rejoinder

Chapter 3 described the anticipatory remarks with which Mises criticized market socialism in 1920 before any detailed schemes had been formulated. Three brief subsequent statements by Mises on this topic will be examined here. Two responses to Mises's original challenge appeared in German in 1922, to which Mises offered a rejoinder the next year in the same journal in which the 1920 challenge was published (translated in 1936 as the appendix to *Socialism*). In 1936 Mises added to the English translation of *Socialism* a section on "the artificial market" that apparently refers to the same "oral tradition" of "younger socialists" in England to which Hayek had responded in 1935. Finally, a section of Mises's *Human Action* (1949) on "Recent Suggestions for Socialist Economic Calculation" responds to the explicit schemes of the later market socialists such as Lange and Dickinson.

In all of these reactions to various proposals for market socialism, Mises maintained the position that there is no way to reconcile social-

---

[15] The noted philosopher Saul Kripke, in his book *Wittgenstein: On Rules and Private Language* (1982, pp. 112–3) has pointed out that "there is perhaps a certain analogy between Wittgenstein's private language argument and Ludwig von Mises's celebrated argument concerning economic calculation under socialism." Kripke's summary of Mises's argument stresses the very features of knowledge as a social process that have been emphasized in this book: "According to Mises, a rational economic calculator (say, the manager of an industrial plant) who wishes to choose the most efficient means to achieve given ends must compare alternative courses of action for cost effectiveness. To do this, he needs an array of prices (e.g. of raw materials, or machinery) set by *others*. If *one* agency set *all* prices, it could have no rational basis to choose between alternative courses of action. (Whatever seemed to it to be right would be right, so one cannot talk about right.)" Particularly in view of Hayek's development of Mises's argument in terms of a "discovery procedure," there seems to be a very close analogy here indeed. Kripke correctly notes that Mises's argument "is now almost universally rejected as a theoretical proposition" and wonders "whether the fact bodes ill for the private language argument." I would argue that on the contrary this fact bodes ill for the standard account of the debate and for some critics of Wittgenstein.

ism (meaning common ownership of the means of production) with the market and the price system. Although very brief, his arguments are broadly consistent with those by Hayek and Robbins, thus lending support to the interpretation presented here that the latter were only restating, not retreating from, Mises's position.

Two of the earliest attempts to answer Mises's challenge by proposing a combination of planning with competition were Karl Polanyi's "Sozialistische Rechnungslegung" [Socialist calculation] (1922) and Eduard Heimann's *Mehrwehrt und Gemeinwirtschaft: Kritische und positive Beiträge zur Theorie des Sozialismus* [Surplus value and collective economy: critical and positive contributions to the theory of socialism] (1922). Mises describes the error of the first as its ambiguity over the assignment of property rights and the error of the second as its assumption "that economic data do not change" ([1923] 1936, p. 516). Both of these errors were to be cited by Robbins and Hayek in their later criticisms of the English market socialists.

Karl Polanyi's scheme admits the difficulty of a truly centralized model and tries to avoid this by relegating the "right of disposing of production" to "associations of producers." At the same time he assigns to the central body, the commune, "ownership" of the means of production. Mises's response is that "ownership is the right of disposal," so that either the commune or the associations must be the ultimate decision makers. If it is the former, we again have the problem of knowledge dispersal under centralized coordination, and if it is the latter we have a syndicalist program that lacks any coordination mechanism at all (pp. 517–18).

Heimann's arguments, Mises says, "resemble Polanyi's on the only point that matters: they are regrettably vague just where they ought to be explicit about the relationship between the individual productive groups . . . and society as a whole" (p. 519). In both of these schemes, production groups are depicted as trading with one another at the same time as they are described as departments within a central planning organization that owns all of the means of production. Mises argues that although such departments may "receive and give as if they were owners" (p. 518), they cannot replicate the function of rivalrous bidding by genuine owners.

The competition of entrepreneurs who, in a social order based on private property, try to use goods and services most profitably, *is replaced* in the planned economy . . . by actions-according-to-plan of the supreme authority. Now it is only by this competition between entrepreneurs, trying to wrest from each other the material means of production and the services of labour, that the prices of the factors of production are formed (p. 520).

Polanyi's problem was a confusion over the locus of ownership, but Mises attributes Heimann's error to an exclusive concern with the state of equilibrium. Like Lange and Taylor, Heimann believed that a simple instruction to observe and adjust current inventory levels would be sufficient to equilibrate the economy. Mises objects to this that "the central problem of economic calculation" is "the renewal of capital and the investment of newly-formed capital" – in other words, what is important is the dynamic aspect of choice, not static problems concerning the optimization of the use of existing capital.

This same attention to dynamic issues underlies Mises's remarks in 1936 about the "artificial market." He argues that "it is not possible to divorce the market and its functions in regard to the formation of prices from the working of a society which is based on private property in the means of production." This, he argues, is because "the motive force of the whole process which gives rise to market prices for the factors of production is the ceaseless search on the part of capitalists and entrepreneurs to maximize their profits by serving the consumers' wishes" (pp. 137–8). Without this "striving" with the prospect of future profit, "the mechanism of the market loses its mainspring, for it is only this prospect which sets it in motion and maintains it in operation" (p. 138).

Thus, to simulate the working of the market process it is not enough to replicate the decisions about matters of "daily business routine," as might appear from "exclusive concentration on the idea of a stationary economic system." One must show how choices are to be made "in an economy which is perpetually subject to change." In order to solve such problems as arise in a changing world, "It is above all necessary that capital should be withdrawn from particular lines of production . . . and should be applied in other lines . . . This is . . . essentially a matter for the capitalists . . . who buy and sell stocks and shares, who make loans and recover them, who make deposits in the banks and draw them out of the banks again, who speculate in all kinds of commodities" (p. 139).

In contrast to the market socialist schemes that assume the data to be available, Mises stresses that "it is the speculative capitalists who create the data" to which the manager has to adjust his business (p. 140).

Moreover, Mises points out that it is not merely a matter of letting the central planning board act as a bank that lends capital to those undertakings that offer the highest return, since, as Hayek had pointed out, the planning board would have to lend to people who have no property of their own, and it would bear all the risk. Mises emphasizes that "the capitalist does not just invest his capital in those undertakings which offer high ... profit; he attempts rather to strike a balance between his desire for profit and his estimate of the risk of loss. He must exercise foresight" (p. 140).

The function that is performed by the profit and loss system cannot be performed by the single will of a central planning bureau but necessarily depends on a divergence of expectations among risk-bearing entrepreneurs who vie with one another for command over resources. When separate owners pit their resources against one another in the pursuit of profit, knowledge is generated without which complex production processes could not be carried out.

These arguments reappear in a section on "The Quasi-market" in Mises's *Human Action* (1949).[16] Again he argues that the "cardinal fallacy" in proposals to simulate competition in the absence of private ownership is their static outlook in which choice is reduced to routine behavior. Such schemes, he says, "consider the structure of industrial production and the allocation of capital to the various branches and production aggregates as rigid, and do not take into account the necessity of altering this structure in order to adjust it to changes in conditions" (1949, p. 707).

Central to Mises's point is his contention that "the capitalist system is not a managerial system; it is an entrepreneurial system" (p. 708). Some socialists contend that because the evolution of large joint stock corporations has separated the functions of ownership and day-to-day control, there would be no difference if all of society were to become the "stockholders," but, in Mises's view, such socialists fail to see the important function of owners behind the scenes. Mises argues that "the speculators, promoters, investors and moneylenders, in determining the structure of the stock and commodity exchanges and of the money market, circumscribe the orbit within which definite minor tasks can be entrusted to the manager's discretion" (p. 708). Although one might imagine the routine tasks of a manager to be reproducible under socialism, the roles of the entrepreneur and speculator are inherently inseparable from the institution of private ownership: "One cannot *play* speculation and investment. The speculators and investors expose their own wealth, their

---

[16] This section of *Human Action* (1949) is substantially the same as had appeared in the 1940 German book *Nationalökonomie* except that *Human Action* includes footnote references to Lange and Dickinson.

own destiny . . . If one relieves them of this responsibility, one deprives them of their very character" (p. 709).

Mises concurs with Hayek's point that it is not possible for the planning board to act as a superbank lending funds to the highest bidder, and indeed states this point in almost the same words: "All those who can bid for these funds have, as is self-evident in a socialist order of society, no property of their own. In bidding they are not restrained by any financial dangers they themselves run in promising too high a rate of interest for the funds borrowed" (p. 709).

This does not, however, reduce to the mere question of "incentives" in the narrow sense of psychological motivation. The "incentives" of the profit and loss system do not merely motivate action; they inform it.

In his critique of trial and error as a solution to the calculation problem, Mises emphasizes this function of profit and loss calculation in dispersing knowledge. He points out that "the method of trial and error is applicable in all cases in which the correct solution is recognizable as such by unmistakable marks not dependent on the method of trial and error itself" (p. 704). Thus Mises contrasts the trial and error of an entrepreneur under capitalism with that attempted by a socialist manager. The former relies on profit and loss statements to inform him whether he is succeeding or not, but the latter, lacking true rivals, also lacks this information. The fundamental issue for Mises, and one, as we have seen, that is almost completely ignored by the market socialists, is the function of economic calculation and the price system as a knowledge dispersal mechanism.[18]

Nowhere in this survey of the responses by Robbins, Hayek, and Mises to the market socialists has there been found any clear evidence of substantive differences among the Austrians in the debate. Although the points of emphasis had changed from those issues stressed in the original Misesian challenge, the leading advocates of socialism at whom the Austrians directed their arguments had also significantly changed their concept of planning. Later writers of the Austrian school may well have learned from the controversy, en-

---

[17] This section was absent from the 1940 book *Nationalökonomie*.

[18] The only reference to the calculation debate in Mises's *Theory of Money and Credit* (added to the 1924 edition) contains a concise summary of the calculation argument, describing it as essentially a problem of knowledge: "The whole structure of the calculations of the entrepreneur and the consumer rests on the process of valuing commodities in money. Money has thus become an aid that the human mind is no longer able to dispense with in making economic calculations" ([1912] 1980, p. 62).

abling them to clarify their ideas, but contrary to the standard account they were making a single sustained argument. And it was an argument that was never understood or answered by Lange and his school.

CHAPTER 7

Conclusion

The main purpose of this study has been to rekindle the fires of the calculation debate by showing that the standard history of the controversy is seriously flawed. According to this standard account, the extreme Misesian challenge in 1920 that planning is "theoretically" impossible stimulated socialists to abandon their Marxian prohibitions and for the first time say something about how planning would work. After the market socialists presented a rigorous theoretical model, Hayek and Robbins are said to have retreated to an "impracticability" argument. Thus, as Abba Lerner put it, the Marxian "thesis" that planning should involve the complete abolition of the market and the price system was met by the Misesian "antithesis" that the market and the price system are indispensable, thus leading to the "synthesis" of market socialism, the combination of planning with the price system, that both sides agreed is workable at least in principle (Lerner 1934b, p. 51). According to this version of the debate, there is little to learn from the controversy, since modern thought has risen above its dogmatic extremes from which each side has retreated and has comfortably reconciled planning with the price system.

Virtually every step of this standard account has been challenged. Although one can locate two "retreats" in the course of the controversy, they were both on the part of the advocates of planning, from the Marxian socialism (discussed in Chapter 2) to the "mathematical" solution (described in Chapter 4), and then to the "competitive" solution (analyzed in Chapter 5). The critics of planning, on the other hand, maintained a single coherent argument that improved with added clarification but changed only in its emphasis, as required by its redirection at the different proposed models of planning. The upshot of the controversy is not a consensus around an intermediate "synthesis" position to which each side retreated, as the standard account would have it, but rather a decidedly unresolved conflict between the advocates and critics of planning, who never saw eye to eye on any of the major issues of contention.

Chapter 2 argued that contrary to the standard account the Marxian perspective on planning amounted to more than a simple prohibition of discussion of the matter. Implicit in Marx's critique of capitalism and in his disputes with the "utopian socialists" is a definite view about certain general characteristics of the socialist economy, a view that is legitimately subject to criticism, even within the Marxian approach. Marx's socialism is an extreme but consistent view that central planning is totally irreconcilable with market institutions of any kind, which are necessarily rivalrous or "anarchic." The fact that this rivalrous or disequilibrium aspect of markets was to become obscured in later contributions to the debate warranted an emphasis on this feature of Marx's analysis.

The third chapter then outlined Mises's initial challenge to central planning. Here it is argued, in effect, that Mises agreed with Marx that markets are inherently rivalrous, that they work only as a consequence of a competitive struggle among incompatible plans. However, Mises went further to point out that the function of this rivalry is to disperse decentralized information in such a way as to bring a degree of coordination to this "anarchy." There is, he argued, no way other than through market prices by which this decentralized information can be marshalled for the purpose of such overall economic coordination. Prices thus act as "aids to the mind" that enable society to engage in far more complex methods of production than could be deliberately planned by a single mind. The specific tool of this market coordination is the orientation of individual entrepreneurs to their profit and loss accounts in terms of money prices. Profit opportunities tend to encourage a more socially coordinated use of resources without requiring any market participant to know more than the information required within his own particular sphere of specialization. Thus economic calculation of profit and loss serves as an unconscious coordinating mechanism for society as a whole, thereby performing a task that is beyond the cognitive ability of any member of society.

Mises was necessarily directing his critique at the dominant form of socialism of the day, Marxism, and thus devoted much of his argument to the point that the price system is necessary for rational calculation and cannot, for example, be supplanted by calculation in units of labor hours. Nevertheless, his critique contains the essential elements of the subsequent critiques of market socialism by Hayek and Robbins. Mises anticipated both the view that the problems could be handled "mathematically" and the attempt to reconcile a "competitive" exchange economy with common ownership of the means of production. The former misunderstands the dynamic nature of the problem, and the latter neglects the fact that it is only through the rivalrous bidding of independent owners of the means of production that prices tend to have the coordinative "meaning" necessary for their function in economic calculation.

The standard account has so thoroughly misunderstood Mises's argument that it has him saying virtually the opposite of what he really said. For Mises, the "static" analysis of equilibrium theory is an important theoretical exercise for showing the nature of the choice problem that must be faced by any economic system, and as such comprises an important part of his own critique of labor hours as the unit of calculation. The depiction of this imaginary world from which all changes have been abstracted is a necessary step toward the demonstration that labor units cannot capture all of the scarcities that have to be taken into account by economic calculation.

However, in the standard account Mises's argument is presented as a denial of this static argument that the same abstract choice problem faces socialist planners as face capitalists. Hence many accounts treat the static "formal similarity" arguments of Wieser and Barone as anticipatory answers to Mises. Chapter 4 began by describing this formal similarity argument, showing that it in no way contradicts Mises's view. The fact that the same logic of choice must apply to socialism as applies to capitalism is not an answer to Mises; it is a partial statement of Mises's challenge that socialist institutions of common ownership in the means of production would preclude a practicable solution to this choice problem.

The early market socialists responded to Mises's challenge with a mathematical solution that takes recourse to the formal similarity argument, as if that argument showed not only the nature of the choice problem to be solved but how it could be solved in practice as well. Chapter 4 described this mathematical solution in two alternative variants: the equation-solving solution and the trial and error solution – as well as a counterargument to one of these, the computation argument. All of these arguments are essentially "static" in the sense that they completely abstract from any complications entailed in the existence of continuous unexpected change. In all three arguments it was assumed that the knowledge necessary for the formulation of the Walrasian equations is available and that the only problem remaining is that of finding, whether by algebra or guesswork, the equilibrium set of prices. Thus the statement of the problem to be solved was significantly modified. An examination of some further work in this direction ("planometrics") concluded that it too suffers from an excessively static formulation of the problem.

The latter part of Chapter 4 presented a critique of this preoccupation with statics by outlining some distinctive features of the Austrian approach. Static analysis plays a secondary role in the analyses of Austrian economists, and their primary interest lies in the institutional environment within which the market process can best function to coordinate the plans of its participants. This view was then used to argue that Lange's celebrated answer to Mises was fundamentally misconceived.

The later market socialists abandoned the mathematical solution and took up the competitive solution. However, Chapter 5 contends that they retained the essentially static formulation of the problem that had characterized their predecessors' arguments. They still assumed that the knowledge that would be necessary to formulate the Walrasian equations was available, if not to the central planning board then at least to the decentralized plant managers. The only discovery they thought it necessary to explain was that of the correct prices, which they presumed could be found by observing the levels of inventory stocks of the various products, adjusting the price up if the stocks were being depleted or down if they were accumulating. This "trial and error" procedure reduces the choice problem to purely routine behavior, avoiding all the problems of alertness to new opportunities, of futurity, and of knowledge dispersal that I argued in Chapter 4 are crucial to any analysis of choice in the real world. Furthermore, despite the fact that this competitive solution relies on decentralized decision making, no discussion was offered about the apparent conflict between this and the idea of common ownership of the means of production. This avoidance of the issues of property rights and of limited knowledge was attributed to an insistence by the market socialists on exclusively describing the optimality conditions that central planning should strive to achieve, rather than any practical, presumably noneconomic issues about the institutional mechanisms by which this ideal might be attained.

The rejoinders by the Austrians to this competitive solution were described in Chapter 6. First, the general statements of the problem to be solved and its relevance to Soviet experience that were presented by Hayek and Robbins were shown to be consistent with Mises's views on these issues. The problem is not one of computing the optimal quantities to produce under the assumption of a complete objective knowledge of the opportunity costs of all options. It is one of dispersing the relevant knowledge in the absence of the process of rivalrous bidding through which the market disperses such information. This conception of the problem also underlies the comments that Robbins and Hayek made in 1934 and 1935 about the possibility of reconciling planning with competition, as well as the criticisms of the competitive solution that Hayek offered later on. Competition necessarily requires private ownership in the means of production in order for it to serve its function as a discovery procedure. The only way in which the market socialists were able to reconcile planning with competition was by reducing the latter to the nonrivalrous state of perfect competition.

The final section of Chapter 6 closed the argument by showing that Mises's own reactions to market socialism are consistent with the Hayek-Robbins critique. Thus there is no basis for the standard view that Hayek and Robbins retreated from Mises's view to a "second line of defense" or that Hayek and Robbins met the market socialists in an intermediate, Lernerian "synthesis" position somewhere between the Marxian and Misesian extremes. If Mises's view that "a socialist system with a market and market prices is as self-contradictory as is the notion of a triangular square" (1949, p. 710) is considered extreme, then so is Hayek's view that "nobody has yet demonstrated how planning and competition can be rationally combined" ([1935] 1948f, p. 179). If anything distinguishes these statements, it is merely their characteristic styles of expression, but neither is reconcilable with the synthesis known as market socialism.

The calculation debate, which is generally treated as a dated clash between extremes that fortunately settled down to a kind of quiet "equilibrium" of consensus, has been seen in this study as a highly relevant confrontation between extremes that unfortunately became diverted into static issues and thus never came to any resolution. It remains in "disequilibrium" today. The initial rivalry between the advocates and critics of central planning was never resolved; it was simply dissipated in confusion. But since the whole controversy revolved around the original challenge by Mises, and since by my interpretation this challenge was never met, it is evident that advocates of economic planning need to address themselves to the central issues raised by the Austrian economists. Despite its confusion, this controversy spawned the discovery of many important ideas by both sides and has raised many fascinating questions for future research. My hope is that this study may help to stimulate contemporary advocates and critics of central planning to return to this intellectual rivalry that so enriched the profession of economics in the 1930s.

References

Ames, Edward. 1967. "Comments." In John Pearce Hardt, Marvin Hoffenberg, Norman Kaplan, et al., eds. *Mathematics and Computers in Soviet Economic Planning*. New Haven: Yale University Press.

Ames, Edward, and Neuberger, Egon. 1977. "Frisch and Tinbergen on Economic Planning." *Journal of Comparative Economics* 1:195–212.

Armentano, Dominick T. 1969. "Resource Allocation Problems under Socialism." In William P. Snavely, *Theory of Economic Systems: Capitalism, Socialism, and Corporatism*. Columbus: Charles E. Merrill, pp. 127–39.

    1978. "A Critique of Neoclassical and Austrian Monopoly Theory." In Louis M. Spadaro, ed., *New Directions in Austrian Economics*. Kansas City: Sheed, Andrews & McMeel, pp. 94–110.

Arrow, Kenneth J., Hurwicz, L., and Uzawa, H. 1958. *Studies in Linear and Non-linear Programming*. Stanford: Stanford University Press.

Balassa, Bela A. 1959. *The Hungarian Experience in Economic Planning*. New Haven: Yale University Press.

    1974. "Success Criteria for Economic Systems." In Morris Bornstein, ed., *Comparative Economic Systems: Models and Cases*. Homewood, Ill.: Richard D. Irwin, pp. 2–18.

Baldwin, Claude David. 1942. *Economic Planning, Its Aims and Implications*. Urbana: University of Illinois Press.

Baran, Paul A. 1952. "National Economic Planning." In B. F. Haley, ed., *A Survey of Contemporary Economics*. Homewood, Ill.: Richard D. Irwin, 2:355–403.

Barone, Enrico. [1908] 1935. "The Ministry of Production in the Collectivist State," trans. Friedrich A. Hayek. In Hayek 1935, pp. 245–90 ("Il ministro della produzione nello stato collettivista").

Baumol, William J. 1958. "Activity Analysis in One Lesson." *American Economic Review* 48:837–73.

    1972. *Economic Theory and Operations Analysis*. Englewood Cliffs, N.J.: Prentice-Hall.

Becker, James F. 1977. *Marxian Political Economy: An Outline*. Cambridge: Cambridge University Press.

Beckwith, Burnham Putnam. 1949. *The Economic Theory of a Socialist Economy*. Stanford: Stanford University Press.

    1955. *Marginal Cost Price Output Control*. New York: Columbia University Press.

Belkin, V. D. 1961. "Kibernetika i ekonomika" [Cybernetics and economics].

In Aksel' Ivanovich Berg, ed., *Kibernetika na sluzhbu kommunizmu* [Cybernetics in the service of communism]. Moscow: State Energy Publishing House, 1:185–202.

Bergson, Abram. 1948. "Socialist Economics." In Howard S. Ellis, ed., *A Survey of Contemporary Economics*. Homewood, Ill.: Richard D. Irwin, 1:412–48.

1967. "Market Socialism Revisited." *Journal of Political Economy* 75:655–73.

Besancon, Alain. 1978. *The Soviet Syndrome*. New York: Harcourt Brace Jovanovich.

1980. "Anatomy of a Spectre." *Survey* 25:143–59.

Bettleheim, Charles. 1975. *Economic Calculation and Forms of Property: An Essay on the Transition between Capitalism and Socialism,* trans. John Tayler. New York: Monthly Review Press.

Blaug, Mark. 1968. *Economic Theory in Retrospect*. London: Heinemann Educational Books.

Bliss, C. J. 1972. "Prices, Markets, and Planning." *Economic Journal* 82:87–100.

Blitzer, Charles R., Clark, Peter B., and Taylor, Lance, eds. 1975. *Economy-wide Models and Development Planning*. Oxford: Oxford University Press.

Blodgett, Ralph H. 1979. *Comparative Economic Systems*. New York: Macmillan.

Böhm-Bawerk, Eugen von. [1888] 1959. *Capital and Interest*. Vol. 2, *The Positive Theory of Capital,* trans. George Huncke. South Holland, Ill.: Libertarian Press.

[1896] 1973. *Karl Marx and the Close of His System*. Clifton, N.J.: A. M. Kelley.

Bornstein, Morris, ed. 1973. *Plan and Market*. New Haven: Yale University Press.

Bradley, Robert, Jr. 1981. "Market Socialism: A Subjectivist Evaluation." *Journal of Libertarian Studies* 5:23–39.

Brozen, Yale, ed. 1975. *The Competitive Economy: Selected Readings*. Morristown, N.J.: General Learning Press.

Brus, Wlodzimierz. 1972. *The Market in a Socialist Economy*. London: Routledge & Kegan Paul.

1975. *Socialist Ownership and Political Systems,* trans. R. A. Clarke. London: Routledge & Kegan Paul.

Brutzkus, Boris. [1922] 1935. *Economic Planning in Soviet Russia,* trans. Gilbert Gardiner. London: Routledge & Sons.

Buchanan, James M. 1969. *Cost and Choice: An Inquiry in Economic Theory*. Chicago: University of Chicago Press.

Buchanan, James M. and Thirlby, G. F., eds. 1973. *L. S. E. Essays on Cost*. New York: New York University Press.

Buick, Adam. 1975. "The Myth of the Transitional Society." *Critique* 5:59–70.

Bukharin, Nicolai I. [1921] 1969. *Historical Materialism: A System of Sociology*. Ann Arbor: University of Michigan Press.

[1920] 1971. *Economics of the Transformation Period.* New York: Bergman.

[1917] 1972. *The Economic Theory of the Leisure Class.* New York: Monthly Review Press.

Bukharin, N. I., and Preobrazhensky, E. [1919] 1966. *The ABC of Communism: A Popular Explanation of the Program of the Communist Party of Russia,* trans. Eden Paul and Cedar Paul. Ann Arbor: University of Michigan Press.

Campbell, Robert W. 1961. "Marx, Kantorovich, Novozhilov: Stoimost' versus Reality." *Slavic Review* 20:402–18.

Cave, Martin. 1980. *Computers and Economic Planning: The Soviet Experience.* Cambridge: Cambridge University Press.

Chenery, Hollis B., and Kretschmer, K. 1956. "Resource Allocation for Economic Development." *Econometrica* 24:365–99.

Coddington, Alan. 1972. "Positive Economics." *Canadian Journal of Economics* 5:1–15.

Dahl, Robert Alan, and Lindblom, Charles E. 1953. *Politics, Economics and Welfare: Planning and Politico-economic Systems Resolved into Basic Social Processes.* New York: Harper & Row.

Dalton, George, 1974. *Economic Systems and Society: Capitalism, Communism and the Third World.* Harmondsworth, U.K.: Penguin Books.

Dantzig, George Bernard. 1963. *Linear Programming and Extensions.* Princeton: Princeton University Press.

Dantzig, George Bernard, and Wolfe, P. 1960. "Decomposition Principle for Linear Programming." *Operations Research* 8:101–11.

1961. "The Decomposition Algorithm for Linear Programs." *Econometrica* 29:767–78.

Debreu, Gerard. 1959. *Theory of Value.* New York: Wiley.

Dickinson, Henry Douglas. 1933. "Price Formation in a Socialist Community." *Economic Journal* 43: 237–50.

1939. *Economics of Socialism.* Oxford: Oxford University Press.

Dobb, Maurice Herbert. 1928. *Russian Economic Development since the Revolution.* New York: Dutton.

1933. "Economic Theory and the Problems of a Socialist Economy." *Economic Journal* 43:588–98.

1935a. "Economic Theory and Socialist Economy: A Reply." *Review of Economic Studies* 2:144–51.

1935b. Review of Brutzkus 1935 and Hayek 1935. *Economic Journal* 45:532–5.

1955. *On Economic Theory and Socialism: Collected Papers.* London: Routledge & Kegan Paul.

Dorfman, Robert. 1953. " 'Mathematical' or 'Linear' Programming: A Nonmathematical Exposition." *American Economic Review* 43:797–825.

Dorfman, Robert, Samuelson, Paul A., and Solow, Robert M. 1958. *Linear Programming and Economic Analysis.* New York: McGraw-Hill.

Drewnowski, Jan. 1961. "The Economic Theory of Socialism: A Suggestion for Reconsideration." *Journal of Political Economy* 69:341–54.

Dunlop, J. T., and Fedorenko, N. P., eds. 1969. *Planning and Markets: Modern Trends in Various Economic Systems.* New York: McGraw-Hill.

Durbin, Elizabeth. 1984. *The Fabians, Mr. Keynes and the Economics of Democratic Socialism.* New York: Routledge & Kegan Paul.

Durbin, Evan Frank Mottram. 1934. *Purchasing Power and Trade Depression.* London: Jonathan Cape.

    1937. "A Note on Mr. Lerner's 'Dynamical' Propositions." *Economic Journal* 47:577–81.

    [1936] 1968. "Economic Calculus in a Planned Economy." In *Problems of Economic Planning.* London: Routledge & Kegan Paul, pp. 140–55.

Eckstein, Alexander, ed. 1971. *Comparison of Economic Systems: Theoretical and Methodological Approaches.* Berkeley: University of California Press.

Eidem, Rolf, and Viotti, Staffan. 1978. *Economic Systems.* New York: Wiley & Sons.

Elliot, John E. 1973. *Comparative Economic Systems.* Englewood Cliffs, N.J.: Prentice-Hall.

Ellman, Michael. 1978. "The Fundamental Problem of Socialist Planning." *Oxford Economic Papers* 30:249–62.

    1979. *Socialist Planning.* Cambridge: Cambridge University Press.

Estrin, Saul, and Holmes, Peter. 1983. *French Planning in Theory and Practice.* London: Allen R. Unwin.

Eucken, Walter. 1950. *The Foundations of Economics: History and Theory in the Analysis of Economic Reality,* trans. T. W. Hutchison. London: William Hodge.

Fadeeva, V. N. 1959. *Computational Methods of Linear Algebra,* trans. C. Benster. New York: Dover.

Fedorenko, Nicolai Prokofevich. 1974. *Optimal Functioning for a Socialist Economy.* Moscow: Progress Publishers.

Felker, Jere L. 1966. *Soviet Economic Controversies: The Emerging Marketing Concept and Changes in Planning, 1960–1965.* Cambridge, Mass.: MIT Press.

Fellner, William John. 1960. *Emergence and Content of Modern Economic Analysis.* New York: McGraw-Hill.

Gale, David. 1960. *The Theory of Linear Economic Models.* New York: McGraw-Hill.

Gamarnikow, Michael. 1968. *Economic Reforms in Eastern Europe.* Detroit: Wayne University Press.

Gatovsky, Lev Markovich. 1963. "The Role of Profit in a Socialist Economy." *Soviet Review* 4:14–22.

Goldman, Marshall I. 1958. "Commission Trade and the Kolkhoz Market." *Soviet Studies* 10:136–45.

    1960. "Marketing: A Lesson for Marx." *Harvard Business Review* 38:79–86.

    1971. *Comparative Economic Systems: A Reader.* New York: Random House.

    1983. *USSR in Crisis: The Failure of an Economic System.* New York: W. W. Norton.

Golob, Eugene O. 1954. *The "ISMS," a History and Evaluation*. New York: Harper & Brothers.

Gottl-Ottlilienfeld, Friedrich von. 1914. *Wirtschaft und Technik. Grundriss der Sozialökonomik*, sec. 2. Tübingen: Abteilung.

Gregory, Theodor E. 1933. "An Economist Looks at Planning." In *Gold, Unemployment and Capitalism*. London: P. S. King & Son, pp. 277–94.

Grossman, Gregory, ed. 1960a. "Soviet Growth: Routine, Inertia, and Pressure." *American Economic Review, Papers and Proceedings* 50:62–72.

1960b. *Value and Plan*. Berkeley: University of California Press.

Gruchy, Alan G. 1966. *Comparative Economic Systems: Competing Ways to Stability and Growth*. Boston: Houghton Mifflin.

Hahn, Frank, and Negishi, Takashi. 1962. "A Theorem of Non-*tâtonnement* Stability." *Econometrica* 30:463–9.

Hall, Robert Lowe. 1937. *The Economic System in a Socialist State*. London: Macmillan.

Halm, George. 1935. "Further Considerations on the Possibility of Adequate Calculation in a Socialist Community," trans. H. E. Batson. In Hayek 1935, pp. 131–200.

Harris, Seymour E. 1949. *Economic Planning: The Plans of Fourteen Countries, with Analysis of the Plans*. New York: Alfred A. Knopf.

Hayek, Friedrich A. 1941. *The Pure Theory of Capital*. Chicago: University of Chicago Press.

[1940] 1948a. "The Competitive Solution." *Economica* 7:125–49. Reprinted in Hayek 1948c, pp. 181–208.

[1937] 1948b. "Economics and Knowledge." *Economica* 4:33–54. Reprinted in Hayek 1948c, pp. 33–56.

1948c. *Individualism and Economic Order*. Chicago: University of Chicago Press.

1948d. "The Meaning of Competition." In Hayek 1948c, pp. 92–106.

[1935] 1948e. "The Nature and History of the Problem." Reprinted in Hayek 1948c, pp. 119–47.

[1935] 1948f. "The Present State of the Debate." Reprinted in Hayek 1948c, pp. 148–80.

[1945] 1948g. "The Use of Knowledge in Society." *American Economic Review* 35:519–30. Reprinted in Hayek 1948c, pp. 77–91.

1973. *Law, Legislation and Liberty*. Vol. 1, *Rules and Order*. Chicago: University of Chicago Press.

1976. *Law, Legislation and Liberty*. Vol. 2, *The Mirage of Social Justice*. Chicago: University of Chicago Press.

1978a. "Competition as a Discovery Procedure." In Hayek 1978b, pp. 179–90.

1978b. *New Studies in Philosophy, Politics, Economics and the History of Ideas*. Chicago: University of Chicago Press.

1979. *Law, Legislation and Liberty*. Vol. 3, *The Political Order of a Free People*. Chicago: University of Chicago Press.

Hayek, Friedrich A., ed. 1935. *Collectivist Economic Planning: Critical Studies on the Possibilities of Socialism.* London: Routledge & Sons.

Heilbroner, Robert L. 1970. *Between Capitalism and Socialism: Essays in Political Economics.* New York: Random House.

Heimann, Eduard. 1918. "Die Sozialisierung" [Towards socialism]. *Archiv für Sozialwissenschaft und Socialpolitik* 45:527–90.

1922. *Mehrwert und Gemeinwirtschaft: Kritische und positive Beiträge zur Theorie des Sozialismus* [Surplus value and collective economy: critical and positive contributions to the theory of socialism]. Berlin: Robert Englemann.

1937. "Planning and the Market System." In Findlay Mackenzie, ed., *Planned Society: Yesterday, Today, Tomorrow.* New York: Prentice-Hall, pp. 703–45.

High, Jack. 1980. "Maximizing, Action and Market Adjustment." Ph.D. diss., UCLA.

Hoff, Trygve J. B. 1949. *Economic Calculation in the Socialist Society,* trans. M. A. Michael. London: William Hodge.

Holesevsky, Vaclar. 1968. "Planning Reforms in Czechoslovakia." *Soviet Studies* 19:544–56.

Hughan, Jessie W. 1932. "Some Features of the Industrial Structure under Socialism." In Harry W. Laidler, ed., *Socialist Planning and a Socialist Program.* New York: Falcon Press, pp. 117–28.

Hunt, E. K., and Schwartz, Jesse G., eds. 1972. *Critique of Economic Theory.* London: Penguin Books.

Hurwicz, Leonid. 1960. "Conditions for Economic Efficiency of Centralized and Decentralized Structures." In Gregory Grossman, ed. *Value and Plan.* Berkeley: University of California Press, pp. 162–75.

1969. "On the Concept and Possibility of Informational Decentralization." *American Economic Review, Papers and Proceedings* 59:513–24.

1971. "Centralization and Decentralization in Economic Processes." In Alexander Eckstein, ed., *Comparison of Economic Systems: Theoretical and Methodological Approaches.* Berkeley: University of California Press, pp. 79–102.

1972. "On Informationally Decentralized Systems." In C. B. McGuire and Roy Radner, *Decision and Organization.* Amsterdam: North-Holland, pp. 297–336.

Hutt, William H. 1940. "Economic Institutions and the New Socialism." *Economica,* 7:419–34.

Itoh, Makoto. 1980. *Value and Crisis: Essays on Marxian Economics in Japan.* New York: Monthly Review Press.

Judy, Richard W. 1967. "Information, Control, and Soviet Economic Management." In John Pearce Hardt, Marvin Hoffenberg, Norman Kaplan, et al., eds., *Mathematics and Computers in Soviet Economic Planning.* New Haven: Yale University Press, pp. 1–48.

Kaldor, Nicholas. 1932. Review of Landauer 1931. *Economic Journal* 42:276–81.

Kantorovich, Leonid Vital'evich. 1965. *The Best Use of Economic Resources.* Cambridge, Mass.: Harvard University Press.

Kaser, Michael. 1965. "Kosygin, Liberman, and the Pace of Soviet Industrial Reform." In *World Today,* no. 21. London: Royal Institute of International Affairs, pp. 375–88.

Kaser, Michael, and Portes, R., eds. 1971. *Planning and Market Relations.* London: Macmillan.

Kautsky, Karl. 1907. *The Social Revolution,* trans. A. M. Simons and M. W. Simons. Chicago: Charles H. Kerr.

Kirzner, Israel M. 1966. *An Essay on Capital.* New York: Augustus M. Kelley.
1967. *The Economic Point of View.* Kansas City: Sheed & Ward.
1973. *Competition and Entrepreneurship.* Chicago: University of Chicago Press.
1978. "The Perils of Regulation: A Market-Process Approach." Law and Economics Center: Occasional Paper. Coral Gables, Fla.: University of Miami School of Law.
1979. *Perception, Opportunity and Profit: Studies in the Theory of Entrepreneurship.* Chicago: University of Chicago Press.

Knight, Frank H. 1936. "The Place of Marginal Economics in a Collectivist System." *American Economic Review, Papers and Proceedings.* 26:255–66.
1940. "Socialism: The Nature of the Problem." *Ethics* 50:253–89.
[1921] 1971. *Risk, Uncertainty and Profit.* Chicago: University of Chicago Press.

Köhler, Heinz. 1966. *Welfare and Planning: An Analysis of Capitalism versus Socialism.* New York: John Wiley & Sons.

Konnik, I. 1966. "Plan and Market in the Socialist Economy." *Problems of Economics* 9:24–35.

Koopmans, Tjalling C., ed. 1951. *Activity Analysis of Production and Allocation.* New York: Wiley.

Koopmans, Tjalling C., and Montias, John Michael. 1971. "On the Description and Comparison of Economic Systems." In Alexander Eckstein, ed., *Comparison of Economic Systems: Theoretical and Methodological Approaches.* Berkeley: University of California Press, pp. 27–78.

Kornai, Janos. 1959. *Overcentralization in Economic Administration: A Critical Analysis Based on Experience in Hungarian Light Industry,* trans. John Knapp. Oxford: Oxford University Press.
1971. *Anti-equilibrium: On Economic Systems Theory and the Task of Research.* Amsterdam: North-Holland.
1974. *Mathematical Planning of Structural Decisions.* Amsterdam: North-Holland.

Kornai, Janos, and Lipták, Tamas. 1965. "Two-level Planning." *Econometrica* 33:141–69.

Kripke, Saul A. 1982. *Wittgenstein: On Rules and Private Language.* Cambridge, Mass: Harvard University Press.

Kuhn, Thomas. 1962. *The Structure of Scientific Revolutions.* Chicago: University of Chicago Press.

Lachmann, Ludwig M. 1977. *Capital, Expectations, and the Market Process: Essays on the Theory of the Market Economy.* Kansas City: Sheed, Andrews & McMeel.

[1956] 1978. *Capital and Its Structure.* Kansas City: Sheed, Andrews & McMeel.

Landauer, Carl. 1923. *Grundprobleme der funktionellen Verteilung des Wirtschaftlichen Werts.* Jena: G. Fischer.

1931. *Planwirtschaft und Verkehrwirtschaft.* Munich: Duncker & Humbolt.

1947. *Theory of National Economic Planning.* Berkeley: University of California Press.

1964. *Contemporary Economic Systems: A Comparative Analysis.* Philadelphia: J. B. Lippincott.

Lange, Oskar Richard. 1934. "Marxian Economics and Modern Economic Theory." *Review of Economic Studies* 2:189–201.

1937. "Mr. Lerner's Note on Socialist Economics." *Review of Economic Studies* 4:143–4.

1945. "Marxian Economics in the Soviet Union." *American Economic Review* 35: 127–33.

[1936] 1964. "On the Economic Theory of Socialism." In Lippincott [1938] 1964, pp. 55–143.

1967. "The Computer and the Market." In C. H. Feinstein, ed., *Socialism, Capitalism and Economic Growth: Essays Presented to Maurice Dobb.* Cambridge: Cambridge University Press, pp. 158–61.

1970. *Introduction to Economic Cybernetics.* New York: Pergamon Press.

1971. *Optimal Decisions: Principles of Programming.* New York: Pergamon Press.

Lange, Oskar Richard, ed. 1962. *Problems of Political Economy of Socialism,* New Delhi: People's Publishing House.

Lavigne, Marie. 1974. *The Socialist Economies of the Soviet Union and Europe,* trans. T. G. Waywell. White Plains, N.Y.: International Arts and Sciences Press.

Lavoie, Don. 1981. "A Critique of the Standard Account of the Socialist Calculation Debate." *Journal of Libertarian Studies* 5:41–87.

1983. "Some Strengths in Marx's Disequilibrium Theory of Money." *Cambridge Journal of Economics* 7:55–68.

1985. *National Economic Planning: What Is Left?* Cambridge, Mass.: Ballinger.

Leeman, Wayne A., ed. 1963. *Capitalism, Market Socialism and Central Planning.* Boston: Houghton Mifflin.

Leichter, Otto. [1923] 1932. *Die Sprengung des Kapitalismus: Die Wirtschaftsrechnung in der sozialistischen Gesellschaft.* Vienna: Verlag der Wiener Volksbuchhandlung.

Lekachman, Robert. 1959. *A History of Economic Ideas.* New York: Harper.

Leontief, Wassily. 1966. *Input-Output Economics*. New York: Oxford University Press.

Lerner, Abba P. 1934a. "The Concept of Monopoly and the Measurement of Monopoly Power." *Review of Economic Studies* 1:157–75.

——— 1934b. "Economic Theory and Socialist Economy." *Review of Economic Studies* 2:51–61.

——— 1935. "A Rejoinder." *Review of Economic Studies* 2:152–4.

——— 1936. "A Note on Socialist Economics." *Review of Economic Studies* 4:72–6.

——— 1937. "Statics and Dynamics in Socialist Economics." *Economic Journal* 47:253–70.

——— 1938. "Theory and Practice in Socialist Economics." *Review of Economic Studies* 6:71–5.

——— 1944. *The Economics of Control: Principles of Welfare Economics*. New York: Macmillan.

Liberman, Evseĭ Grigor'evich. 1966a. "The Plan, Direct Ties and Profitability." *Problems of Economics* 8:27–31.

——— 1966b. "Profitability of Socialist Enterprises." *Problems of Economics* 8:3–10.

——— 1967. "Are We Flirting with Capitalism? Profits and 'Profits.' " In Shanti S. Tangri, ed., *Command versus Demand: Systems for Economic Growth*. Boston: D. C. Heath, pp. 90–99.

——— 1968. "The Role of Profits in the Industrial Incentive System of the USSR." *International Labour Review* 97:1–14.

——— 1972. *Economic Methods and the Effectiveness of Production*. White Plains, N.Y.: International Arts and Sciences Press.

Liberman, E. G., and Zhitnitskii, Z. 1968. "Economic and Administrative Methods of Managing the Economy." *Problems of Economics* 11:3–11.

Liebhafsky, Herbert Hugo. 1963. *The Nature of Price Theory*. Homewood, Ill.: Dorsey.

Lippincott, Benjamin E., ed. [1938] 1964. *On the Economic Theory of Socialism*. New York: McGraw-Hill.

Little, Ian Malcolm David. 1950. *Critique of Welfare Economics*. Oxford: Clarendon Press.

Loucks, William N. 1957. *Comparative Economic Systems*. New York: Harper & Brothers.

Luch, R. D. 1959. *Individual Choice Behavior: A Theoretical Analysis*. New York: John Wiley & Sons.

Lutz, Vera. 1969. *Central Planning for the Market Economy: An Analysis of the French Theory and Experience*. London: Longmans, Green.

McCloskey, Donald N. 1983. "The Rhetoric of Economics." *Journal of Economic Literature* 21:481–517.

McFarlane, Bruce J., and Gordijew, I. 1964. "Profitability and the Soviet Firm." *Economic Record* 40:554–68.

Machlup, Fritz. 1958. "Equilibrium and Disequilibrium: Misplaced Concreteness and Disguised Politics." *Economic Journal* 68:1–24.

1959. "Statics and Dynamics: Kaleidoscopic Words." *Southern Economic Journal* 26:91–110.

1976. "Closing Remarks." In Laurence S. Moss, ed., *The Economics of Ludwig von Mises: Toward a Critical Reappraisal*. Kansas City: Sheed & Ward, pp. 111–16.

Mack, Ruth Prince. 1971. *Planning on Uncertainty*. New York: Wiley-Interscience.

McNulty, Paul J. 1967. "A Note on the History of Perfect Competition." *Journal of Political Economy* 75:395–9.

1968. "Economic Theory and the Meaning of Competition." *Quarterly Journal of Economics* 82:639–56.

Makower, Helen. 1957. *Activity Analysis and the Theory of Economic Equilibrium*. New York: St. Martin's Press.

Malinvaud, Edmond. 1961. "On Decentralization in National Planning." Working Paper no. 36. Berkeley: University of California Press.

1967. "Decentralized Procedures for Planning." In Edmond Malinvaud and M. O. L. Bacharach, eds., *Activity Analysis in the Theory of Growth and Planning*. London: Macmillan, pp. 170–208.

Mandel, Ernest. 1970. *Marxist Economic Theory*, trans. Brian Pearce. New York: Monthly Review Press.

Marcuse, Herbert. 1961. *Soviet Marxism: A Critical Analysis*. New York: Random House.

Marglin, Stephen A. 1963. *Approaches to Dynamic Investment Planning*. Amsterdam: North-Holland.

Marschak, Jakob. 1923. "Wirtschaftsrechnung und Gemeinwirtschaft: Zur Mises'schen These von der Unmöglichkeit sozialistischer Wirtschaftsrechnung." *Archiv für Sozialwissenschaft und Sozialpolitik* 51:501–20.

Marx, Karl. [1847] 1963. *The Poverty of Philosophy*. New York: International Publishers.

[1867] 1967a. *Capital: A Critique of Political Economy*. Vol. 1, *The Process of Capitalist Production*. New York: International Publishers.

[1885] 1967b. *Capital: A Critique of Political Economy*. Vol. 2, *The Process of Circulation of Capital*. New York: International Publishers.

[1894] 1967c. *Capital: A Critique of Political Economy*. Vol. 3, *The Process of Capitalist Production as a Whole*. New York: International Publishers.

[1859] 1970. *A Contribution to the Critique of Political Economy*. New York: International Publishers.

[1962] 1971. *Theories of Surplus Value*. Pt. 3. Moscow: Progress Publishers.

[1953] 1973. *Grundrisse: Foundations of the Critique of Political Economy*, trans. Martin Nicolaus. New York: Random House.

[1871] 1974a. "The Civil War in France: Address of the General Council." In D. Fernbach, ed., *The First International and After: Political Writings*. Random House, New York: vol. 3, pp. 187–268.

[1891] 1974b. "Critique of the Gotha Programme." In *The First International and After: Political Writings*, vol. 3, pp. 339–59.

Marx, Karl, Engels, Friedrich, and Lenin, Vladimir Ilyich. 1972. *Anarchism and Anarcho-syndicalism.* Moscow: Progress Publishers.

Meade, James E. 1976. *The Just Economy: Principles of Political Economy.* London: Allen & Unwin.

Mises, Ludwig von. 1923. "Neue Beitrage zum Problem der sozialistischen Wirtschaftsrechnung." *Archiv für Sozialwissenschaft und Sozialpolitik* 51:488–500.

    1928. "Neue Shriften zum Problem der sozialistischen Wirtschaftsrechnung." *Archiv für Sozialwissenschaft und Sozialpolitik* 60:187–90.

    [1920] 1935. "Economic Calculation in the Socialist Commonwealth," trans. S. Adler. In Hayek 1935, pp. 87–103. "Die Wirtschaftsrechnung im sozialistischen Gemeinwesen." *Archiv für Sozialwissenschaft und Sozialpolitik* 47:86–121.

    [1922] 1936. *Socialism: An Economic and Sociological Analysis,* trans. J. Kahane. London: Jonathan Cape. (*Die Gemeinwirtschaft.* Jena: G. Fischer.)

    1949. *Human Action: A Treatise on Economics.* London: William Hodge.

    [1929] 1977. *A Critique of Interventionism.* New Rochelle, N.Y.: Arlington House.

    [1912] 1980. *The Theory of Money and Credit,* trans. H. E Batson. Indianapolis: Library Press.

Misra, Baidyanath. 1972. *Capitalism, Socialism and Planning.* New Delhi: Oxford University Press and IBH Publishing.

Montias, John Michael. 1963. "Socialist Operational Price Systems: Comment." *American Economic Review* 53:1085–93.

    1967. "Soviet Optimizing Models for Multiperiod Planning." In John Pearce Hardt, Marvin Hoffenberg, Norman Kaplan, et al., eds., *Mathematics and Computers in Soviet Economic Planning.* New Haven: Yale University Press, pp. 201–45.

Morgan, Theodore. 1964. "The Theory of Error in Centrally Directed Economic Systems." *Quarterly Journal of Economics* 78:395–419.

Murrell, Peter. 1983. "Did the Theory of Market Socialism Answer the Challenge of Ludwig von Mises? A Reinterpretation of the Socialist Controversy." *History of Political Economy* 15:92–105.

Myrdal, Gunnar. 1960. *Beyond the Welfare State: Economic Planning and Its International Implications.* New Haven: Yale University Press.

Negishi, Takashi. 1962. "The Stability of a Competitive Economy: A Survey Article." *Econometrica* 30:635–69.

Nemchinov, V. S., ed. 1964. *The Use of Mathematics in Economics,* trans. Alec Nove. Edinburgh: Oliver & Boyd.

Neuberger, Egon. 1966. "Libermanism, Computopia, and the Visible Hand: The Question of Informational Efficiency." *American Economic Review, Papers and Proceedings* 56:131–44.

Neuberger, Egon, and Duffy, W. 1976. *Comparative Economic Systems: A Decision-making Approach.* Boston: Allyn & Bacon.

Neurath, Otto. 1919. *Durch die Kriegswirtschaft zur Naturalwirtshaft.* Munich: G. D. W. Callwey.

Nove, Alex. 1958a. "The Politics of Economic Rationality: Observations on the Soviet Economy." *Social Research* 25:127–44.

    1958b. "The Problem of 'Success Indicators' in Soviet Industry." *Economica* 25:1–13.

    1966. "Planners' Preferences, Priorities and Reforms." *Economic Journal* 76:267–77.

Novozhilov, Valentin Valentinovich. 1969. *Problems of Measuring Outlays and Results under Optimal Planning.* New York: International Arts and Sciences Press.

Nutter, G. Warren. 1974. "Markets without Property: A Grand Illusion." In Eirik G. Furubotn and Svetozar Pejovich, eds., *The Economics of Property Rights.* Cambridge, Mass.: Ballinger, pp. 217–24.

    1983. *Political Economy and Freedom.* Indianapolis: Liberty Press.

O'Driscoll, Gerald P. 1977. *Economics as a Coordination Problem: The Contributions of Friedrich A. Hayek.* Kansas City: Sheed, Andrews & McMeel.

Ostrom, Vincent. 1976. "Some Paradoxes for Planners: Human Knowledge and Its Limitations." In *The Politics of Planning: A Review and Critique of Centralized Economic Planning.* San Francisco: Institute for Contemporary Studies, pp. 243–54.

Parker, Alan. 1963. "On the Application of Mathematics in Soviet Economics." *Yale Economic Essays* 3:471–86.

Pejovich, Svetozar. 1976. "The End of Planning: The Soviet Union and East European Experiences." In *The Politics of Planning: A Review and Critique of Centralized Economic Planning.* San Francisco: Institute for Contemporary Studies, pp. 95–113.

Pickersgill, Gary M., and Pickersgill, Joyce E. 1974. *Contemporary Economic Systems: A Comparative View.* Englewood Cliffs, N.J.: Prentice-Hall.

Pierson, Nikolaas Gerard. [1902] 1912. *Principles of Economics,* trans. A. Wotzel, vol. 2. London: Macmillan.

    [1902] 1935. "The Problem of Value in the Socialist Community," trans. G. Gardiner. In Hayek 1935, pp. 41–85.

Plant, Arnold. [1937] 1974. "Centralize or Decentralize?" In *Some Modern Business Problems.* London: Longmans, Green. Reprinted in *Selected Economic Essays and Addresses.* London: Routledge & Kegan Paul, pp. 174–98.

Polanyi, Karl. 1922. "Sozialistische Rechnungslegung" [Socialist calculation]. *Archiv für Sozialwissenschaft und Sozialpolitik* 49:377–420.

    1924. "Die funktionelle Theorie der Gesellschaft und das Problem der sozialistischen Rechnungslegung. (Eine Erwiderung an Prof. Mises und Dr. Felix Weil)." *Archiv für Sozialwissenschaft und Sozialpolitik* 52:218–28.

Polanyi, Michael. 1951. *Logic of Liberty.* Chicago: University of Chicago Press.

1958. *Personal Knowledge: Towards a Post-critical Philosophy.* Chicago: University of Chicago Press.

1969. *Knowing and Being.* Chicago: University of Chicago Press.

Popper, Karl R. 1972. *Objective Knowledge: An Evolutionary Approach.* London: Oxford University Press.

Porwit, Krzysztof. 1967. *Central Planning: Evaluation of Variants,* trans. Jozef Stadler. Oxford: Pergamon Press.

Radner, Roy. 1968. "Competitive Equilibrium under Uncertainty." *Econometrica* 36:31–58.

Rakovskii, M. 1968. "Introducing Economic-Mathematical Methods in Planning Practice." *Problems of Economics* 10:14–21.

Recktenwald, Horst Claus. 1978. "An Adam Smith Renaissance anno 1976? The Bicentenary Output: A Reappraisal of His Scholarship." *Journal of Economic Literature* 16:56–83.

Reekie, W. Duncan. 1979. *Industry, Prices and Markets.* New York: John Wiley & Sons.

Reese, David A. 1980. "Alienation and Economics in Karl Marx." Ph.D. diss., Virginia Polytechnic Institute.

Revesz, G. 1968. "Regulation of Enterprise Profits under the New System of Control and Management." *Acta Oeconomica* 3:23–40.

Rima, Ingrid H. 1972. *Development of Economic Analysis.* Homewood, Ill.: Richard D. Irwin.

Rivett, Kenneth. 1955. "The Definition of Economics." *Economic Record* 31:215–31.

Rizzo, Mario J. 1978. "Knight's Theory of Uncertainty: A Reconsideration." Paper presented at the annual meeting of the American Economic Association.

Rizzo, Mario J., ed. 1979. *Time, Uncertainty and Disequilibrium: Exploration of Austrian Themes.* Lexington, Mass.: Lexington Books.

Robbins, Lionel. 1934a. *The Great Depression.* New York: Macmillan.

1934b. "Production." *Encyclopedia of the Social Sciences.* 12:462–7. New York: Macmillan.

[1932] 1935. *An Essay on the Nature and Significance of Economic Science,* 2d ed. London: Macmillan.

1971. *Autobiography of an Economist.* London: Macmillan.

1976. *Political Economy, Past and Present.* New York: Columbia University Press.

Roberts, Paul Craig. 1970. "War Communism: A Re-examination." *Slavic Review* 29:238–61.

1971. *Alienation and the Soviet Economy.* Albuquerque: University of New Mexico Press.

Roberts, Paul Craig, and Stephenson, Matthew A. 1973. *Marx's Theory of Exchange, Alienation and Crisis.* Stanford: Hoover Institution Press.

Roper, Willet Crosby, Jr. 1931. *The Problem of Pricing in a Socialist State.* Cambridge, Mass.: Harvard University Press.

Rothbard, Murray N. 1962. *Man, Economy, and State: A Treatise on Economic Principles.* Los Angeles: Nash.

1976. "Ludwig von Mises and Economic Calculation under Socialism." In Laurence S. Moss, ed., *The Economics of Ludwig von Mises: Toward a Critical Reappraisal.* Kansas City: Sheed & Ward, pp. 67–77.

Scarf, Herbert E. 1960. "Some Examples of Global Instability of the Competitive Equilibrium." *International Economic Review* 1:157–72.

Schumpeter, Joseph A. [1942] 1950. *Capitalism, Socialism and Democracy.* New York: Harper & Row.

1954. *History of Economic Analysis.* New York: Oxford University Press.

Seligman, Ben B. 1971. *Main Currents in Modern Economics.* Vol. 1, *The Revolt against Formalism.* Chicago: Quadrangle.

Sengupta, Jati K. 1972. *Stochastic Programming: Methods and Applications.* Amsterdam: North-Holland.

Shackle, George Lennox Sharman. 1955. *Uncertainty in Economics and other Reflections.* Cambridge: Cambridge University Press.

1972. *Epistemics and Economics: A Critique of Economic Doctrines.* Cambridge: Cambridge University Press.

Sharpe, Myron E., ed. 1965. *The Liberman Discussion: A New Phase in Soviet Economic Thought.* White Plains, N.Y.: International Arts and Sciences Press.

Sherman, Howard J. 1969a. "The 'Revolution' in Soviet Economics." In Alex Simirenko, ed., *Social Thought in the Soviet Union.* Chicago: Quadrangle, pp. 222–68.

1969b. *The Soviet Economy.* Boston: Little, Brown.

Sik, Ota. 1967a. *Plan and Market under Socialism.* White Plains, N.Y.: International Arts and Sciences Press.

1967b. "Socialist Market Relations." In C. H. Feinstein, ed., *Socialism, Capitalism and Economic Growth: Essays Presented to Maurice Dobb.* Cambridge: Cambridge University Press, pp. 133–57.

1976. *The Third Way: Marxist-Leninist Theory and Modern Industrial Society,* trans. M. Sling. White Plains, N.Y.: International Arts and Sciences Press.

Sikes, Earl R. 1940. *Contemporary Economic Systems: Their Analysis and Historical Background.* New York: Henry Holt.

Sirkin, Gerald. 1968. *The Visible Hand: The Fundamentals of Economic Planning.* New York: McGraw-Hill.

Snavely, William P. 1969. *Theory of Economic Systems: Capitalism, Socialism, and Corporatism.* Columbus: Charles E. Merrill.

Solo, Robert A. 1967. *Economic Organizations and Social Systems.* Indianapolis: Bobbs-Merrill.

Steele, David Ramsey. 1978. "The Impossibility of Communism." Unpublished manuscript, University of Hull, England (portions published in the *Journal of Libertarian Studies* 5:7–22, 99–111).

Suranyi-Unger, Theo. 1952. *Comparative Economic Systems.* New York: McGraw-Hill.

Swann, M. J. 1975. "On the Theory of Optimal Planning in the Soviet Union." *Australian Economic Papers* 14:41–56.

Sweezy, Alan. 1936. "The Economist in a Socialist Economy." In *Explorations in Economics: Notes and Essays Contributed in Honor of F. W. Taussig.* London: McGraw-Hill, pp. 422–33.

Tangri, Shanti S., ed. 1967. *Command versus Demand: Systems for Economic Growth.* Boston: D. C. Heath.

Taylor, Fred M. [1929] 1964. "The Guidance of Production in a Socialist State." In Benjamin E. Lippincott, ed., *On the Economic Theory of Socialism.* New York: McGraw-Hill, pp. 41–54.

Thirlby, G. F. 1973a. "Economists' Cost Rules and Equilibrium Theory." In Buchanan and Thirlby 1973, pp. 273–87.

1973b. "The Ruler." In Buchanan and Thirlby 1973, pp. 163–98.

1973c. "The Subjective Theory of Value and Accounting Cost." In Buchanan and Thirlby 1973, pp. 135–61.

Tisch, Kläre. 1932. "Wirtschaftsrechnung und Verteilung im zentralistisch organisierten sozialistischen Gemeinwesen." Ph.D. diss., University of Bonn.

Tschayanoff, Alexander. 1923. "Zur Frage einer Theorie der nichtkapitalistischen Wirtschaftssysteme." *Archiv für Sozialwissenschaft und Sozialpolitik* 51:577–613.

Turetskii, Sh. 1967. "Price and Its Role in the System of Economic Methods of Management." *Problems of Economics* 10:3–14.

Uno, Kōzō. 1980. *Principles of Political Economy: Theory of a Purely Capitalist Society,* trans. T. Sekine. New York: Harvester Press.

Vaughn, Karen. 1980a. "Does it Matter That Costs Are Subjective?" *Southern Economic Journal* 46:702–15.

1980b. "Economic Calculation under Socialism: the Austrian Contribution." *Economic Inquiry* 18:535–54.

Veblen, Thorstein. 1919. *The Place of Science in Modern Civilization, and Other Essays.* New York: Viking Press.

Vorhies, W. Francis. 1982. "Marx and Mises on Money: The Monetary Theories of Two Opposing Political Economies." Ph.D. diss., University of Colorado.

Wakar, Aleksy, and Zielinsky, Janusz. 1963. "Socialist Operational Price Systems." *American Economic Review* 53:109–27.

Ward, Benjamin N. 1960. "Kantorovich on Economic Calculation." *Journal of Political Economy* 68:545–56.

1967a. "Linear Programming and Soviet Planning." In John Pearce Hardt, Marvin Hoffenberg, Norman Kaplan, and Herbert S. Levine, eds., *Mathematics and Computers in Soviet Economic Planning.* New Haven: Yale University Press, pp. 147–200.

1967b. *The Socialist Economy: A Study of Organizational Alternatives.* New York: Random House.

1971. "Organization and Comparative Economics: Some Approaches." In Alexander Eckstein, ed., *Comparison of Economic Systems: Theoretical and Methodological Approaches*. Berkeley: University of California Press, pp. 103–33.

Weber, Max. [1921] 1978. *Economy and Society: An Outline of Interpretive Sociology*. Berkeley: University of California Press.

Weil, Felix. 1924. "Gildensozialistische Rechnungslegung. Kritische Bemerkungen zu Karl Polanyi: 'Sozialistische Rechnungslegung' in diesem Archiv 49/2, S.377 ff:." *Archiv für Sozialwissenschaft und Sozialpolitik* 52:196–217.

Weitzman, Martin. 1970. "Iterative Multi-level Planning with Production Targets." *Econometrica* 38:50–65.

White, Lawrence H. 1978. "Entrepreneurial Price Adjustment." Paper presented at the Washington, D.C. annual meeting of the Southern Economic Association.

1984. *Free Banking in Britain*. Cambridge: Cambridge University Press.

Wicksteed, Philip H. [1910] 1933. *The Common Sense of Political Economy*. London: Routledge & Kegan Paul.

Wieser, Friedrich von. [1914] 1927. *Social Economics*, trans. A. Ford Hinrichs. London: Allen & Unwin. (*Theorie der gesellschaftlichen Wirtschaft*. Tübingen: J. C. B. Mohr).

[1899] 1956. *Natural Value*, trans. C. A. Malloch. New York: Kelley & Millman. (*Der natürliche Werth*. Vienna: A. Hölder).

Wilczynski, J. 1970. *The Economics of Socialism: Principles Governing the Operation of the Centrally Planned Economies in the USSR and Eastern Europe under the New System*. London: Allen & Unwin.

1973. *Profit, Risk and Incentive under Socialist Economic Planning*. New York: Harper & Row.

Wiseman, Jack. 1973a. "The Theory of Public Utility Price: An Empty Box." In Buchanan and Thirlby, 1973, pp. 245–71.

1973b. "Uncertainty, Costs, and Collectivist Economic Planning." In Buchanan and Thirlby 1973, pp. 227–43.

Wootton, Barbara. 1935. *Plan or No Plan*. New York: Farrar & Rinehard.

1945. *Freedom under Planning*. Chapel Hill: University of North Carolina Press.

Zaleski, Eugene. 1967. *Planning Reforms in the Soviet Union, 1962–1966: An Analysis of Trends in Economic Organization and Management*. Chapel Hill: University of North Carolina Press.

1971. *Planning for Economic Growth in the Soviet Union, 1918–1932*. Chapel Hill: University of North Carolina Press.

1980. *Stalinist Planning for Economic Growth, 1933–1952*. Chapel Hill: University of North Carolina Press.

Zassenhaus, Herbert. [1934] 1956. "On the Theory of Economic Planning." *International Economic Papers* 6:88–107.

Zauberman, Alfred. 1976. *Mathematical Theory in Soviet Planning: Concepts, Methods, Techniques.* Oxford: Oxford University Press.

Zauberman, Alfred, Bergstrom, A., Kronsjö, T., et al. 1967. *Aspects of Plano-metrics.* New Haven: Yale University Press.

Index

accounting, *see* profit and loss accounting
aggregation, 170, *see also* central planning; macroeconomic variant
alertness, *see* choice, aspects of
alienation, 36, 39
Ames, Edward, 15, 94n
anarchy of capitalist production, 20, 28, 34–47, 53n, 54, 60, 62n, 66–8, 82n, 84, 154–5, 167, 180
Armentano, Dominick T., 12, 20n, 22n
Arrow, Kenneth J., 94n
Austrian Economics Newsletter, 146n
Austrian school, 2n, 3, 5–6, 7, 22–5, 33, 35, 51n, 64–6, 67, 83–4, 92, 93n, 100–16, 129, 132, 134, 148, 170, 182

Bakunin, Michael, 34
Balassa, Bela A., 17n, 25n
Baldwin, Claude David, 6n, 18
banking, 35n 163, 164–6, 175
Baran, Paul A., 17n
Barone, Enrico, 12, 13, 14, 16, 21, 48, 78–85, 88, 91, 92, 100, 108, 112, 115, 118–19, 124, 152, 181
Baumol, William J., 94n
Becker, James F., 60n
Beckwith, Burnham Putnam, 19n
Belkin, V. D., 95
Bergson, Abram, 2–3, 12n, 142
Bergstrom, A., 94n
Besancon, Alain, 156n
Bettleheim, Charles, 60n
Blanc, Louis, 34–5
Blaug, Mark, 94n
Bliss, C. J., 12, 17n, 19n
Blitzer, Charles R., 24n
Blodgett, Ralph H., 11n, 17n
Böhm-Bawerk, Eugen von, 6, 64n, 67, 133
Bornstein, Morris, 19n
Bradley, Robert, Jr., 20n
Bray, John, 34
Brozen, Yale, 22n
Brus, Wlodzimierz, 19n, 25n

Brutzkus, Boris, 2n, 155, 157
Buchanan, James M., 20n, 102n
Buick, Adam, 46–7
Bukharin, Nicolai I., 6n, 40, 42, 43n
bureaucracy, *see* socialism, bureaucratic problems of

calculation, *see* economic calculation
calculation argument, 6, 8–9, 23, 28, 30n, 32, 45, 48–77, 83, 111, 118, 144, 151, 156, 159–60, 173n, 177
calculation debate, 1, 5, 26–7
  alleged retreats in 4–5, 14–15, 20, 21, 26, 48, 50, 90–1, 117, 121n, 135, 145–58, 161, 174, 177–8, 183
  alternative account of, 20–2, 28
  German variant of, 6, 117n, 162–6, 173–6
  importance of, 1
  standard account of, 2–20, 28, 79, 86, 112n, 117, 166, 173n, 178, 179
Campbell, Robert W., 94n
Cannan, Edwin, 3n, 133
capital, 52n, 63–4, 65, 73n, 81, 112, 122, 128, 142, 147, 155–60, 163–5, 175
capital structure, 51, 55–6, 63–4, 73–4, 126, 129, 132
capitalism, 7, 9, 16, 29, 115n, 118
Cave, Martin, 15, 94
central planning, 2, 4, 10, 22–7
  macroeconomic theory of, 8, 133n, 142
  market-socialist theory of, *see* competitive solution
  Marxian theory of, 8–11, 20, 23, 28–9, 31, 34, 39–47, 48, 50, 53, 60, 63, 74, 86, 138, 146, 151, 154, 155, 165, 166–7, 179–80
Chamberlin, Edward, 129
chaos, 35–7, 49n, 81, 155n, 158, 167
Chenery, Hollis B., 94n
choice, aspects of, 104–8, 125, 127, 135
  alertness, 105–7, 108n, 127, 131, 132, 144, 159, 182

choice, aspects of (*cont.*)
  futurity, 57, 59, 65, 71, 73, 100n,
    104–5, 106, 107, 108n, 109, 127,
    132, 141–2, 144, 147, 159, 164,
    165, 166, 176, 182
  maximization, 16, 18, 20, 49, 54, 57,
    81–3, 94, 101, 104, 106, 107, 114–
    16, 122, 125, 131–2, 151, 159, 169,
    175
Clark, John Bates, 51n
Clark, Peter B., 24n
classical economics, 22–3, 35–6, 38, 80–
  1, 100n, 101
Coddington, Alan 32n
commodity fetishism, 53n
common ownership of the means of
  production, *see* producers goods, centralized allocation of
communism
  as imaginary equilibrium construct,
    80–5
  first phase of, 46–7, 68
  second phase of, 46
competition, 3, 4, 22–3, 45, 49, 118–19,
  121, 140, 145, 149, 150, 154, 160,
  161, 171–3
  as a discovery procedure, 10, 26–7,
    62, 73, 123–4, 137, 139, 169n,
    170–3, 182–3
  imperfect and monopolistic, 129n
  perfect, 12, 16, 21, 104, 106–7, 119–
    22, 128–9, 139–40, 161, 172,
    183
  under socialism, 5, 163, 164–6, 180
  rivalrous, *see* rivalry
competitive solution, 9–10, 75–7, 95,
  117–44, 145, 150, 158–60, 162–6,
  166–73, 179, 182
  marginal cost pricing in, 107, 118–32,
    134n, 140, 142, 146, 151, 159, 162,
    163–4, 171
  superbank variant, 163, 164–6, 175–7
  trial and error in, 93, 118–32, 161,
    167, 169, 177, 182
  "World of Competing Monopolies"
    variant, 163–4
complexity, 19, 22–4, 36, 39, 51, 53, 58,
  60–7, 72–4, 91, 94, 96, 99, 115, 123,
  126, 147–9, 158, 167, 176, 180
computation argument, 21, 79–80, 90–
  2, 117–19, 128, 133, 144, 160, 168n,
  181
computers, 15, 66–7, 86, 94–8, 124
conscious planning, *see* central planning,
  Marxian theory of

consumer goods
  market allocation of, 8, 11, 74–7,
    114n, 121, 146, 147, 150, 158, 162
  centralized allocation of, 8, 19, 74
contracts, 115n
coordination process, 22–4, 35–7, 41,
  54, 55n, 60, 86, 108, 111, 113, 115,
  122, 125, 129, 144, 160, 165, 173,
  174, 180, 182
Crusoe, Robinson, 52–3, 60–1, 80

Dahl, Robert Alan, 12n, 13, 16, 17n,
  19n
Dalton, George, 16, 19n
Dantzig, George Bernard, 94n
Debreu, Gerard, 109
delegation of authority, 55n, 137, 165–
  6, 176–7
depression, 133n, 145, *see also* trade
  cycles
development, 157
Dickinson, Henry Douglas
  Hayek's critique of, 152, 166–71
  Mises's critique of, 173, 176n
  on the competitive solution, 118,
    125n, 126–7, 132, 135–9, 145, 163
  on entrepreneurship, 137–9
  on the equation-solving solution, 21,
    79–80, 86n, 88–90, 100, 133
  on equilibrium, 113n, 115n, 131n, 140
  on knowledge, 134
  on risk, 135–7
  on trial and error, 93, 96
  response to Mises by, 2, 13–14
disequilibrium, 18, 35–6, 47, 56, 57,
  82n, 97–8, 104–8, 112, 115, 125, 159,
  169, 180
division of labor, 41–3, 62n, 174
Dobb, Maurice Herbert, 8, 10–11, 12n,
  17n, 18, 49, 88, 113, 115n, 125n,
  128n 139
Dorfman, Robert, 94n
Drewnowski, Jan, 4–5, 7, 12n
Duffy, W., 18
Dunlop, J. T., 19n
Durbin, Elizabeth, 133n, 146n
Durbin, Evan Frank Mottram, 2, 88n,
  118, 125n, 132, 133–5, 139, 140
dynamics, 21, 49, 51n, 57, 59, 65, 73,
  78, 79, 87, 91, 97, 99, 110, 116, 119,
  125, 135, 141, 144, 149, 151, 159–60,
  164, 169, 175, 180

Ebeling, Richard M. 146n
Eckstein, Alexander, 1, 19

economic calculation, 3, 16
  in natura, 51, 63, 74, 155
  under capitalism, 48–60, 119–21, 180
  under socialism, 4, 12, 60–7, 121–2
economics, methods of, 2, 32n, 67, 84–
  5, 103, 109–11, 113, 120n, 170
efficiency, 3, 16, 17, 35, 54, 55n, 148,
  157, 173, *see also* Pareto-optimality
Eidem, Rolf, 12, 17n, 24n
Elliot, John E., 1, 12n, 13, 15n, 17n
Ellman, Michael, 20n
Engels, Friedrich, 34
entrepreneurs, 14, 25–6, 49, 75–6, 85,
  106, 110, 129, 137–9, 150, 158–60,
  166, 174, 176, 177, 180
entrepreneurship, *see* market process
equation-solving solution, *see* mathematical solution
equilibration process
  by entrepreneurial action, 41, 56, 75,
    98, 100n, 108–15, 118, 129–31,
    164, *see also* coordination process
  by Walrasian auctioneer, 18, 24, 85,
    86, 94–5, 97–9, 107, 118, 120–4,
    127, 129–31, 134, 144, 167, 168n
equilibrium
  as abstract imaginary construction, 5n,
    59, 65, 80–5, 88, 118, 172
  as actually attained, 13, 35, 88–9, 93,
    96, 121–2, 127, 129, 130–1, 161,
    168, 181
  as inherently unattainable, 22–3, 37,
    44, 47, 56, 65, 91, 127, 181
  competitive, as goal of central plan-
    ning, 22, 25, 119, 133–4, 140
  determinateness of, 11, 14, 16, 48,
    115, 161
  no calculation problem in, 12, 20, 56
  no role for money in, 44, 46–7, 59
  preoccupation with, 78, 84, 88, 139,
    144, 164, 169, 175
  tendency to, *see* equilibration process
Estrin, Saul, 108n
ethics, 18, 54, 154n
Eucken, Walter, 20n
evaluations
  consumer, 50–1, 54, 55, 58, 60–1, 64,
    66, 72, 75, 87, 147, 149
  primary, 50–1
  producer, 50–62, 64, 66, 71–2, 73–4,
    75, 82n, 87–8, 147
evolution of capitalism into socialism,
  23, 30–3, 40, 62n, 96, 176
expectations, *see* choice, aspects of,
  futurity

Fadeeva, V. N., 94n
Fedorenko, Nicolai Prokofevich, 19n,
  94n
Felker, Jere L., 6, 25n, 94n
Fellner, William John, 94n
firm, economic theory of the, 41, 43,
  62n, 138n, 164
formal similarity argument, 16, 21, 48,
  79–84, 86, 88, 100, 112n, 113, 118–
  24, 133n, 152, 181
Friedman, Milton, 32n
futurity, *see* choice, aspects of

Gale, David, 94n
Gamarnikow, Michael, 25n
Gatovsky, Lev Markovich, 25n
Goldman, Marshall I., 12, 13n, 14, 25n,
  157
Golob, Eugene O., 19n
Gordijew, I., 25n
Gottl-Ottlilienfeld, Friedrich von, 55n
Gray, John, 34
Gregory, Theodor E., 20n
Grossman, Gregory, 25n, 94n
Gruchy, Alan G., 17

Hahn, Frank, 94n
Hall, Robert Lowe, 19n
Halm, George, 6n, 20n
Harris, Seymour E., 13, 15n
Hayek, Friedrich A.
  on the calculation argument, 2–27,
    95, 132, 145, 149–58, 174, 179–83
  on the competitive solution, 28, 48,
    50, 77, 117, 160–6, 166–71
  on complexity, 64n, 167–73
  on the computation argument, 90–2,
    133, 160
  on the equation-solving solution, 90
  on equilibrium, 65, 78–80, 100, 109
  on knowledge, 62, 86, 89–90, 115,
    126, 141, 160–6, 171–3, 180
  on law, 112–13
  on the market process, 43n, 55n
  on Marxian socialism, 39n
  on risk, 135, 165–6, 177
  on trial and error, 96–8, 119, 125
Hegel, Georg Wilhelm, 31
Heilbronner, Robert L., 14
Heimann, Eduard, 6n, 19n, 174–6
Hicks, John, 78
High, Jack, 24n
Hilferding, Rudolf, 67
Hobbes, Thomas, 43n
Hoff, Trygve J. B., 6n, 20n

Holesevsky, Vaclar, 25n
Holmes, Peter, 108n
Hughan, Jessie W., 31n
Hunt, E. K., 17n
Hurwicz, Leonid, 94n, 95
Hutt, William H., 20n

incentives, 15, 18–19, 102n, 139, 142,
    143–4, 149, 151, 159, 170–1, 177
indicative planning, 108n
inflation, 58n
information, *see* knowledge
initiative, 42, 129, 138–9, 151, 163, 166
institutions, 19, 20, 36, 46, 54, 81, 111–
    13, 131, 134, 135, 137, 142, 143, 153,
    155–6, 182
interest rate, 38, 70–4, 81–2, 100n, 111,
    136, 177
interventionism, 34, 37–9, 76n, 134n,
    150
Itoh, Makoto, 33n

Judy, Richard W., 95

Kahane, J., 146n
Kaldor, Nicholas, 6n
Kantorovich, Leonid Vital'evich, 94n
Kaser, Michael, 19n, 25n
Kautsky, Karl, 32
Keynes, John Maynard, 133n
Kirzner, Israel M., 20n, 22n, 23, 24n,
    64n, 104–6, 129, 138n, 148n, 159n
Knight, Frank H., 2, 12n, 20n, 135, 137
knowledge, 10, 15, 26, 32, 36, 50, 66–7,
    72, 73, 97n, 102, 122, 133, 136, 139,
    142, 143, 145, 161, 171–3, 176, 177n
    as contextual, 103–4, 137
    as decentralized, 93, 119, 124, 126–8,
        138, 142, 158, 160, 162, 165, 170,
        171–2, 180, 182
    as "given" data, 55n, 57, 62, 64, 85,
        86–7, 89, 93, 98n, 99, 101, 102,
        111, 114, 115, 119, 126, 134, 139,
        160, 161–2, 164, 171–2, 175, 181–
        2
    dispersal of, 24, 62–3, 75, 78, 79, 83,
        89–93, 98, 103, 115, 119, 123,
        125–6, 134, 135, 144, 160–1, 171–
        2, 174, 177, 180, 182
    tacit or implicit, 3, 7, 14, 17n, 98n,
        103, 127, 137, 143, 162
Köhler, Heinz, 10, 12, 13, 14n, 15n, 16,
    17n, 18, 94n, 152
Konnik, I., 19n
Koopmans, Tjalling C., 12, 94n

Kornai, Janos, 19, 24n, 25n, 93n, 94
Kretschmer, K., 94n
Kripke, Saul A., 173n
Kronsjö, T., 94n
Kuhn, Thomas, 5, 26

labor, 39, 159
    centralized allocation of, 68, 74, *see
        also* labor time solution
    heterogeneity of, 67, 68, 70–3
    market allocation of, 74–7, 150, 158,
        174
    simple or abstract, 72–4
labor theory of value, *see* value
labor time solution, 6n, 20–1, 46, 67–
    74, 82n, 180–1
Lachmann, Ludwig M., 22n, 64n
Lakatos, Imre, 26
Landauer, Carl, 6n, 12, 13, 15, 18, 19n
Lange, Oskar Richard
    on choice, 104, 107, 125
    on the competitive solution, 1, 2, 19n,
        28, 117–32, 133, 135, 158, 162,
        163, 166–71, 173, 176n, 178
    on Dickinson's answer to Mises, 90
    on equilibrium, 78–9, 88, 108, 117–
        24, 129–30
    on Hayek's and Robbins's practical ar-
        gument, 9, 12, 16, 21, 95, 97, 145,
        152, 161
    on knowledge, 50, 101, 119, 121–3,
        126–7, 170
    on Marxian socialism, 11n, 146n
    on Mises's "theoretical" argument, 13,
        14, 49, 85, 100, 111–12, 114–16,
        182
    on rules, 18, 121–2, 123, 134n, 139,
        140, 164, 171
    on trial and error, 25, 94n, 96, 125–
        32, 168, 175
Lavigne, Marie, 11
Lavoie, Don, 2n, 8n, 35n
law, 112–13, 115n, 122n, 142–3, 150–1,
    163
Leeman, Wayne A., 19n
Leichter, Otto, 6n
Lekachman, Robert, 10, 13, 14n, 16
Lenin, Vladimir Ilyich, 34, 49n, 153, 155
Leontief, Wassily, 55n
Lerner, Abba P.
    on calculation argument, 12, 13n, 14,
        133n, 139–44, 172, 179, 183
    on competitive solution, 2, 118, 125n,
        132, 139–44, 163
    on consumer goods market, 8

Lerner, Abba P. (*cont.*)
  on Dickinson's response to Mises, 88,
    139
  on perfect competition, 129n, 139–40
  on rules, 16, 134n, 139–43
  on subjective value, 102
  on trial and error, 128n
Liberman, Evsei Grigor'evich, 25n
Libermanism, *see* market socialism, lib-
  eral reform movement
Liebhafsky, Herbert Hugo, 16
Lindblom, Charles E., 12n, 13, 16, 17n,
  19n
Lippincott, Benjamin E., 112n
Liptak, Tamas, 94n
Little, Ian Malcolm David, 13
Loucks, William N., 17n
Luch, R. D., 24n
Lutz, Vera, 108n

McCloskey, Donald N., 32n
McFarlane, Bruce J., 25n
Machlup, Fritz, 62n, 78, 93n
Mack, Ruth Prince, 24n
McNulty, Paul J., 22n
Makower, Helen, 94n
Malinvaud, Edmond, 94n
managers, 138n, 159, 162, 165, 171,
  176, 177
Mandel, Ernest, 11n, 19n
Mandeville, Bernard, 43n
Marcuse, Herbert, 19n
marginal cost pricing, *see* competitive
  solution
marginal cost, principle of, 88n, 120,
  128n, 134, 139–42, 164
Marglin, Stephen A., 94n
market process, 22–7, 36, 56, 64, 72, 85,
  95, 101–2, 124, 131, 171–2, 175, 182
market socialism, Lange-type theoretical
  models of, *see* competitive solution
market socialism, liberal reform movement, 25n, 163n
Markham, Jesse, 17
Marschak, Jakob, 6n, 94n
Marshall, Alfred, 3, 5n, 6, 108–9, 131,
  133, 134
Marx, Karl, 11n, 28–47, 52–3, 60–1,
  68, 71–2, 82n, 111, 179, 183
Marxism, 3, 5–6, 7, 19, 23, 25, 28–47,
  67, 69, 74, 77, 146, 149, *see also* central planning, Marxian theory of
mathematical solution, 25, 79–80, 85–
  99, 125, 146, 147, 160, 161–2, 166–7,
  179, 180–1

equation-solving variant, 14–15, 21,
  79–80, 85–91, 119, 124, 128, 135,
  167, 181
trial and error variant, 16, 21, 79–80,
  86–7, 88, 92–9, 119, 125, 167, 181
Mayer, Hans, 148n
Meade, James E., 19n
Menger, Carl, 6, 64n, 112–13
Mises, Ludwig von
  market socialist responses to, 85–92,
    100, 114–16, 119, 123, 132, 139–
    40, 144, 172
  on the calculation argument, 2–27,
    40n, 48–67, 111, 117–18, 135,
    145–63, 173n, 179–83
  on choice, 104–5
  on equilibrium theory, 48, 56, 59, 65,
    78–80
  on institutions, 112–13
  on knowledge, 62–3, 66, 123, 173n
  on the market process, 64–5, 138n
  on market socialism, 74–7, 96n, 173–
    8
  on Marxian socialism, 28, 30n, 32–3,
    60–74, 82n
  on methods of economics, 109–10
  on money, 44, 49, 58–9, 74
  precursors of, in calculation debate,
    2n, 83
Misra, Baidyanath, 12, 13n, 14, 18, 152
money, 58–9, 112–13
  absence of, in equilibrium, 84n, 115n
  absence of, under socialism, 10–11,
    29, 34, 46–7, 49, 50, 60, 68, 155
  as common denominator for economic
    calculation, 57–8, 72–3, 74–7, 162,
    177n, 180
  Marxian theory of, 10, 44
monopoly, 62n, 138, 141, *see also* competition
Montias, John Michael, 12, 19n, 94n
Morgan, Theodore, 24n
Murrell, Peter, 20n
Myrdal, Gunnar, 19n

nationalization of industries, 76–7
Negishi, Takashi, 94n
Nemchinov, V. S., 94n
neoclassical school, 3, 5–6, 7, 12, 19, 22,
  24, 25, 32, 33, 35, 44, 47, 49, 51n, 54,
  55n, 56, 57, 64, 67, 100–16, 133, 135,
  159n, 160, 161, 168n, 170, 172
Neuberger, Egon, 15, 18, 25n
Neurath, Otto, 6n
New Economic Policy, 153, 155–6

Nove, Alex, 25n
Novozhilov, Valentin Valentinovich, 94n
numeraire, 59, 115
Nutter, Warren G., 20n, 156n

O'Driscoll, Gerald P., 20n
optimization, *see* choice, aspects of
Ostrom, Vincent, 20n
Owen, Robert, 46
ownership, 3, 12, 13, 18–19, 25, 36, 42,
    50, 54, 59, 78, 111–12, 119, 125, 130,
    135, 137–8, 142–3, 146–7, 151, 158,
    160, 162–6, 174–7, 180–2

Pareto, Vilfredo, 11, 12, 48, 83, 85, 133,
    160
Pareto-optimality, 12, 16, 17, 54, 55n,
    111, 120, 122, 140, 173
Parker, Alan, 94n
Pejovich, Svetozar, 20n
Pickersgill, Gary M., 13, 18
Pickersgill, Joyce E., 13, 18
Pierson, Nikolaas Gerard, 2n, 90n
Pigou, A. C., 133
planning, *see* central planning
planometrics, 93–9, 107, 130, 181, *see
    also* mathematical solution, trial and
    error variant
Plant, Arnold, 20n, 55n
Polanyi, Karl, 6n, 174–5
Polanyi, Michael, 20n, 26, 95, 103–4,
    155n, 156n
Popper, Karl R., 7
Portes, R., 19n
Porwit, Krzysztof, 19n
post-Keynesian school, 19
Preobrazhensky, E., 6n, 42n
prices, 3, 114, 115n, 119, 125n, 153,
    154, 155, 179
    as parametric, 12, 24, 49, 114, 119,
        121–3, 128–9, 134, 143, 159, 168
    "false," 97–8, 130
    regularities of, 35
    rivalrous underpinnings of, 23–4, 40,
        42–4, 49, 50, 56, 68, 124, 134, 144,
        147, 174–5, 181
    under capitalism, 24, 43, 58–60, 61–
        4, 72, 77, 87, 115, 137
    under socialism, 10, 16, 20, 75–7, 86,
        137, 156, 162, 168, 174, 182
primitive economics, 52, 60, 153
private ownership of the means of pro-
    duction, *see* producers goods, market
    allocation of

producers goods
    centralized allocation of 19, 21, 25,
        30, 51, 74–6, 112, 115, 146, 160,
        163, 164–5, 174, 180–2
    market allocation of, 42, 112, 147,
        158, 160, 162, 164, 174
    profit and loss accounting, 24, 34, 38,
        42–4, 53-7, 62, 95, 103–5, 111, 113,
        121–3, 125n, 129, 130, 136–9, 144,
        147, 151, 155, 158–64, 175–7, 180
property, *see* ownership
Proudhon, Pierre–Joseph, 34
psychology, 18–19, 143, 177
pure logic of choice, *see* choice, aspects
    of, maximization

Radner, Roy, 17n
Rakovskii, M., 94n
Recktenwald, Horst Claus, 22n
redistribution, 96
Reekie, Duncan W., 22n
Reese, David A., 20n, 46
rent, 38, 81–2, 111, 136
reproduction, 33, 35
responsibility, *see* delegation of authority
Revesz, G., 25n
Ricardo, David, 38
Rima, Ingrid H., 13
risk, 15, 42, 135–7, 138, 139, 142, 144,
    159–60, 165, 166, 171, 176
rivalry, 8, 22–7, 39–47, 56, 60, 62, 64, 74–
    5, 78, 81, 85, 86, 102, 118, 123, 125, 130,
    136, 155–6, 158–9, 160, 164–5, 167,
    169n, 171, 180, 182–3, *see also* prices,
    rivalrous underpinnings of
Rivett, Kenneth, 148n
Rizzo, Mario J., 24n
Robbins, Lionel
    on the calculation argument, 2–3, 14,
        21, 79, 117, 145–9, 152, 153, 174,
        179, 182
    on the competitive solution, 9–10, 12,
        16, 77, 158–60, 162, 177, 180, 183
    on the computation argument, 80,
        90–2, 133
    on equilibrium, 110
    on knowledge, 126, 161
Robbinsian optimization, 105–7, 158–9,
    see also choice, aspects of, maximiza-
    tion
Roberts, Paul Craig, 20n, 46, 95, 155n,
    156n
Robinson, Joan, 129
Roper, Willet Crosby, 86n
Rothbard, Murray N., 20n, 62n

rules, 121, 123, 127–8, 133, 134n, 139–143, 150–1, 159, 163, 164, 171
  enforceability of, 121n, 142, 165

Samuelson, Paul A., 94n
scarcity, 11, 24, 35, 59, 65, 68–70, 82, 100n, 122, 181
Scarf, Herbert E., 94n
Schumpeter, Joseph A., 2, 5n, 12n, 13, 14n, 15n, 18, 51n, 152
Schwartz, Jesse G., 17n
Seligman, Ben B., 13, 14n, 152
Sengupta, Jati K., 24n, 94n
Shackle, George Lennox Sharman, 17n, 24n, 78, 104, 106, 111
Sharpe, Myron E., 25n
Sherman, Howard J., 11–12, 14n, 15, 16, 25n, 94n
Sik, Ota, 25n, 94n
Sikes, Earl R., 16, 17–18
Sirkin, Gerald, 20n
Smith, Adam, 36, 43n
Snavely, William P., 12
socialism, 7, 9, 16, 21, 29, 115n, 118
  bureaucratization problems of, 17, 166
  political problems of, 8
  practical experience of, 1, 4–5, 7, 13, 33, 94n, 145, 152–8
  utopian, 29, 30, 34–9
sociology, 143
Solow, Robert A., 18
Solow, Robert M., 94n
Soviet Union, 5, 10, 11, 13, 16, 20, 95, 145, 152–8, 182
speculation, 141–2, 175–6, *see also* uncertainty
spontaneous order, 37, 42–3, 55n, 74, 82n, 95, 118, 128, 136, 144, 147
Stalinist-style five-year plans, 153, 155, 156n, 157
standardization of production, 168–9
statics, 9, 12, 16, 20, 21, 25, 51n, 56, 59, 65, 66, 78–116, 119, 130, 139–40, 158, 159, 161, 169, 174, 176, 181
Steele, David Ramsey, 20n, 46, 153n, 155n
Stephenson, Matthew A., 46
subjectivism, *see* value, subjective theory of
supply and demand, 122n, 127–32, 167–8, 175, 182
Suranyi-Unger, Theo., 17, 19
Swann, M. J., 94n
Sweezy, Alan, 11n, 12, 17n
syndicalism, 6n, 34–7, 76, 174

Tangri, Shanti S., 12, 13n, 15n, 152
Taylor, Fred M., 2, 16, 79–80, 86–8, 90, 93, 96, 114, 118–19, 122, 134, 152, 175
Taylor, Lance, 24n
technological vs. economic choice, 54–5, 57, 72, 147–8, 149
Thirlby, G. F., 20n, 101n
time, 69n, 70–4, 78, 108, 111, 132, 141–2, *see also* dynamics
Tisch, Kläre, 6n, 86n
trade cycles, 35n, 40, 126, 132
trial and error, *see* mathematical solution; competitive solution
Trotsky, Leon, 49n
Tschayanoff, Alexander, 6n
Turetskii, Sh., 19n

uncertainty, 12, 18, 57, 59, 78, 104, 108n, 109–10, 135–9, 159, 160
Uno, Kōzō, 33
utopian socialism, 29–39, 48, 60, 180
Uzawa, H., 94n

value
  applicability of theory under socialism, 6, 33, 60n
  objective or labor theory of, 60n, 67, 69, 71, 80–1, 83, 100n, *see also* labor time solution
  subjective theory of, 51, 54, 59, 60n, 61, 67, 81–2, 93n, 100–4, 114, 168, 170–1
  under capitalism, 36, 38
Vaughn, Karen, 20n, 101n
Veblen, Thorstein, 17n
Viotti, Staffan, 12, 17n, 24n
Vorhies, Francis W., 28n

wages, 38, 72, 136
Wakar, Aleksy, 19n
Walras, Leon, 3, 5n, 6, 12, 14, 80, 83, 85, 89, 91, 92n, 100, 119, 128, 133, 181
Walrasian auctioneer, *see* equilibration process
War Communism, 10, 20, 49, 95, 153, 155, 157
War Socialism, 49
Ward, Benjamin N., 2–3, 15n, 94n, 98, 99
Weber, Max, 2n
Weil, Felix, 6n
Weitzman, Martin, 94n

welfare economics, 1, 11, 19, 135, 139–
40, 143, 172
White, Lawrence H., 24n, 35n
Wicksteed, Philip H., 114
Wieser, Friedrich von, 6, 48, 51n, 78–
85, 100, 115, 118, 124, 181
Wilczynski, J., 25n, 94n, 96n
Wiseman, Jack, 20n
Wittgenstein, Ludwig, 173n

Wolfe, P., 94n
Wootton, Barbara, 19n
worker's control, 35, 76

Zaleski, Eugene, 25n, 156
Zassenhaus, Herbert, 6n
Zauberman, Alfred, 94n
Zhitnitskii, Z., 25n
Zielinsky, Janusz, 19n